THE SPORT AND FITNESS SECTOR

AN INTRODUCTION

**EDITED BY
BEN OAKLEY AND MARTIN RHYS**

 Routledge
Taylor & Francis Group

LONDON AND NEW YORK

 The Open University

First published 2008
by Routledge
2 Park Square, Milton Park, Abingdon, Oxon OX14 4RN

Simultaneously published in the USA and Canada
by Routledge
270 Madison Ave, New York, NY 10016

Routledge is an imprint of the Taylor & Francis Group, an informa business

Published in association with The Open University, Walton Hall, Milton Keynes, MK7 6AA

Typeset in Zapf Humanist and Eras by
RefineCatch Limited, Bungay, Suffolk
Printed and bound in Great Britain by
MPG Books Ltd, Bodmin

British Library Cataloguing in Publication Data
A catalogue record for this book is available from the British Library

Library of Congress Cataloging-in-Publication Data
A catalog record for this book has been requested

ISBN10: 0–415–45404–2 (hbk)
ISBN10: 0–415–45405–0 (pbk)

ISBN13: 978–0–415–45404–9 (hbk)
ISBN13: 978–0–415–45405–6 (pbk)

CONTENTS

LIST OF ILLUSTRATIONS

FIGURES

TABLES

ACKNOWLEDGEMENTS

The publishers would like to thank the following for permission to reprint their material:

CHAPTER 2

Taylor & Francis Ltd. for permission to reprint C. Gratton and P. Taylor, (figure) 'Private/commercial sector sport and leisure', *Economics of Sport and Recreation, Second Edition*, 2000, p. 4. www.tandf.co.uk. © Taylor & Francis, 2000.

Taylor & Francis Ltd. for permission to reproduce L. Robinson, (table) 'Local authority sport and recreation services', *Managing Public Sport and Leisure Services*, 2004, pp. 37–57. www.tandf.co.uk. © Taylor & Francis, 2004.

CHAPTER 3

The Department of Culture, Media and Sport for permission to reprint P. Carter, (figure) 'Indicative sports funding flows: a simplified national model', *Review of National Sport Effort and Resources*, 2005, p. 21. © Crown Copyright, 2005.

CHAPTER 4

Experian Ltd. for permission to reprint MOSAIC UK, (map) 'Mosaic Map showing Drive Time for a Health Club in Oxford', http://www.business-strategies .co.uk/Products%20and%20services/Micromarketing%20data/Consumer% 20segmentation/Mosaic/Mosaic%20UK.aspx, 2006. © Experian Ltd., 2006.

CHAPTER 5

The Department of Culture, Media and Sport and the Strategy Unit for permission to reprint 'Why do we care: benefits and the role for Government', *Game Plan: A Strategy for Delivering Government's Sport and Physical Activity Objectives*, 2002. © Crown Copyright, 2002.

CHAPTER 6

The National Coaching Foundation for permission to reprint G. Cooke, 'Pathways to success: a model for talent development', *Supercoach*, 8, 5, 1997, pp. 10–11. © The National Coaching Foundation, 1997.

CHAPTER 7

The Institute for Sport and Recreation Management for permission to reprint M. Collins, 'Sports participation in decline?', *Recreation*, November, 2004, pp. 26–28. © The Institute for Sport and Recreation Management, 2004.

CHAPTER 8

Sport England for permission to reprint Sport England, *The Framework for Sport in England*, 2002. © Sport England, 2002.

Sport England for permission to reprint N. Rowe, R. Adams and N. Beasley, *Driving up Participation in Sport: The Social Context, the Trends, the Prospects and the Challenges*, 2004. © Sport England, 2004.

Sport England for permission to reprint N. Rowe and S. Moore, (figure) 'Trends in participation in sport (excluding walking) – decline in participation by age – comparing 1990 to 2002', *Research Briefing Note: Participation in Sport – results from the General Household Survey 2002*, 2002. © Sport England, 2004.

Sports Council Wales for permission to reprint Sports Council Wales, (table) 'Stock of sports facilities in Wales at three points over the last 35 years', *Internal Analysis (2007)*, 2007. © Sports Council Wales, 2007.

CHAPTER 9

Taylor & Francis Ltd. for permission to reprint L. Robinson, 'Managing public sport and leisure services', *Managing Public Sport and Leisure Services*, 2004, pp. 37–57. www.tandf.co.uk. © Taylor & Francis, 2004.

Prentice Hall for permission to reprint H. Mintzberg, (table) 'Managerial roles', *The Nature of Managerial Work*, 1979. © Prentice Hall, 1979.

Taylor & Francis Ltd. for permission to reprint J. S. Batsleer, (figures) 'The rational approach to decision making' and 'The bounded approach to decision making', in J. David, R. Hedley, and C. Rochester (eds.), *An Introduction to the Voluntary Sector*, 1994. www.tandf.co.uk. © Taylor & Francis, 1994.

CHAPTER 10

HMSO for permission to reprint A. Blair, *Healthy Living: Whose Responsibility*, 2006, http://www.number-10.gov.uk/output/Page9921.asp. © Crown Copyright, 2006.

CHAPTER 11

Adventurous Activities Licensing Authority for permission to reprint AALA, *From Lyme Bay to Licensing: Past, Present and Future – the Development of Current Regulation of Outdoor Adventure Activities*, 2001. © AALA, 2001.

CHAPTER 15

Oxygen Consulting for permission to reprint N. Wright, 'Managing a monumental crisis' in R. Algar (ed.), *Mastering Health Club Management*, 2006, pp. 172–187. © Oxygen Consulting, 2006.

CHAPTER 16

The Open University for permission to reprint material from OU Business School Certificate in Management Programme, B630 *Managing Customers and Quality*, Book 1 *Understanding your Customers*, 2001. © The Open University, 2001.

Prentice Hall Europe for permission to reprint P. Doyle, (figure) 'Stakeholders and their expectations', *Marketing Management Strategy, Second Edition*, 1998, p. 12. © Prentice Hall Europe, 1998.

CHAPTER 17

The Open University for permission to reprint material from OU Business School Certificate in Management Programme, B630 *Managing Customers and Quality*, Book 1 *Understanding your Customers*, and Book 2 *Meeting Customers Needs*, 2001. © The Open University, 2001.

Kelley School of Business for permission to reprint L. L. Berry, V. A. Zeithaml and A. Parasuraman, (figure) 'The roots of customer satisfaction', and (table) 'Competitors of customer orientation', in 'Quality counts in services too', *Business Horizons*, May–June, 1985, p. 47. © Kelley School of Business, 1985.

Massachusetts Institute of Technology for permission to reprint A. Parasuraman, L. Berry and V. A. Zeithmal, (figure) 'The zone of tolerance' in 'Understanding customer expectations of service', *MIT Sloan Management Review*, Spring, 1991, p. 42. © Massachusetts Institute of Technology, 1991.

CHAPTER 18

American Marketing Association for permission to reprint A. Parasuraman, V. A. Zeithaml and L. L. Berry, (figure) 'The quality gaps model', in 'A conceptual model of service quality and its implications for future research', *Journal of Marketing*, 49, 4, September, 1985. © American Marketing Association, 1985.

CHAPTER 20

The Open University for permission to reprint material from OU Business School Certificate in Management Programme, B630 *Managing Customers and Quality*, Book 3 *Valuing your Customers*, 2001. © The Open University, 2001.

CHAPTER 21

American Psychological Association for permission to adapt D. N. Lombard, T. N. Lombard and R. A. Winett, (figure) 'Frequent professional contact' in 'Walking to meet health guidelines: the effect of prompting frequency and prompt structure', *Health Psychology*, 14, 1995, pp. 164–170. © APA, 1995.

Bellwether Publishing Ltd. for permission to reprint C. Thompson, (figure) 'Effects of perceived activity choice upon exercise behaviour', in 'The effects of perceived activity choice upon frequency of exercise behaviour', *Journal of Applied Social Psychology*, 10, 5, 1980, p. 440. © Bellwether Publishing Ltd, 1980.

CHAPTER 23

Oxygen Consulting for permission to reprint D. Minton, 'Profit from getting close to your members', in R. Algar (ed.), *Mastering Health Club Management*, 2006, pp. 24–31. © Oxygen Consulting, 2006.

CHAPTER 24

Oxygen Consulting for permission to reprint D. Green, 'Turning members into raving fans', in R. Algar (ed.), *Mastering Health Club Management*, 2006, pp. 80–100. © Oxygen Consulting, 2006.

THE SPORT AND FITNESS SECTOR: AN INTRODUCTION

Ben Oakley and Martin Rhys

INTRODUCTION

This book is the inaugural text developed by The Open University in the subject area of sport and fitness. It has been stimulated by the continued development of the sector and of undergraduate courses in the subject, including vocationally focused foundation degrees. The book is being used as a 'Reader' on the Open University module E112 *Introduction to Sport, Fitness and Management*, which is part of the Foundation Degree in Sport, Fitness and Health. The text is therefore slightly different to other academic work in this field in that its remit is very much to link with the world of work since this is the purpose of foundation degrees in the UK; it also differs in that it is partly designed for a distance learning audience, which means that clarity, for a wide range of readers, is particularly important.

The terms 'sport' and 'fitness' have been used together in this book to capture the idea of the range of settings and motivations that may be involved in such activities and to explicitly include the health and fitness sector. When we talk of 'fitness' we mean the activities associated with health and fitness facilities, those connected with physical activity, health and casual participation in training. This recognition of fitness provision represents a recurring theme of the book: that health and fitness facilities offer a number of employment opportunities and this recognition is blended with the broader interest that many may have in sport. The book addresses sport and fitness as a distinct and significant part of the economy, signalled by the term 'sector'; those with a commercial background often talk about it as an 'industry'.

The sport and fitness sector connects with people on a range of levels. Some of the largest national television audiences are generated by coverage of sporting events and this shared experience is a phenomenon that makes it a unique part of most nations' popular culture. Whilst sport and fitness at an elite level connects with a wide range of collective public interests, it also plays an important role for many people at the individual level. A majority of people regard personal fitness as a source of personal pride and self-esteem (Carter, 2005), though individual involvement in sport and fitness may well go beyond straightforward personal participation. Consider the person who acts as a volunteer for a local sports club or helps out when a major event is run in their locality; evidence suggests that of all the voluntary roles that people fulfil in society sport and recreation volunteering is the most popular (Sport England, 2003).

Looking ahead, it seems likely that growth in the sport and fitness sector will be affected by recognition of physical activity's links to health. Worldwide, many governments are tackling public health issues by placing greater emphasis on physical activity, which raises sport and fitness up the political and funding agendas. In the UK, the opportunity to host the 2012 Olympic Games provides a rare opportunity to increase sport and fitness participation. The Sports Industry Research Centre (2007) reports that if participation increases by 4 per cent in the years before and after the Olympic Games the whole sector will strongly expand. Individual sport or fitness participation is the most important long-term factor behind the growth of the sector and there are considerable efforts by the government and many other agencies to drive sports and fitness participation up as part of the legacy of the 2012 Olympics.

BACKGROUND TO SPORTS STUDIES

Sport and fitness has become one of the most popular subjects to study at university. The demand for sports-related courses has resulted in more than 40,000 student applications per year in the UK.

In the late 1970s only a few institutions offered degrees in sports-related subjects, and these were traditionally based in physical education teacher training departments. As the field developed, staff from science departments were redeployed to teach programmes in what became known as 'sports science'. These courses tended to be oriented around the laboratory-based elements of biology, chemistry, biomechanics, medicine and later psychology and nutrition. Further routes in the development of sports courses have come from management departments, where the curriculum has tended to focus on sport/leisure/recreation management with particular reference to the disciplines of management and economics. Other courses have incorporated expertise from university departments of sociology, politics, law and history; these courses have often used the generic title of 'sports studies'.

Since 2000, the focus of such degrees has begun to shift from sport to exercise, perhaps unsurprisingly given the level and significance of recent government initiatives aimed at encouraging healthy lifestyles and an active population (Tong, 2005). There is currently a far greater range of expertise and specialism than there was in the 1970s, such as sports development, sports injuries, sports therapy, sports coaching, exercise prescription, health and exercise. It is inevitable that this will be reflected in the wide range of subjects, drawn from a number of disciplines, which make up sports-related degrees. This book follows the trend by taking a multi-disciplinary approach toward the subject of sport and fitness, using definitions, concepts, theories and methods from a range of disciplines, including management, politics, sociology, economics, history and law.

CHOICE OF TOPICS

In keeping with the vocational focus of this book, we will concentrate on some of the most important topics for employers and their staff, and address these in some depth. In order to ensure relevance, we have consulted with leading employers and a government training council called SkillsActive which develops 'national occupational standards', and employee surveys, such as *Working in Fitness* (SkillsActive, 2006).

The *Working in Fitness* survey in particular provided strong indicators of what would be desirable content for an introductory text of this nature, given the potential readership of new or intending new staff to the health and fitness industry. In the survey 1,200 staff working in the sector were asked the question 'How important are the following skills in your job?' They were asked to respond on a scale from 'very important' to 'not at all important'. Figure 0.1 shows the results of this question.

Although this survey is identifying 'skills', academic books can underpin such competences with knowledge and understanding. Looking at the above survey results, we suggest that communication skills and customer handling skills are strongly linked and for this reason the topic of valuing customers is addressed in some detail as a major section of this book (see Section 3, p. 177). A further item which features strongly in these results is health and safety skills. This is an important issue when working in sport and fitness, and is supported by

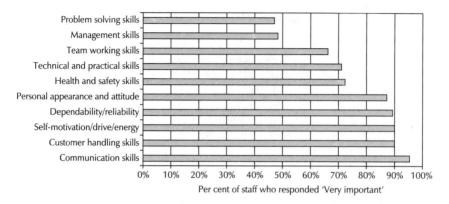

Figure 0.1 Summary of top ranking skills identified by fitness staff as being important

Source: SkillsActive (2006).

employers' comments. Therefore background awareness of regulation and legal frameworks, particularly how they relate to safety issues, is also addressed in some depth in the book, with a whole section devoted to it (see Section 2, p. 121). Students will also develop the analytical and problem solving skills from using this book, and the theme of management skills recurs throughout the text.

STRUCTURE OF THE BOOK

The book is structured in three main sections, each considered to be of paramount importance to new and potential recruits to employment within the sport and fitness sector. Within each section, a range of contributors provide expert knowledge in their particular field of expertise. The three main sections are:

1   *Putting sport and fitness in context*: This section investigates the background and organisational context of the sport and fitness sector, including recent industry trends, government policies and sporting/social trends. This section is a logical starting point for those in the early stages of undergraduate study of the subject and inevitably has a UK bias.
2   *Regulation and legal responsibilities*: This section assesses the need for regulation in various aspects of sport and fitness and explores the ways in which different forms of regulation have evolved. Those in the workplace need grounding in health, safety and welfare awareness and the contributory legal

frameworks. These concepts are carefully addressed in an accessible way, partly in a sport or fitness facility operational context.

3   *Valuing customers of sport and fitness facilities*: This section addresses the generic question of how to satisfy and retain customers, an ability which most employers have at the top of their list of desirable qualities among employees. Wherever possible, the generic nature of the subject matter is particularised to address issues within the sport and fitness sector.

The sequencing of chapters has been carefully chosen so that each section starts with chiapters which introduce the background to and/or definitions in the field of knowledge. These ideas and understandings are then extended in later chapters in each section. At the start of each section there is an editorial introduction that explains the outline content of each chapter. There is also a little background information about the author(s) that will help readers to understand the particular perspective that they are writing from.

A particular strength of the book is the broad mix of authorial voices behind the different chapters. These range from established academics from leading sports universities and key organisations, such as the different UK Sports Councils, commercial managers and hands-on facility managers, and include a regulatory perspective from a former prime minister. We believe that readers will find that the variety of ideas and perspectives enhances their knowledge and awareness of the sector.

REFERENCES

Carter, P. (2005) *Review of National Sport Effort and Resources*, London: Department of Culture Media and Sport.

SkillsActive (2006) *Working in Fitness, 2006*, available from: www.skillsactive.com/resources/research, accessed August 2007.

Sport England (2003) *Sport Volunteering in England, 2002*, London: Sport England.

Sports Industry Research Centre (2007) *Sport Market Forecasts 2007–2011: Summary*, joint publication between SIRC and Sport England, available from: www.sportengland.org/smforecast_2007to2011.doc.

Tong, R. (2005) 'Sport and exercise science: past, present and future', *Link 12 – Newsletter of the Hospitality, Leisure, Sport and Tourism Network (HLSTN)*, pp. 17–18.

ABOUT THE EDITORS

Ben Oakley is the Head of Award for the Open University's new Foundation Degree in Sport, Fitness and Health and is also contributing to other sports-related courses. His sporting interests have taken a prominent role in past jobs, and he has been a successful international windsurfer and later full-time Olympic coach for the Games held in Korea (1988) and Spain (1992). He has lectured in sports policy at universities in Portsmouth, Southampton and Rennes, and was a member of Sport England's Regional Sports Board, which makes decisions about the distribution of National Lottery funds to local projects.

Martin Rhys is a Staff Tutor in Education at The Open University (OU) in Wales. He has served on several OU course teams, including Exploring the English Language and English Grammar in Context. He has been a freelance broadcast journalist in television and radio, having broadcast on rugby, soccer and cricket. His sporting pursuits have included cricket, rugby, soccer, squash, golf and tennis.

SECTION 1

PUTTING SPORT AND FITNESS IN CONTEXT

INTRODUCTION

The purpose of this section of the book is to build the foundation for studying sport and fitness and give an overview of the sector, its organisation and the opportunities and challenges it faces in the future. Therefore in the early chapters key terms are defined and the language and concepts involved in the provision of sport and fitness facilities are introduced. Then the chapters move on to consider how the sector is structured, in terms of the main organisations involved and how it is funded using tax payers' money, the National Lottery and money from commercial sources. The claimed wider social benefits of sport and the concept of sport development are then discussed before the facts about who takes part in sport and fitness are addressed. The section ends by considering social trends that might affect sport and fitness participation in the future and with an evaluation of the management skills needed to lead sport and fitness organisations. A more detailed description of each chapter and the background of the authors are given below.

The first two chapters are authored by **Mick Green** of Loughborough University (School of Sport and Exercise Sciences). Green, a former professional footballer for Exeter City in the 1970s, is now a lecturer in sports management and policy. In Chapter 1 he outlines and discusses the varied meanings of the terms *leisure*, *sport*, *physical activity* and *recreation*. This is followed in Chapter 2 by an explanation of the different settings in which sport and fitness is practised, exploring how the underlying motives differ between public, private and voluntary sectors.

In Chapter 3, **Ben Oakley** of The Open University considers the influence of sports organisations on participants, from the familiar (a person using a local authority swimming pool) to the more rarefied (the organisation and funding of elite sport squads at international levels). The chapter aims to respond to the question posed in the title: 'Who's in charge?'

Chapter 4 is written by two members of staff from the Leisure Database Company, **David Minton** (a cycling and Tour de France enthusiast) and **Jenny Stanley** (who enjoys walking and tennis). David is the director of this company, which is a leisure market research company providing data and analysis for strategic decision-making. The chapter focuses on ownership and financial trends in the health and fitness industry and as a result has a fairly commercial focus, in contrast to the previous chapter (which has a public sector focus).

Chapter 5 is an edited version of a public sector document: a pivotal 2002 UK government strategy document called *Game Plan*. It assesses the evidence for the alleged benefits of sport and fitness. The academic discipline of the government authors is economics, so they are interested in the evidence, efficiency and effectiveness of the sport 'system' and its impacts on wider society.

Chapter 6 briefly introduces the idea of sport development and also the use of visual models. Its author, **Geoff Cooke**, is a former coach of the England Rugby team (1987–1994), and when this was written he was leading the then National Coaching Foundation (now SportsCoach UK). This piece was written in 1997, one year after the disastrous showing by the British team at the 1996 Atlanta Olympic Games. You may notice this reflected in the rather opinionated content.

Chapters 7 and 8 are linked since they are both about the rates of sports participation and the variety of patterns that exist within different social groups. The author of Chapter 7 is **Mike Collins**, Visiting Professor at the University of Gloucestershire; formerly of Loughborough University and Head of Research, Planning and Strategy at the Sports Council (now Sport England). This chapter, written shortly after UK statistics on sports participation were released, outlines unequal patterns of participation, looking in particular at categories such as gender, ethnicity, age and socio-economic group membership. Chapter 8 follows on by looking forward to trends over the next 20 years. Authors **Martin Rhys** and **Indra Sinka** (both Open University Education Staff Tutors) adapt research from two main sources (Sport England research summaries) in order to consider the effect of specific social trends on sport and fitness participation over the next couple of decades, along with the associated problems posed for policy makers and organisers.

Chapter 9 is written by **Leigh Robinson** (a water-polo player and former manager of the Great Britain and England women's water polo teams). She now works at Loughborough University (School of Sport and Exercise Sciences) as a lecturer in sports management. In this chapter she unpicks and explains the range of skills needed to manage sports and leisure facilities.

CHAPTER 1

DEFINING SPORT, RECREATION, PHYSICAL ACTIVITY AND LEISURE

Mick Green

INTRODUCTION

It should be noted at the outset that the task of providing clear definitions for 'sport', 'recreation', 'physical activity' and 'leisure' is fraught with problems. Not only is there a lack of agreement on clear definitions for each of these terms on their own but the picture is also further complicated by the blurring of the boundaries between all four. For example, Gratton and Taylor argue that 'Sport is a part of a broad range of activities that we call leisure' (2000, p. 6). However, leisure researchers have struggled for many years to answer a simple question: 'What is leisure?'

In many ways, what 'leisure' means to one person will be different from what it means to somebody else. In short, the same activity can be leisure to one person but non-leisure to another. For example, for one person, gardening, jogging and walking might be perceived as leisure activities/pursuits. Yet, for another person, the previous list might be perceived as:

- gardening – a 'job to be done';
- jogging – a fitness activity; and
- walking – just a means of travel.

One of the key questions to be answered is how to distinguish between sport and more general leisure and recreation activities (Gratton and Taylor, 2000, p. 7). Some activities, such as rugby, hockey and cricket, are clearly recognised as sport. Going to the cinema, going out for a meal and reading are other activities done in leisure time that are clearly non-sports. It is at the margin that problems arise. Are darts, snooker, pool and fishing, for example, sports, recreations, or leisure activities? It might be argued that they are sports since they are covered by sports programmes on television and newspaper coverage is in sports sections. They are also all competitive. However, they involve little or no physical exertion, so they do not meet the criterion of 'physical activity' in the much-quoted definition of sport in the Council of Europe's (1992) *European Sports Charter*:

> 'Sport' means all forms of physical activity which, through casual or organised participation, aim at expressing or improving physical fitness and mental well-being, forming social relationships or obtaining results in competition at all levels.
>
> (Council of Europe, 1992)

At this stage, it is important to note that 'leisure' is the broader sphere within which we can make some sense of the other terms that concern us in this chapter, i.e. sport, recreation and physical activity (Gratton and Taylor, 2000). As a starting point, Haywood *et al.*'s review of four consistently recurring themes in the attempts to define 'leisure' provide an organising framework for a better understanding of the term. These are now described briefly in turn.

LEISURE

Leisure as residual time

Within this definition, leisure is viewed as time free from obligations, or as discretionary time to use in essentially freely chosen ways, when paid work and other obligatory activities have been done. This view of leisure is problematic for reflecting a 'man-made' view of society, with little account given to evaluating women's leisure experiences when many still have the major responsibility for childcare and housework (Kay, 2000).

Leisure as activities

This view is clearly seen as a range of activities which people choose to take part in during their free time. The emphasis here, though, is on the *nature* of the activities chosen, e.g. sports, dancing, television, arts, holidays. Although this may be an easily understood and commonsense way of thinking about leisure, it tends to downplay certain forms of activity that are harder to categorise such as religion, DIY and charity work.

Leisure as functional

This view encourages us to think about leisure activities as performing useful functions both at an individual level and for society as a whole. This view of leisure differs from our first two definitions insofar as it is less concerned with time and activity and more concerned with how it is *used*.

Leisure as freedom

Historically, the definition of leisure as 'freedom' focused on pursuits enjoyed primarily by the aristocracy and the wealthy 'upper classes', such as the fine arts, literature, theatre, ballet, opera and classical music. This view of leisure presents us with a picture of wealthy people idling away their time in activities that enhanced their quality of life. On the other hand, this view presents an elitist picture of what is ' "worthwhile", "fulfilling" [and] "meaningful" ' for the majority of the population (Haywood *et al.*, 1995, p. 9).

To sum up this section, as Roberts maintains, 'Leisure is highly context dependent' (1999, p. 1). What leisure is can vary between individuals, groups and even countries. It is therefore important for us to understand the different views of leisure, and the related notions of sport, recreation and physical activity.

SPORT, RECREATION AND PHYSICAL ACTIVITY

Sport

Writers on the topic of defining sport agree that there are a number of characteristics that help us to categorise sport and to distinguish it from related activities like recreations and hobbies (see, for example, Gratton and Taylor, 2000). Four themes in particular emerge from this literature.

1   There must be some physical dimension involved, e.g. running, jumping, throwing, psycho-motor skills. Archery and shooting do not require hard physical activity but they do involve expert hand–eye co-ordination and so qualify as sport. On this measure, darts and lawn bowls are also categorised as sport but chess, Scrabble and poker are not.
2   There should normally be a competitive element involved. So vigorous activities like recreational swimming and strenuous walking do not qualify

as sports but less energetic activities such as competitive golf and curling do.

3   The activity has to be structured and have a framework of institutional organisation. In other words, there will be an agreed-upon set of rules which are normally regulated by an organisation such as a national governing body of sport like the Scottish Football Association or England Netball.

4   There should be a criterion of general acceptance that an activity is sporting by the media (e.g. newspapers, broadcasters) and sports organisations such as the Sports Councils in the UK.

The value of thinking about these criteria in this way is that it allows for a distinction to be made between sport and related areas of activity like games, pastimes and recreations. At least one of the main objectives in defining sport in this way is that it helps decide 'who is in and who is out when it comes to things like who is eligible for grants and assistance' (Stewart et al., 2004, pp. 19–20), in particular those provided by governmental sports organisations.

Recreation

On the issue of how 'recreation' has been defined, perhaps the best way to differentiate between sport and recreational activity is to look at the *form* of the activities and the social *contexts* in which they occur.

With regard to the form of the activity, running is an example that can be conceived of either as a sport, when it takes place within the rules and structure of a competitive athletics meet, or conversely as a physical form of recreation, when people take up jogging, where there is no competitive element, people set their own goals and determine what counts as success or failure. In terms of different social contexts, the same activity *form* can be a sport or simply a physical recreation depending on the *context* of its practice. Swimming, for example, can be engaged in as a fun, relaxing day out for all the family. Equally, the same activity can be highly regularised and rigidly formalised, where participants swim primarily to achieve a winning result or to better a past performance.

The objectives of those who participate are considered to be appropriate or inappropriate according to the relative social context of the organisation of the sport. Thus, to be playful when engaged in a formally organised sport is as inappropriate as taking a 'win-at-all-costs' attitude in an informal recreation setting. In summary, the context of sporting activity is therefore identified by its level of organisation and by participants' motives and objectives. As

Haywood *et al*. note, 'the characteristics of "sports" in contrast to mere physical recreation *demand* that participants are motivated to achieve particular goals or objectives – and these can only be met if the activity is formally organised' (1995, p. 44).

Physical activity

Attempts to define 'physical activity' are less complex than other areas since it partly has a scientific basis. For example, a 1996 report by the Surgeon General in the United States defined physical activity as 'bodily movement produced by the contraction of skeletal muscle that increases energy expenditure above the basal level' (US Department of Health and Human Services, 1996, p. 20). This technical definition is further explained in terms of the inter-relationship between 'physical activity' and sport, recreation and leisure: 'Common categories include occupational, household, leisure time, or transportation. Leisure-time activity can be further subdivided into categories such as competitive sports, recreational activities (e.g. hiking, cycling) and exercise training' (US Department of Health and Human Services, 1996, p. 20).

In the UK, the government has outlined a long-term aim for 2020 'to increase significantly levels of sport and *physical activity*' and set a target for 30 per cent of the 'population to be reasonably active (for example 30 minutes of moderate exercise five times a week) by 2020' (DCMS/Strategy Unit, 2002, p. 80, emphasis added). It is significant here that government is less concerned with defining what is and what is not 'sport proper' (Haywood *et al.*, 1995, p. 42) and more concerned with promoting forms of physical activity that 'needs to be of moderate intensity, i.e. raises [individuals'] breathing rate' (DCMS/Strategy Unit, 2002, p. 7) For example, research commissioned by Sport Scotland that investigated *Increasing Demand for Sport and Physical Activity for Girls* stated:

> To avoid confusion that can arise when the word 'sport' is used so broadly, we do sometimes use the term 'sport and physical activity', or simply 'physical activity' when the emphasis may infer much broader aspects of a physically active lifestyle, such as walking to school.
>
> (Biddle *et al.*, 2005, p. 22)

There is strong evidence in the above observations of the functional use of activities that was described under the 'leisure as functional' heading above, that is, to increase physical activity participation rates for future health benefits for all the population. This is important because a recognition is growing of the need to invest in initiatives for increasing physical activity levels that improve *health, fitness* and *well-being* in order to enhance our *quality of life* (Sport England, 2006). Quality of life is a broad term that refers to all aspects of a person's life, including physical health; psychological well-being; social well-being; financial well-being; family relationships; friendships; work; leisure; and so on. Recent changes in NHS plans point towards a focus on the whole of health and well-being, not only on preventing illnesses such as heart disease, obesity and cancer. These health plans, often in partnerships with organisations such as Sport Councils (explained in Chapter 3), therefore involve physical activity initiatives that aim not only to prevent such illnesses but also to help improve the emotional and mental well-being of the population.

SUMMARY

This chapter highlights the complexity of providing clear definitions for sport, recreation, physical activity and leisure. What is clear, however, is the amount of overlap between the way these terms are and have been used. One of the strongest trends in recent years is an increased emphasis by the government's sport and health agencies on encouraging all citizens to become much more physically active in order to improve overall levels of health, fitness and well-being.

REFERENCES

Biddle, S., Coalter, F., O'Donovan, T., MacBeth, J., Nevill, M. and Whitehead, S. (2005) *Increasing Demand for Sport and Physical Activity for Girls*, Edinburgh: Sportscotland.

Council of Europe (1992) *The Council of Europe's Work on Sport, 1967–91, Volume 1*, Strasbourg: Council of Europe.

Department for Culture, Media and Sport (DCMS)/Strategy Unit (2002) *Game Plan: A Strategy for Delivering Government's Sport and Physical Activity Objectives*, London: DCMS/Strategy Unit.

Gratton, C. and Taylor, P. (2000) *Economics of Sport and Recreation*, 2nd edn, London: E. & F. Spon.

Haywood, L., Kew, F., Bramham, P., Spink, J., Capenerhurst, J. and Henry, I. P. (1995) *Understanding Leisure*, 2nd edn, Cheltenham: Stanley Thornes.

Kay, T. A. (2000) 'Leisure, gender and family: the influence of social policy', *Leisure Studies*, 19(4): 247–265.

Roberts, K. (1999) *Leisure in Contemporary Society*, Wallingford: CABI.

Sport England (2006) *Sport Playing Its Part: The Contribution of Sport to Healthier Communities*, London: Sport England.

Stewart, B., Nicholson, M., Smith, A. and Westerbeek, H. (2004) *Australian Sport: Better by Design? The Evolution of Australian Sport Policy*, London: Routledge.

US Department of Health and Human Services (1996) *Physical Activity and Health: A Report of the Surgeon General*, Atlanta, GA: US Department of Health and Human Services.

CHAPTER 2

THE THREE SECTORS OF PROVISION
Public, private and voluntary

Mick Green

INTRODUCTION

In the UK and in many other countries the provision or 'supply' of sport, leisure, fitness and recreation services is characterised by a complex mixture of three main types of provider: the public sector, the private sector and the voluntary sector. With regard to *public sector* provision, central government and local authorities are the primary providers of sport and fitness opportunities; public (tax payers') money is used to fund these services for the public benefit. Over the past 30 years or so, the *private*, or *commercial, sector*, has emerged as an increasingly significant player in provision. From the growth in the numbers of health and fitness centres, gymnasiums and local five-a-side football pitches, to the influence and involvement – in various areas of the broader leisure industry – of global companies such as Nike, BSkyB and Rank (e.g. casinos and bingo) – the primary motive of such provision is to generate profit for owners and share-holders. Finally, the *voluntary sector* (made up of a number of different types of *not-for-profit* provider), plays a substantial role in providing opportunities ranging 'from the recreational to the competitive elite' (Gratton and Taylor, 2000, p. 125), and which at times may cross-cut opportunities provided by the public and private sectors. Local clubs and national governing bodies (NGBs) of sport are good examples of such provision and their main motive is to serve the interests of their users, often using voluntary labour.

The aim of this chapter therefore is to present an overview of the nature and structure of these three sectors of provision, and to show how, at times, opportunities and services in these areas are provided by a complicated mixture of organisations and agencies from all three sectors. As Gratton and Taylor note, 'it is not always so easy in practice to put clear divisions between the commercial [private] sector and the government [public] and voluntary sectors' (2000, pp. 154). It is important to acknowledge that organisations in each of the sectors will have different reasons or rationales for providing opportunities: what follows then also provides a consideration of the ways in which each of the sectors may *constrain* the nature of opportunities available.

THE PUBLIC SECTOR

The public sector essentially comprises government authorities (at national and local levels) and government-related agencies and infrastructure (Chapter 3 discusses this in greater detail). This section concentrates on the chief providers: local authorities or, as they are sometimes known, the local council.

As Robinson (2004) sets out in detail, local authorities are key to public sector provision of sport and recreation. The scale and nature of provision at local authority level is clear from Table 2.1. The relative prominence of provision by local authorities is also clearly outlined in the government's sports strategy document *Game Plan*, where they were recognised as being:

> key providers and enablers of sport and recreation services to local communities, working in partnership with the voluntary and

Table 2.1 Local authority sport and recreation services

Sport and recreation	*Countryside recreation*
Playing fields	Country parks
Golf courses	National parks
Bowling greens	Camping/caravan sites
Marinas	Picnic areas
Swimming pools	Water sport areas
Stadiums/running tracks	
Sports halls	*Education-related services*
Ice rinks	Adult education centres
Leisure centres	Youth clubs
Informal recreation	*Housing, community and social services*
Play areas	Play centres
Open spaces	City farms
Urban parks and gardens	Allotments
Beaches, lakes and rivers	Day centres
	Community centres
	Holiday camps

Source: adapted from Robinson (2004).

mick green

private sectors. They are the biggest providers of sport facilities and provide opportunities through sports development teams and officers who work with the voluntary sector, schools and community.

(DCMS/Strategy Unit, 2002, p. 40)

The rationale for the provision of opportunities at local authority level is broadly similar to that at other levels of governmental intervention. The word intervention is used since their involvement is based on two main arguments. First, local authorities provide services for those who cannot afford opportunities offered by the private and voluntary sectors. Gratton and Taylor (2000) provide a comprehensive overview of the reasons for public provision, and it is clear that a primary motivation for state provision is to enable access for all citizens to sport and recreation opportunities through price subsidies and targeted programming.

The second main argument can be linked to the discussion in Chapter 5, around the functional uses of sport; the argument being that participation in these activities is potentially beneficial for society as a whole. This line of reasoning suggests that there are external (other than sporting or recreational) benefits to be realised, such as the potential to improve health, reduce crime, improve social cohesion, enhance educational standards and contribute to lifelong learning (DCMS/Strategy Unit, 2002). These social goals have, both historically and in contemporary policy, provided a justification for the provision and subsidy of public sport and recreation services.

The delivery of local authority provision has changed in recent years. There is an increasing trend within local authorities to contract out the running of their centres to private suppliers due to the compulsory competitive tendering legislation introduced in 1993. Examples of large companies specialising in this field are DC Leisure and Leisure Connection. The interesting alternative to this private route is something that has been called a 'third' way, i.e. not public, not private but the leisure trust or social enterprise model, in which a trust is established to oversee the operation of local centres in which any profit has to be reinvested into the enterprise. Greenwich Leisure Ltd (GLL) in London and Edinburgh Leisure in Scotland are both large organisations which are run on these principles (see Box 2.1 for further explanation and a case study of GLL).

BOX 2.1: LEISURE TRUSTS

A trust is a not-for-profit distributing organisation. This means it retains surplus funds for the purpose of the trust rather than distributes them to shareholders. It may or may not have charitable status. Local authorities can transfer their leisure services to a trust (new or established), which manages the facilities on behalf of the council through a board of trustees. The council generally retains ownership of the facilities which are leased to the trust. The trust receives an annual grant or management fee to make up the difference between its income from user charges and the cost of operating the service (Audit Commission, 2006, p. 2). The council still has a major influence in the provision of leisure even though a trust is running the facility. A close relationship is maintained between council and trust in terms of development plans, price setting, key performance indicators and opening hours, to name a few.

THE GREENWICH LEISURE LIMITED (GLL) STORY

Greenwich Leisure Limited (GLL) is an innovative staff led 'leisure trust' with a social enterprise structure. They manage over 50 leisure centres within the M25 area in partnership with nine London Boroughs. They reinvest any surpluses back into services and training. The Secretary of State for Trade and Industry commented on the operations of GLL:

> The team at GLL have shown that it is not only possible to combine private sector entrepreneurial flair with strong public sector commitment to deliver public benefit, it can also be highly successful.
>
> (no date, adapted from GLL website, 'About us',
> available from: www.gll.org.uk, accessed 1 March 2007)

The early years

In 1993 Greenwich Council faced severe budget cuts, and proposed a 30 per cent cut in the funding of leisure centres. The service impact of this was the closure of two or three leisure centres and a 28 per cent loss of permanent staff. A review recommended a not-for-profit organisation to manage the council's leisure facilities, with continued influence rather than control from the council.

A Society for the Benefit of the Community, registered under the Industrial & Provident Societies (IPS) Act, was recommended and adopted. This structure held particular appeal due to the possibility for staff ownership of the society. The existing seven leisure centres were transferred to the new organisation – Greenwich Leisure Limited (GLL) – in July 1993. The new organisation quickly proved to be a great success in the London Borough of Greenwich. Instead of cuts, new jobs were created and new services delivered in the existing centres. In addition three new facilities have been built since 1993 – two leisure centres and a health and fitness centre.

Membership levels at the centres in Greenwich rose rapidly from an initial 7,000 at the time of the transfer (1993) to around 70,000 paid memberships in 2004.

Ownership and empowerment

GLL is owned by the contracted staff (who become members by purchasing one share). GLL is guided by a management board, which is appointed on an annual basis by the staff members at the general meeting. The board has representation from a number of stakeholders, including customers, council, trade union and the workforce. This stakeholder mix has helped create empowerment, enthusiasm and ownership at all levels of the organisation. In turn this has led to improved commitment and motivation of staff, resulting in an improved quality of service for customers.

Promoting social inclusion

GLL have successfully introduced many 'inclusive' initiatives into its partnerships to promote the leisure centre and encourage more people to visit them, regardless of their ethnicity, gender, disability or financial background. This social inclusion agenda is as important to them as ensuring a value-for-money service.

Staff and training

GLL's training and development opportunities are amongst the best in the leisure industry. GLL, in partnership with Greenwich Community College, operate a leisure college. In addition to courses available for the communities they serve, the leisure college provides training for GLL's 800 full time staff and over 3,000 part time and casual staff.

THE PRIVATE SECTOR

The significance of private (commercial) sector provision is underscored by Gratton and Taylor when they state that 'the commercial [private] sector of sport . . . is the most dynamic sector of the . . . sports market' (2000, p. 142). Indeed, more broadly, it is now not unusual to talk about the 'sport and leisure industries', and it is the private sector organisations that account for a major share of sport and leisure-related economic activity and employment. Figure 2.1 provides an overview of the two main divisions in private sector involvement, that is, the supply of sport/leisure *goods* and the supply of sport/leisure *services*. The key difference between a commercial organisation and a public or voluntary organisation is that the primary objective of the commercial operator is to achieve financial profit or an adequate return on investment. The other sectors may also make profits but they are established for other reasons. Chapter 4 analyses the health and fitness industry, which is highly commercialised.

The remainder of this part of the chapter concentrates on some of the key developments in private sector provision. The objective of these commercial organisations is to make a profit by serving the public with 'what they want'. Yet, how can we be sure that what is provided – be it five-a-side football or ten-pin bowling – is what the public really wants or needs? Some would argue that the public are 'persuaded', primarily through increasingly sophisticated advertising and marketing campaigns, that they want or need these goods/services. In order for these commercial operators to track market trends, fashions and consumer preferences in a highly volatile and dynamic marketplace, they use up-to-date trend data provided by private market research companies such as the Mintel International Group (known as Mintel) and the Henley Centre, as well the General Household Survey (published by the Office of National Statistics).

As Mintel (2003a), for example, reported, the last 30 years have seen radical changes in the way that many people communicate, travel, eat and drink, entertain themselves in the home and keep themselves fit. With regard to the last item, private health clubs have been a major growth area in recent years. Another Mintel report, *The Leisure Business – UK* (Mintel 2003b), found that 'Spending by consumers at these [health and fitness] clubs rose by 62 per cent between 1998 and 2002 to reach £1,753 million. To give this perspective, it is five times the amount spent on going to the theatre, and twice the size of the spectator sport market. Mintel's (2003a) consumer research also found that health and fitness club users are divided almost equally between those who are members of private sector facilities (e.g. dedicated stand-alone clubs,

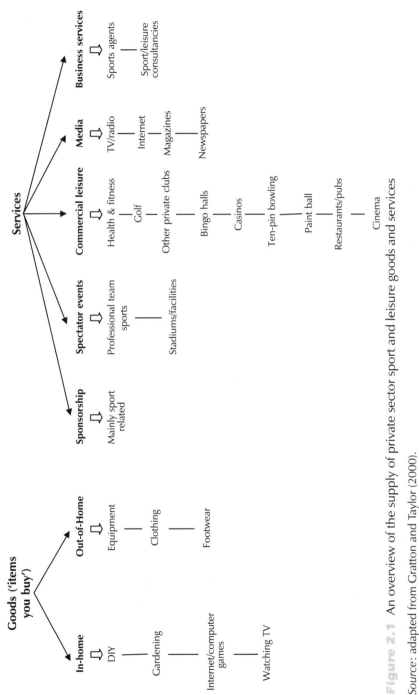

Figure 2.1 An overview of the supply of private sector sport and leisure goods and services

Source: adapted from Gratton and Taylor (2000).

those in hotels and conference facilities) and public sector facilities (e.g. clubs in leisure centres/swimming pool complexes). This balance reflects the fact that there is considerable demand for both types of club and that they can co-exist comfortably alongside one another, each appealing to different types of consumer.

In-home leisure and entertainment is also a growing area. Torkildsen (2005, p. 199) shows that 'leisure in the home' and 'home entertainment' are the two areas where spending by consumers has increased faster than for any out-of-home activity. Gardening, DIY, watching TV and, increasingly, computer games and 'surfing the net' are the main activities for household spending and the most popular activities that people participate in at home.

THE VOLUNTARY SECTOR

According to Torkildsen (2005, p. 164), voluntary sector provision can be viewed in two ways. On the one hand, the sector is viewed as consisting of not-for-profit providers: a collection of sports clubs, national governing bodies (NGBs) of sport, societies, charities, associations of many kinds with sport and recreation as a significant element. Another view is that it consists of a body of volunteers: people doing unpaid work in their own leisure time, using their energy, skills and often their money because it gives satisfaction and because they want to. From this perspective, volunteering – providing service to other people – can be seen as a leisure activity in itself.

In terms of sports provision the most important voluntary organisations are the thousands of sports clubs that operate locally throughout the UK. These, and the NGBs of which they are a part, are the backbone of competitive sport – without sports clubs many people would find it difficult to pursue their specialised sporting interests (such as Ultimate (frisbee)); nor would there be the competitions and training through which talented individuals work their way up to elite representative levels. Sports clubs are often encouraged by the public sector, and National Lottery funding, to also address social objectives such as increasing participation amongst minority groups, but they have generally not been very effective at such tasks.

It is not possible to provide an accurate picture of numbers and types of other voluntary organisations, given the lack of definitive research in this area. Voluntary bodies vary greatly from local groups to national and international organisations. Several different types of grouping can, however, be identified, and some of these are listed in Figure 2.2, but there are numerous overlaps

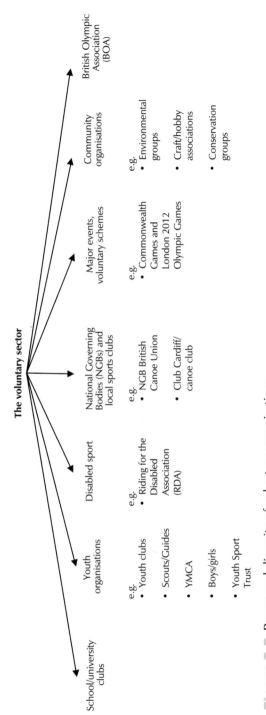

The voluntary sector

School/university clubs

Youth organisations

e.g.
- Youth clubs
- Scouts/Guides
- YMCA
- Boys/girls
- Youth Sport Trust

Disabled sport

e.g.
- Riding for the Disabled Association (RDA)

National Governing Bodies (NGBs) and local sports clubs

e.g.
- NGB British Canoe Union
- Club Cardiff/ canoe club

Major events, voluntary schemes

e.g.
- Commonwealth Games and London 2012 Olympic Games

Community organisations

e.g.
- Environmental groups
- Craft/hobby associations
- Conservation groups

British Olympic Association (BOA)

Figure 2.2 Range and diversity of voluntary organisations

between groupings. Figure 2.2 is neither exhaustive nor an attempt at classification or categorisation; it is simply a means of showing the range and diversity of voluntary organisations in the broad field of sport and recreation.

Moreover, as Roberts notes, 'Anyone who is dissatisfied with the range of commercial [or public] provisions can look to voluntary associations' (1999, p. 188). These voluntary bodies will do anything for which their members have sufficient enthusiasm. And, as Roberts also observes, 'This is the engine that drives the voluntary sector' (1999, p. 188). Voluntary organisations aim to cater for their members' needs and are based largely around sports, hobbies and literally anything else where there is enthusiasm shown by (usually) groups of like-minded people to come together for enjoyment in a shared interest. Thus this major sector for providing sport and recreation opportunities is characterised by independent ownership and the lack of a profit motive. Finally, although some voluntary organisations are committed to supplying sport on a continual basis, such as NGBs and sports clubs, others are more temporary, e.g. to supply volunteers for the running of specific major sports events such as the 2002 Manchester Commonwealth Games and the 2012 Olympic Games in London.

SUMMARY

This chapter presents an overview of the three main sectors that provide sport and leisure services and opportunities: public, private and voluntary. At times it is difficult to draw definite lines between the three sectors, for example in the case of the new leisure trusts at local authority level (see Box 2.1). Public sector provision is based mainly on the idea that sport/leisure opportunities are good for us all and consequently many services are heavily subsidised. In contrast, companies in the private sector provide sport/leisure services in order to make a financial profit. Organisations in the voluntary sector that provide sport/leisure services might make a profit but it is not their prime motive for involvement. Instead, voluntary organisations give people the chance to participate in whatever activity is popular in a particular place and also an opportunity to serve the organisation, which many people see as fulfilling and as adding to their overall quality of life.

REFERENCES

Audit Commission (2006) *Public Sports and Recreation Services: Making Them Fit for the Future*, London: Audit Commission.

Department for Culture, Media and Sport (DCMS)/Strategy Unit (2002) *Game Plan: A Strategy for Delivering Government's Sport and Physical Activity Objectives*, London: DCMS/Strategy Unit.

Gratton, C. and Taylor, P. (2000) *Economics of Sport and Recreation*, 2nd edn, London: E. & F. Spon.

Mintel (2003a) *Health and Fitness Clubs*, London: Mintel Group.

Mintel (2003b) *The Leisure Business – UK*, London: Mintel Group.

Roberts, K. (1999) *Leisure in Contemporary Society*, Wallingford: CABI.

Robinson, L. (2004) *Managing Public Sport and Leisure Services*, London: Routledge.

Torkildsen, G. (2005) *Leisure and Recreation Management*, 5th edn, London: Routledge.

CHAPTER 3

WHO'S IN CHARGE?

The organisation and funding of sport and fitness

Ben Oakley

INTRODUCTION

To most people playing sport or attending a gym, it hardly matters how sport or fitness is organised or how it is funded; their main concerns are that there is a sound and safe facility for them to use, nearby and at reasonable cost. However, to those studying or working in the field, it clearly does matter that the organisational structures of sport or fitness are understood. Without this foundation knowledge it is difficult to appreciate the dynamics of both how the field works and the context in which decisions are made. This chapter therefore explains some of the main organisational relationships and funding mechanisms, including the National Lottery, that operate in the UK. Throughout the chapter it would be useful to refer to Figure 3.1, Indicative sports funding flows: a simplified national model, since it will help put into perspective some of the relationships and funding that are discussed. The figure mainly addresses public and voluntary sector funding but also recognises the input of private funds; this is indicated by a dividing line towards the right hand side of the figure. The chapter itself is organised in two parts since there is so much information presented: the first part discusses public sector sport, including Sports Councils, whilst the second part considers elite sport and a range of other influential organisations. It should be noted that when the text discusses 'sport' the term is used in the very widest way to include the health and fitness activities mentioned in the chapter heading.

So let us return to a person participating locally in a formal sport setting, broadly speaking using one of the types of facilities at the foot of Figure 3.1; they are likely to be doing so at a public (community), educational, voluntary (club) or private sector facility. Sports participation statistics tell us the most popular activity is swimming (see Chapter 7). If ten random people who had been swimming

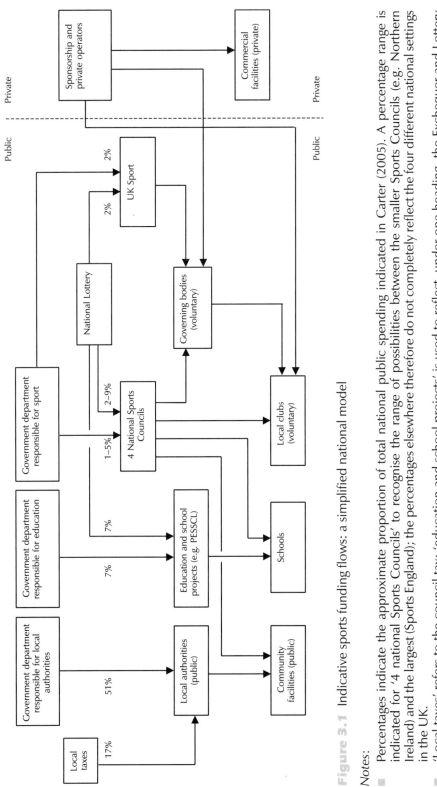

Figure 3.1 Indicative sports funding flows: a simplified national model

Notes:

■ Percentages indicate the approximate proportion of total national public spending indicated in Carter (2005). A percentage range is indicated for '4 national Sports Councils' to recognise the range of possibilities between the smaller Sports Councils (e.g. Northern Ireland) and the largest (Sports England); the percentages elsewhere do not completely reflect the four different national settings in the UK.

■ 'Local taxes' refers to the council tax; 'education and school projects' is used to reflect, under one heading, the Exchequer and Lottery funding of this sphere of activity.

■ 'Government departments' have not been named to reflect the range of titles used for departments in the four nations of the UK.

Source: adapted from Carter (2005, p. 21).

in the last four weeks were stopped and interviewed in a town centre, which sector would you expect them to have used for swimming? It could have been at a private health and fitness facility; or it could have been at a voluntary club that had its own pool; or it could have been at a public, local authority pool. There is of course another possibility: they could have been informally participating outside all of these structures at a friend's house or at a local piece of water (river, sea, reservoir). However, this discussion will focus on the organisation and funding of sport which relies on *formal* settings and organisations. The most likely answer to the above mini-survey is likely to have been the public sector setting. We will focus our attention initially on this sector due to the importance of such facilities, from swimming pools to skate parks amongst many others, in providing widespread provision accessible to most of the population.

PART 1: PUBLIC SECTOR SPORT

Local level

As suggested above, the key organisations in the provision of sporting opportunities in the public sector are local authorities, e.g. Oxford City Council. Local authorities all provide, often through a leisure services department and contracted providers, a range of local community facilities, amenities and services (as discussed in Chapter 2). These are represented in the bottom left corner of Figure 3.1.

BOX 3.1: LOCAL AUTHORITIES

There are in fact three different types of local authority in the UK with slightly differing roles. A local area would be served by one of these:

- the district authority (the most common, particularly outside large cities);
- the unitary authority (individual cities or areas);
- the metropolitan authority (large cities such as Glasgow).

Overlapping with this local focus are the larger separate administrative blocks of counties in England (the name 'county' is also used in Wales and Scotland but they are one combined organisation, e.g. Cardiff and County Council). The separate English county councils normally do not provide leisure centres etc. but do undertake a great deal of work in providing access to countryside recreation and/or providing sports development opportunities across their areas.

The challenge for these different types of local authorities (including English counties) is that sports provision is not a mandatory requirement, as is, for example, overseeing the collection of rubbish. Sport is a discretionary service. The local authority can therefore decide the importance placed and money spent on sport. Local authority budgets are negotiated year by year, so long-term planning and investment in facilities take place in a difficult and sometimes uncertain financial climate.

Whilst most sport facilities tend to be a drain on resources and need subsidising by their local authorities (and therefore tax payers), the health and fitness components of such facilities (i.e. gyms) are normally very profitable. For example, gyms and exercise classes are often sufficiently successful to create enough income to help support larger financially draining facilities such as a sports hall or swimming pool.

National level

Government departments

The funding of much of the work of local authorities comes from tax payers via a department of the national government. In general, national government departments (represented at the top of Figure 3.1) in the different nations of the UK have a tendency to change their titles as political priorities and sensibilities change. For example, in England the department which funded local authorities changed from the Office of the Deputy Prime Minister to, the rather more encompassing title, Department of Communities and Local Government. They, like their counterparts in the other nations, distribute large sums of money to help deliver local services: one of which, albeit discretionary, is sport.

What is interesting here is that this Communities and Local Government department is completely separate from the main UK government department which oversees and funds UK sporting interests. Sport is part of the UK Department of Culture, Media and Sport (DCMS) and has to work with completely separate departments to influence funding issues in local authorities. The DCMS thus attempts to determine strategic priorities for sport in the UK (e.g. the principles of National Lottery funding, Olympic preparations) whilst also having to work with a number of other departments to realise its goals. Figure 3.2 illustrates this.

31

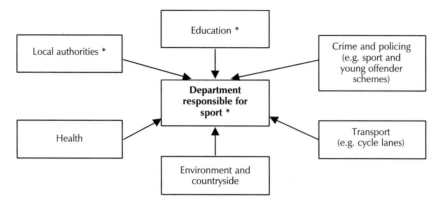

Figure 3.2 The range of government departments that could have an input into national sports policy

Note:
* There is only space to represent these three departments in Figure 3.1.

Claims are made about how sport can help address a range of other social issues such as health, crime prevention, educational achievement and community regeneration (see Chapter 5). The function of any national department with responsibility for sport is therefore to try to pull together these different interests and 'uses' of sport to offer what has been termed 'joined-up thinking'. For example, few would disagree that the greatest influence on the perception and shape of sport for young people is through physical education at school. Yet for a lead body like the DCMS to influence this it has to work with the four national departments responsible for education. Thus Figure 3.2 illustrates the range of departments that a single national government department with responsibility for sport has to work with to create a 'joined-up' approach to sport.

Sports Councils

Many people participating locally in sport may have heard of a Sports Council; many local facilities were initially constructed using grants from a Sports Council and there are a number of commemorative plaques that advertise Sports Council input. Since 1994, which marked the start of the National Lottery, funding has predominantly been from this source. In a nutshell, Sports Councils act as a link between government and other organisations, with their main role being to distribute the money raised from the National Lottery games (the DCMS oversees the whole Lottery mechanism).

In all, there are four national Sports Councils (England, Wales, Scotland and Northern Ireland) and a fifth UK Sports Council which focuses on elite sport only (of which more later). In 1997, when the current system was adjusted, a more media friendly name was adopted by some councils: hence we have Sport England, Sport Scotland and UK Sport. Each national government 'sponsors' its Sports Council through funding.

The very first UK-wide Sports Council was established in 1965; it was independent of government and this is known by a metaphor: that Sports Councils are at 'arm's length', or distinctly separated, from government. This arm's-length separation (government from sport) arose from the strongly held 1960s principles that British amateur sport must be apart from politics and commercial influences. It was argued then that government should have minimal involvement in sport. However, since that time Sports Councils have become far closer to government and the independence of the state from sport has been largely eroded.

Interestingly, the debate about how much government should get involved in sport has been played out in a number of other countries with some contrasting approaches. In the USA, for example, sport is seen entirely as a private matter. There is very little public funding of sport and the popular (and commercialised) competitive university and college sport system lies at the core of American sport. In France the opposite is true: sport is viewed as such an important field of activity that, like many other spheres of French social policy, it was felt too risky to leave it to the vagaries of market forces. Instead, there is a very strong interest and investment from government (e.g. the Stade de France is largely funded by public money, in contrast to Wembley stadium), but higher tax rates are used to pay for this policy approach. International comparisons of sports provision with the UK help one understand the domestic 'system'.

Sports Council funding

One of the Sports Council's primary roles is to distribute proceeds from the National Lottery. Sport is one of the 'good causes' (like heritage and the arts) which the National Lottery Acts of 1993 and 1998 stipulated should receive benefit from the Lottery. The UK Parliament also allocates the proportion of the total funds of each of the four national Sports Councils according to population; resulting in 83 per cent to England, 9 per cent to Scotland, 5 per cent to Wales and 3 per cent to Northern Ireland (Oakley and Green, 2001). The Lottery Acts laid down principles for how the funding process should be administered, and one of the requirements is that each nation should have clear strategies for its

Lottery investments. It is therefore instructive to look at the goals and vision laid out for each nation, normally in the 'about us' sections of their websites. The common themes appear to be:

- to increase participation in sport and physical activity, with a focus on priority groups such as women, those living in deprived areas;
- retaining people in sport by investments in the sporting infrastructure of school and club sport, coaching, volunteering, local communities;
- recognition and support for elite success (see elite section on pp. 35–38).

Policy documents often refer to *capital* and *revenue* funding. In the period 1994–1997, the Lottery was only permitted to fund capital projects: items, normally buildings or equipment, that leave a tangible legacy and have a long working life and, incidentally, ones on which a plaque can be placed. Revenue funding, on the other hand, often supports a coach or community worker or talented athlete to work towards agreed goals – each year they need funding, in contrast to the one-off purchase (build) cost of capital projects. You might like to consider an ongoing debate in sport concerning whether buildings or people help raise participation levels most effectively.

Sports Councils also receive tax payers' money, sometimes known as *Exchequer* funding since it comes indirectly from the Treasury. This used to be the sole support for sport from government; since the establishment of the Lottery, the proportion from the Exchequer is relatively small compared with Lottery funds. Whereas in the early days of independent Sports Councils (1960–1970s) Exchequer money was largely handed down with modest conditions, in the modern era government sets stringent targets and *service agreements* for the use of such funding. There is increasing monitoring in all parts of the public sector about how tax payers' money is spent, from local authorities even through to the DCMS itself.

Sports Council devolved decision-making

The title of the former pre-devolution (1997) Conservative department responsible for sport, tourism and the arts – the Department of National Heritage – indicates the previous way of thinking: the notion that there is a single, unitary, British national heritage. Some people in UK nations vehemently disagree with this idea. There was widespread dissent from such a notion throughout the UK, particularly in the Celtic nations, and one of the first things New Labour did in 1997 was to change the department's title to DCMS. The term devolution is all about the delegation of power and decisions from central control (London) to nations and regions. It follows that a decision about whether a community skatepark in Stirling, Swansea, Strabane or Scarborough receives Lottery funding should be made locally rather than in a remote London office. Devolution mostly came about after the election of the Labour administration in 1997.

The implications of devolution post-1997 were to allow far more decision-making to each of the three Celtic nations within the UK. However, devolution principles were also adopted within England, where somewhere like the North East has very different sporting needs to the South East. Hence Sport England developed a regional network which funds (using Exchequer and Lottery money) 45 County Sports Partnerships, e.g. Hampshire County Sports Partnership. These are important local organisations that pull together interests such as local authorities, county councils, clubs, National Governing Bodies (see p. 38), local education authorities and school sport, health authorities and the private sector. Their primary role is to deliver the first of the Sports Council's strategic priorities listed above – 'increasing participation in sport and physical activity'. Similarly organised local partnerships exist in Wales and Scotland but they have increased emphasis in England due to the amount of funding, the size of the country and the strong existing county structure.

SUMMARY

This section has outlined the rather complex way in which government interacts with sport. Figure 3.1 shows the indicative percentage of funds flowing from different public sources and re-emphasises the important role played by local authorities: some two-thirds $(17 + 51 = 68$ per cent) of national public spending on sport is used by local authorities in providing sporting opportunities. The word indicative, used in the title, suggests that the figures only 'indicate' the rough proportions – far more local authority funding comes from national government (51 per cent) than is raised by local council tax (17 per cent). The other main contributor is money from the National Lottery, which when you add up the allocations to education and national Sports Councils amounts to up to one-fifth of the total national public funding of sport.

PART 2: ELITE SPORT AND OTHER ORGANISATIONS

This section considers elite sport (partly represented in Figure 3.1 by UK Sport and National Governing Bodies) and other influential organisations, including some discussion of the private sector. The range of other organisations is not represented in Figure 3.1.

Elite sport

It is perhaps becoming clear that the control of sport is often a matter of dispute: who controls elite sport is also a vexed question. First, it would help to identify what is meant by elite sport. Professional sports such as football, rugby, cricket, tennis are played at an elite level but are self-financing commercial (private) operations and therefore not within the scope of this discussion. By elite sport we mean sport which is associated with organisations supporting those aspiring to national representative honours, most often at Commonwealth and Olympic Games; this involves the public, private and voluntary sectors.

The lead agencies at UK level are UK Sport (a 'public' Sports Council) and the British Olympic Association (BOA), a voluntary organisation. In simple terms, UK Sport funds, with National Lottery input, the training and preparation of athletes via NGBs. UK Sport also co-ordinates the UK's anti-doping programme. In contrast, the BOA prepares the selection procedures, acclimatisation and sends the team (up to 500 people) to the Winter and Summer Games, with the British Paralympic Association (BPA) supporting them for the Paralympic Games at the same venue.

BOX 3.2: THE SPECIAL OLYMPICS

There is also a Special Olympics for athletes with learning difficulties, organised completely separately.

Whilst the BOA raises millions of pounds from companies to pay for Olympic participation, it does not receive any tax payers' money. It is categorised as a voluntary organisation – its primary motive is not profit driven. It also values its independence from government. An example of this was in 1980 when it ignored the government demands for a boycott of the Moscow Olympic Games in protest against the invasion of Afghanistan by the USSR.

Figure 3.3 outlines the mix of inputs and organisations involved at UK level. The role of NGBs (see also p. 38) is paramount in elite sport since it is they who have the specialist knowledge, identify and nurture young talent, employ

ben oakley

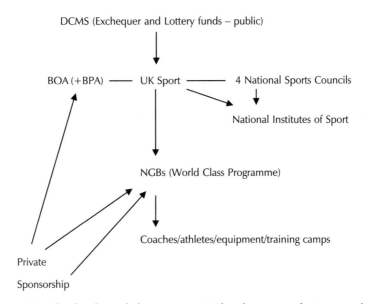

DCMS (Exchequer and Lottery funds – public)

BOA (+BPA) ———— UK Sport ———— 4 National Sports Councils

National Institutes of Sport

NGBs (World Class Programme)

Coaches/athletes/equipment/training camps

Private

Sponsorship

Figure 3.3 The funding of elite sport at UK level – a mix of private, voluntary and public sector inputs

the coaches and propose selection criteria. These aspects are all developed in what is known as a World Class Performance Plan, which UK Sport approves for funding with strict performance targets. The sports that deliver the most medals receive the highest funding; athletics, cycling, rowing and sailing have recently accounted for some 60 per cent of UK medals and these sports top the public funding of elite sport and therefore have rather more influence than other sports.

Another name appears in Figure 3.3, that of National Institutes of Sport, e.g. Scottish Institute of Sport, English Institute of Sport (EIS). The title suggests a state-of-the-art building in one place, but this is only partly true. It is a series of top class facilities and services (e.g. fitness testing, nutritionists) based on the *needs of each sport* and often connected with top universities. For example, British success in the winter sports discipline of bobsleigh is connected with expertise and a specialist starting track built at Bath University for £350,000 in 1999. Cycling uses a velodrome in Manchester, sailing uses a Weymouth facility and so on. Welsh, Scottish and Northern Ireland Sports Councils fund their own institutes, whilst the EIS is funded by UK Sport.

The main challenge in co-ordinating UK sporting squads and teams is that there is also the national representative level, where Wales, Scotland, Northern

37

Ireland and England compete, with their own national pride at stake, in events such as the Commonwealth Games or in football and other team sports. The national Sports Councils and sports institutes, especially Wales and Scotland, place great importance on a strong showing at these events, and for UK teams some funding and political tensions often emerge. The structures of the devolution agenda post-1997 have strengthened such national representation. For example, considerable debate has consistently stalled the proposed formation of a UK football team for the Olympics. No other country in the world has four nations, each with their own sporting teams – the UK is really in a unique position, mainly due to its leading role in the historical development and dissemination of sport in the nineteenth century.

Other major organisations

National Governing Bodies (NGBs)

The NGBs, in addition to their high profile role in developing Olympians, train, accredit and regulate the teaching of their sport. Anyone who has been taught to swim in formal lessons will be influenced by the guidelines and training that their swimming teacher has been through. Furthermore, anyone who has competed in swimming in a formal setting will probably be a member of a club who will abide by the rules of swimming developed by the NGB (in collaboration with the international federation for the sport).

Figure 3.4 helps to understand the role of an NGB in the funding, influence and delivery of its sport to end users (the general public). The boxes titled 'quality and safety standards' and 'clubs' in the delivery section of the figure represents the instructional and competition activities explained above for swimming. NGBs also engage in a number of other activities. A useful 'what if' exercise is to consider what might happen if an NGB suddenly ceased to exist.

Collectively NGBs have quite a powerful voice. The Central Council for Physical Recreation (CCPR) is effectively a form of 'trade union' that represents the interests of NGBs and voluntary clubs in England. The other UK nations have similar bodies, called the Scottish Sports Association, the Welsh Sports Association and the Northern Ireland Sports Forum.

Youth Sports Trust (YST)

This charity established in 1994, has been very influential in developing TOP Play and TOP Sport programmes to enhance the teaching of physical education

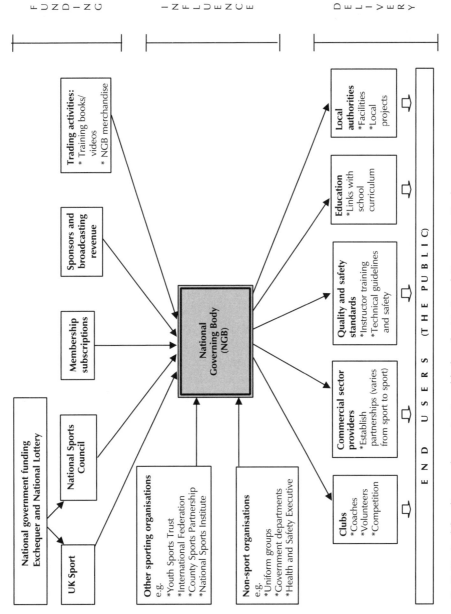

FUNDING

INFLUENCE

DELIVERY

National government funding Exchequer and National Lottery

UK Sport

National Sports Council

Membership subscriptions

Sponsors and broadcasting revenue

Trading activities:
* Training books/videos
* NGB merchandise

Other sporting organisations
e.g.
*Youth Sports Trust
*International Federation
*County Sports Partnership
*National Sports Institute

Non-sport organisations
e.g.
* Uniform groups
*Government departments
* Health and Safety Executive

National Governing Body (NGB)

Clubs
*Coaches
*Volunteers
*Competition

Commercial sector providers
*Establish partnerships (varies from sport to sport)

Quality and safety standards
*Instructor training
*technical guidelines and safety

Education
*Links with school curriculum

Local authorities
*Facilities
*Local projects

END USERS (THE PUBLIC)

Figure 3.4 Typical funding and organisational links of a National Governing Body

(PE) in primary and secondary schools. TOP is used as an attractive name and does not refer to anything in particular. The YST has become so successful an independent organisation that it is now used by the London-based Department responsible for Education to co-ordinate the investment and bringing together of school sport and clubs by using School Sport Partnerships (SSPs). The SSPs work with County Sport Partnerships (in England), or their national equivalents, to try to provide a co-ordinated approach to school sport.

The private sector

The private sector is represented in Figure 3.1 on the right side of the figure, in which there is recognition of both:

- the sponsorship of individuals, clubs and parts of NGB activity; and
- the existence of a range of private operators who run some local facilities, particularly in the health and fitness industry.

The importance of local fitness facilities and the private sector's involvement in this area is the subject of Chapter 4. The total annual funding inputs into both sponsorship and commercial facilities are very difficult to quantify in monetary terms but they have a substantial impact. In fact governments are particularly keen to encourage private sector sponsorship of local or inclusive sport and fitness projects; a number of schemes, such as 'Sportsmatch', operate to enhance grassroots sport by offering what is termed 'matching funding'. If a company puts £10,000 into a scheme the government will, subject to certain criteria, match it with another £10,000, doubling the funds to a total of £20,000. This example of different sectors or organisations working together to achieve similar goals is known as partnership working and is particularly effective in pooling expertise and human and financial resources. An example of an organisation that works with a range of partners is the Fitness Industry Association (FIA), which leads the area of fitness.

The Fitness Industry Association

As the not-for-profit trade organisation for the health and fitness sector, the FIA promotes campaigns, runs training events and education programmes about best practice within the industry. It aims to represent the industry at a range of levels and influence government policy. It also works towards raising standards in the industry. As part of their membership of the FIA, all facilities work to comply with a code of practice, which is a set of performance standards covering health and safety, staff training and customer care. Membership is from both the public and private sectors and each year research is conducted to produce the *State of the UK Fitness Industry Report*, which is used to inform decision-making. The FIA works closely with the Register of Exercise Professionals, which is discussed in Chapter 12.

Professionalisation: sport and fitness workers

Sport is a relatively new field of working (c.40 years) compared to professions such as medicine, law or education. There are earlier examples of professional sports performers but here the focus is on those involved in delivering sport and fitness opportunities. The challenge is how to change a growing area of work, such as this, into a recognised 'profession', with the enhanced status this brings. SkillsActive is partly involved in this area; it is a government funded agency known as a *sector skills council* that is responsible for enhancing the development of skills and training in the leisure sector. Organisations representing sports facility managers, sports development officers and fitness instructors are working towards developing the professional status of the industry with training, representation and levels of recognition.

At the time of writing this area was under scrutiny by the DCMS and others since three bodies exist, working in slightly different areas, as their titles suggest,

- the Institute of Sport and Recreation Management (ISRM);
- the Institute of Sport, Parks and Leisure (ISPAL);
- the Register of Exercise Professionals (REPs) (closely linked to SkillsActive)

Discussions on an amalgamation between the ISRM and ISPAL foundered in 2006. It is possible that there may be changes to these arrangements over time but increasing the 'professional' status of the field remains a priority.

CONCLUSION

Throughout this chapter a number of organisations have been mentioned and the complexities of who is in control have, to some extent, been simplified for the sake of clarity. In the UK our long stable democracy has encouraged the development of often small clubs, interest groups and independent organisations. More recently the UK's democratic tradition has been expressed in the development of devolved governments. This diversity and plurality of interests in the UK can be seen as a strength (the large number of different cultural traditions and sports played compared to other countries) as well as an obstacle (trying to organise these diverse interests).

A number of harsh words have been written about the organisation of sport in the UK in the past. Adjectives such as 'complex', 'fragmented' and 'inefficient' often appear when people comment on the arrangements. Indeed, even a UK government sports minister had this to say:

> We have 112 recognized sports in Britain. We also have 397 governing bodies, five Sports Councils and four ministers. It's nonsense. By June, I intend to do something to rationalize this structure. Until that happens sport has its hands tied.
>
> (Banks, quoted in Miller, 1998)

Sports ministers have always struggled to 'do something' about it since they do not sit at the highest levels of government; nor do they control the main budgets of the Sports Councils or local authorities. However, times are changing and the hosting of the 2012 Olympic Games in London is acting as a catalyst for change: sport and health issues are rising up the political agenda and the role of different bodies is being clarified. If sport and health promotion were to change from being a discretionary to a mandatory local public service, subject to the considerable scrutiny that this would bring (as it does in education and health), it would help transform current arrangements.

Indeed this is happening to some extent since local authority providers are grappling with the introduction of comprehensive performance assessment (CPA). The CPA is the performance management framework used by the Audit Commission and government to measure local authority performance and drive improvement in the sector. The (functional) importance of sport, recreation and leisure services is highlighted by the Audit Commission's report *Public Sports and Recreation Services*: 'The CPA will assess councils' contribution to improving the health of their communities, meeting the needs of young people and their overall performance in cultural services. Sports and recreation provision contribute to all these elements of CPA' (2006, p. 11). This is a major step forward in the importance placed on sport and fitness. Note, in particular, the way it is phrased above: 'health of their communities and meeting the needs of young people'. This suggests the future focus of local authorities will be the use of sport to meet these types of target since they will be heavily criticised if they do not reach the goals set.

Finally, to respond to the initial question 'Who's in charge?', the answer is that there is no one lead organisation in control. This is due partly to devolution and partly to the tradition of letting sport govern itself; this has resulted in a number of organisations claiming to be in charge of their own areas. In future, the most effective arrangement would be to find a way of combining the work of the three most important organisations in grassroots sport, summarised in both Figures 3.1 and 3.4: local authorities, National Governing Bodies and their clubs, and the education system. If only it were that simple.

REFERENCES

Audit Commission (2006) *Public Sports and Recreation Services: Making Them Fit for the Future*, London: Audit Commission.

Carter, P. (2005) *Review of National Sport Effort and Resources*, London: Department of Culture, Media and Sport.

Miller, D. (1998) 'Nothing Wrong with the Aim as Banks Loose Cannon Fires off Broadside', *Daily Telegraph*, 24 February.

Oakley, B. and Green, M. (2001) 'Still playing the game at arm's length? the selective re-investment in British sport 1994–1999', *Managing Leisure*, 6(2), pp. 74–94.

CHAPTER 4

THE HEALTH AND FITNESS INDUSTRY

Trends and commercial realities

David Minton and Jenny Stanley

The health and fitness industry is often more profitable than other activities in leisure centres. As a result its commercial potential has been taken up by a range of operators some of whom are part of large multi-site branded chains with a range of shareholders. This chapter largely focuses on the commercial realities of this industry in both the public and private sector and the trends that have emerged over recent years. It starts by considering the market structure: who uses the facilities and the parts of the UK where they are more prevalent. Throughout comparisons are made between private and public provision; this is particularly highlighted in terms of the different types of ownership models. The second part of the chapter considers the costs of operating such facilities and the income opportunities. The aim of studying the current state of the industry and emerging trends is to help give readers the background to understand and interpret future developments. Most of the statistics and figures are drawn from the Fitness Industry Association *State of the UK Fitness Industry Report* (2006); where other sources are used these are indicated.

MARKET STRUCTURE

Over the last 15 years the health and fitness industry has grown rapidly and it is now moving into a more mature stage. The commercial environment of the health and fitness industry is still in a period of change as competition increases, consumers become more assertive and operators adapt to the developing health needs of the nation. However, with 11.3 per cent of the population members of the UK's 5,400 fitness facilities this is a significant consumer industry.

Market trends revealed in Figure 4.1 show continued year on year growth, albeit at a slower rate than the peak years of 1999–2002. This growth has been in both

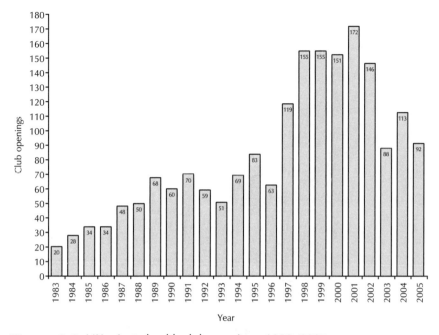

Figure 4.1 UK private health club openings, 1983–2005

total memberships and new facilities opening but with changes in the profile of the industry away from the founding small independent operators towards the multi-site branded operators. These multi-site branded operators run 46 per cent of the UK private clubs but serve 69 per cent of all UK private fitness members and generate 75 per cent of the value of the private club market, estimated on membership fees only. The multi-site operators tend to run larger, more diverse facilities. The average total memberships at independently operated clubs stood at about 800 at the beginning of 2006, whilst the average total memberships for multi-club operators were 2,100. These statistics therefore demonstrate the dominant position of multi-site branded operators and the scale of their operations.

Analysis of the location of all private and public facilities highlights that 87 per cent of the UK population live within two miles of a fitness facility. This indicates a good distribution of facilities with plenty of capacity for increased memberships and further population penetration. Figure 4.2 highlights the greater nationwide coverage provided by the public sector facilities compared to private operators who are more concentrated on the main urban areas. For instance, look closely at Scotland and Wales and the differences become apparent.

45

the health and fitness industry

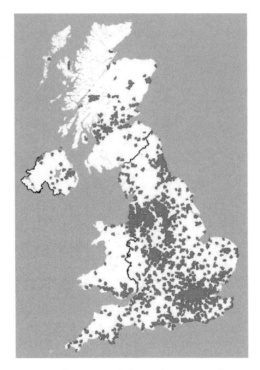

Figure 4.2(a) Areas with private clubs within two miles

The health and fitness phenomenon started in London and the South East and has spread throughout the UK, with private facility concentrations in the urban, affluent areas. London continues to be the most significant region, accounting for 14 per cent of all private clubs, whilst London and the South East combined account for 41 per cent of the market worth, as shown in Table 4.1.

Despite the seemingly good distribution of facilities across the UK population further analysis has revealed that the distribution may not yet be targeting sufficiently the lower socio-economic groups with which the government wishes to engage. Dr Melvyn Hillsdon, of the University of Bristol, published a geographical study into equitable access to exercise facilities in the UK (Hillsdon et al., 2007). The findings suggested that the availability of exercise facilities declines with area deprivation. The greater the level of deprivation in an area, the lower the density of both public and private facilities per 1,000 population.

In addition, it has also been highlighted that people in deprived neighbourhoods have a reduced capacity to travel to facilities as a consequence of less access to cars and public transport (Hillsdon et al. 2007). Research from the National

Figure 4.2(b) Areas with public gyms within two miles

Table 4.1 Regional summary of private clubs with market value (2006)

Region	Total clubs (%)		Total members (%)		Market value (%)	
East Midlands	204	(7%)	260,218	(6%)	£135 million	(5%)
Eastern	276	(9%)	386,066	(9%)	£226 million	(9%)
London	415	(14%)	846,111	(20%)	£652 million	(26%)
North East	151	(5%)	161,608	(4%)	£73 million	(3%)
North West	382	(13%)	594,783	(14%)	£288 million	(12%)
Northern Ireland	48	(2%)	60,005	(1%)	£32 million	(1%)
Scotland	200	(7%)	261,557	(6%)	£145 million	(6%)
South East	435	(14%)	599,385	(14%)	£377 million	(15%)
South West	264	(9%)	269,135	(6%)	£140 million	(6%)
Wales	105	(3%)	118,490	(3%)	£62 million	(2%)
West Midlands	261	(9%)	389,138	(9%)	£197 million	(8%)
Yorkshire	289	(10%)	348,338	(8%)	£163 million	(7%)
All clubs	3,030	(100%)	4,294,834	(100%)	£2.49 billion	(100%)

Audit of Fitness Consumers (Leisure Database Company 2006) has shown that people from lower income groups take less exercise and are the least likely to make use of publicly available health facilities such as gyms in leisure centres. The audit shows that middle class families are eight times more likely to use publicly available health and fitness facilities than less affluent social groups.

The audit also reveals that there are slightly more female health club members (53 per cent) than male. Clubs are still attracting the younger markets over the older groups. Over three-quarters of members are under 45 years old and almost half of all members are under 35 years old. Most members are financially high achievers, with 36 per cent earning over £30,000. Over half, 56 per cent, of all members are single and 66 per cent have no children.

OWNERSHIP MODELS

Of the 5,400 fitness facilities the market is split 56 per cent in private ownership and 44 per cent in public ownership, by number of clubs.

Private sector models

The private sector has been subject to consolidation since 2000. Acquisition and merger activity was seen for a number of reasons: from competitor operators aspiring to grow, private equity houses desiring to make good returns and other leisure companies buying into the health and fitness sector to offer broader propositions and improve group profits.

The top 30 branded health and fitness operators manage 32 per cent of the private health clubs. Their ownership structure, indicative of the multi-club sector, is as follows:

Stock listed operators	3%
Private equity owned clubs	11%
Private companies	18%
Total	*32%*

Stock listed operators

There are a small number of operators who are stock listed, at the time of writing, including JJB Health Clubs. One widely known stock listed operator until mid-2007 was David Lloyd Leisure. It was owned by and was part of the larger Whitbread Group, which is a publicly listed company on the stock exchange; members of the public can buy a share of the business. In fact Whitbread have diversified away from their original activity of brewing beer. They also own Costa Coffee, Premier Travel Inns and Beefeater/Brewers Fayre Restaurants, all of whom are part of the broader leisure industry. The financial benefits and administrative efficiency of owning a portfolio of companies are known as the 'economies of scale'. Therefore Whitbread's strategy of integration across the leisure sector provided the David Lloyd Leisure clubs with management and marketing expertise tried and tested in a variety of successful service operations.

Private equity investors

In contrast to public investment, a number of operators have private investors, often not individuals but investment companies which speculate that money can be made from their investment. Private equity investors have injected a new growth phase in the health and fitness sector since 2000 by providing funding or 'expansion capital'. Large growing businesses, although turning over large sums of money in takings, also have high costs, so there is limited money left for expansion. Private equity investors supply this expansion capital in return for a proportion of the business and are seeking annual returns on their investment in excess of 20 per cent. These types of arrangements have helped to speed up the consolidation of the industry.

Some of the operators in private equity ownership include:

- Fitness First
- LA Fitness
- Total Fitness
- Cannons

Private equity investors see opportunities in the health and fitness sector such as:

- ability to increase profits through improved management, systems and operations;
- further growth.

Fitness First's strategy for further growth is an international approach based on low price. They focus purely on the single delivery of fitness facilities and have not diversified. Fitness First have taken the approach of expanding their brand globally in Italy, Germany, Spain, France, Netherlands, Australia, Hong Kong,

India, Thailand, United Arab Emirates (UAE) and China, and are showing the most significant growth of all the major branded operators. Commentators have suggested that the level at which they price their product, the 'price point', is critical to the success of their strategy.

However, these private equity owned businesses create an ever changing situation in health and fitness provision, since the private equity investors seek exit strategies to cash in on their investment whilst others wait in the wings looking for a favourable price to buy into a business. Private Equity investors look for brands where the performance is below the total values of the assets. Holmes Place was an example of a company whose price was undervalued; it was taken from public ownership into private equity ownership in May 2003. The price paid was 25 pence per share, compared to the same share price in August 1999 peaking at 370 pence per share. In 2006 Holmes Place was sold by private equity owners to Virgin Active.

Private companies

There are a number of large companies owning a portfolio of businesses which include health club chains, companies such as the Alternative Hotel Group, who own both the De Vere hotels and therefore their health clubs, and Greens Health and Fitness Clubs. Another example is Virgin Active, which is owned by the Virgin Group.

Since mid-2007 David Lloyd Leisure has been sold by stock-listed Whitbread to the private company London and Regional.

The private sector can be understood further by analysing the features and differences of single-site operators compared with multi-club operators.

Multi-club operators compared to single-site operators

The private health and fitness sector is clearly divided into independent single-site operators and multi-club operators, the latter generally being the more successful business model based on volume of members attracted to these facilities, average membership fees and income generation.

Multi-club operators

46 of all UK private clubs are run by multi-club operators. Their facilities tend to be larger and more diverse, with higher membership attraction, average total

membership numbers being 50 per cent higher than the UK market average. Average membership at multi-club operator sites is 2,100. Membership growth from 2005 to 2006 showed a 1 per cent increase.

Independent single-site operators

In 2006, 54 per cent of all private health clubs were owned by independent single-site operators. Recent trends suggest that the market is getting tougher for small independent operators. The largest number of club closures occurs in this segment of the market.

Although the small independent operators run just over half of the UK private health and fitness clubs they only account for 31 per cent of the total fitness members in the UK and only earn 25 per cent of the total market value. Their club facilities and membership bases tend to be smaller; this is reflected in the fact that less than one-third of all health and fitness employees work for independent private clubs.

Public sector management models

Whereas the main distinction in private sector provision is in the types of owner-ship, the public sector is characterised by differences in the way facilities are run, i.e. different management models. The public sector provision of health and fitness is delivered through local authority owned leisure centres, which are operated under a number of different management models, namely:

Direct service organisations – the local authority in-house management	46%
Charitable trusts (e.g. Greenwich Leisure)	19%
Privately owned leisure management contractors (e.g. DC Leisure)	15%
Education (linked to schools or universities)	15%
Other	5%

Of the 4000+ UK public Leisure centres 53 per cent are on their own stand-alone site and 47 per cent are based at an educational establishment such as a secondary school, university or higher education site and open to the public for part of the normal opening times. Two-thirds of all leisure centres have fitness facilities, with more leisure centres each year extending their service offering by converting existing space into new fitness facilities or building on new space for fitness provision.

The public sector fitness provision is also witnessing ongoing growth driven by:

- national government initiatives to counter public health issues such as obesity (see pp. 57–58);
- national and local government social inclusion policies;
- increased consumer demand.

Nearly 4.7 per cent of the population (nearly 2.5 million people) are members of public fitness facilities. With 'pay and play' usage offered in the public sector the true usage population penetration is probably significantly higher. Membership levels have been increasing steadily, and to keep pace the number of new fitness facilities opening in the public sector has also been increasing; for example 33 new public sector sites with gym facilities opened in 2005.

FINANCE

Trends in operating costs

It is revealing to consider the operating costs of facilities and here the information is supplied by Leisure Connection, which operates over 60 public leisure centres throughout the UK. The operating costs associated with a public leisure facility vary. The averages are presented in Table 4.2. The information contained in Table 4.2 is a brief overview of the trends over the past few years.

Utilities

The main area of expenditure which has seen varying trends is utilities, i.e. gas, electricity and water supplies. In the decade after the millennium there has been a dramatic upward trend in the costs of heating and powering facilities. At the time of writing total increases have seen utility costs almost double.

The utilities market remains volatile and this has led to a majority of leisure operators purchasing their utilities through a broker who attempts to optimise the prices paid.

Table 4.2 Leisure centre operating costs as a percentage of total costs

Expenditure area	Percentage of total costs
Salaries (monthly paid staff)	47%
Wages (casual staff paid weekly)	15%
Other staff costs	1%
Utilities	19%
Equipment & materials	5%
Repairs & maintenance	7%
Other premises costs	3%
Advertising & marketing	1%
Communications	1%
Capital costs	1%

Source: Leisure Connection (2006).

Staff costs

The trend for staff costs has continued to be upward and it remains the number one cost associated with leisure facility operation. The upward trend has continued with the main element being the continued increase in the minimum wage and the associated points of the Working Time Directive. Other issues affecting the increase are:

- health and safety legislation and guidance:
    - lifeguard numbers on poolside
    - lone working.
- competition for recruitment from other industries – the leisure industry has been widely regarded as one of the lowest paying sectors.
- training – to ensure that recruitment remains positive, training is now seen not only as a tool to improve performance, but also as an effective tool in recruitment.

Insurance

Although this cost area is variable, the general trend is an upward one. The main reason for this is the increase in premiums and the excess due to the 'claim culture' becoming more commonplace.

Although this area remains small in comparison to the total costs of operating the facilities, an upward trend has also been evident. The main reason for this is the increased competition within the leisure sector. More of the main players within the industry are now using more costly mediums to sell their services, with national newspapers, television and radio being used.

Repairs and maintenance

With the current leisure stock ageing, higher investment to repair and maintain facilities has become necessary.

Trends in income

Most health and fitness operations have stable cashflows since most of the revenue is generated on a monthly membership fee basis collected mainly through direct debit systems.

Pricing, as measured by membership fees, has been upheld despite increasing competitive pressure. In 2005, 34 per cent of UK clubs increased their membership fees, whilst only 9 per cent of clubs decreased theirs. However, the market is likely to be subject to further price pressure. 'No frills' strategies have worked in other consumer sectors such as the EasyJet brand and are starting to enter into the health and fitness market too. McFit from Germany are successfully employing this strategy.

Figure 4.3 illustrates the wide spread of UK adult monthly membership fees in 2006. Typically multi-club operators tend to have higher average membership fees than the independent operators, 35 per cent higher at the start of 2006.

Secondary income is generated from members and guests and is categorised by income from anything other than membership fees. Typically secondary income for operators is derived from sales of food, beverages, retail space, beauty products and personal training.

Smaller fitness-only type clubs would typically range between 5 and 10 per cent of revenues being generated from secondary spend. More commercial fitness operators could hope to earn over 10 per cent of membership fee levels in secondary spend primarily because of aggressive promotion of personal training services, whilst the large multi-facility/premium-end operators would earn

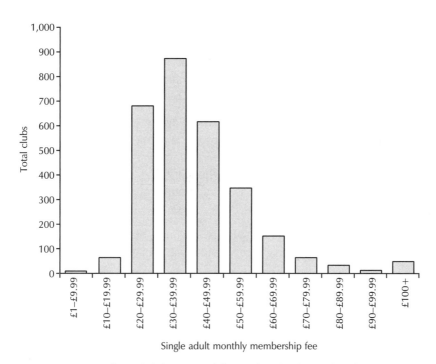

Figure 4.3 Number of clubs using different levels of membership fees (2006)

15–25 per cent extra revenue from secondary services, some exceptional operators even getting close to 30 per cent extra revenue from secondary spend. Revenues in these cases are being driven by sales of beauty products, personal training, retail clothing and shoe areas, special events and courses.

UNDERSTANDING AND WIDENING THE MEMBERSHIP BASE

As a relatively young industry the health and fitness sector is new to realising the importance of detailed analysis of their consumers. Profiling and segmenting membership bases are new management tools for a club's market positioning and are discussed in detail in Chapter 23.

Analysis of member data using profiling techniques can be further used to widen the membership base by identifying more potential members from the local area. The first step in this process is to establish the catchment area and then analyse the demographics of this catchment. By taking all members' postcodes and analysing these alongside the club's postcode, it is possible to work out the distance each member travels to get to the club as the crow flies and to establish drive times, taking into account roads and average speeds. This gives a core catchment area for a club, which the current membership base is drawn from. Plotting the member locations on a map illustrates where clusters of members are living and enables target marketing approaches to be planned.

An example of a member dot map is shown in Figure 4.4, which shows where existing members live and where any gaps in the market are. The gaps may be due to local demographics, i.e. the types of people who live in these areas do not have a high interest in health and fitness. If this is not the case and these areas do contain people who are potential members, they can be targeted in mailing campaigns.

Information on catchment demographics can then be drawn from the core catchment area. These highlight the residential, workforce, age and gender

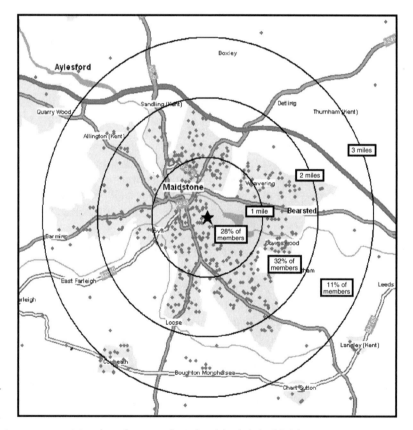

Figure 4.4 Member dot map for a health club in Maidstone

david minton and jenny stanley

details of the local area which indicate the growth opportunities for an operator. Using a geo-demographic system such as MOSAIC UK, the make-up of the local population can be reported on and illustrated by maps.

MOSAIC UK is Experian's classification system, classifying all UK consumers into 61 types and aggregating them into 11 groups. The classification has been devised under the direction of Professor Richard Webber, a leading authority on consumer segmentation. MOSAIC paints a rich picture of UK consumers in terms of their socio-demographics, lifestyles, culture and behaviour.

An example of a MOSAIC map is shown in Figure 4.5. This map highlights a 3-mile radius (using a circle) and a 15-minute drive-time (using the shaded area) around an example site just outside Oxford. Note how the drive-time presents a completely different pattern to the circle, based on the road network. Drive-times are common indicators of potential market used across the health and fitness industry, with 15–30-minute drive-time catchment areas often being used.

By comparing the profiles of existing members with catchment demographics, the current catchment penetration rates can be calculated. The current performance and market potential in the local area can then be assessed. Operators may employ companies like the Leisure Database Company to undertake their profiling and demographics analysis for them.

GOVERNMENT POLICY

In the preparation and aftermath of the Olympics in 2012 there will be considerable focus on getting the nation active. There is both a political desire and an economic necessity to reverse the increases in obesity and reduce the increasing strain this places on the nation's health. At the same time there is also a drive to get children active, swelling the base of participation and talent spotting future Olympic champions.

Participation in sport and higher levels of physical activity has already been accepted as an outcome for making communities healthier. The Chief Medical Officer's report published in April 2004 and the Public Health White Paper speak of the ideals of a more active and sporting nation.

Funding sport and driving increases in participation are at the core of many UK and national government policy priorities. DCMS, Health, Education and the Home Office (law and order/policing) all have funding programmes to boost general and specific target group participation levels.

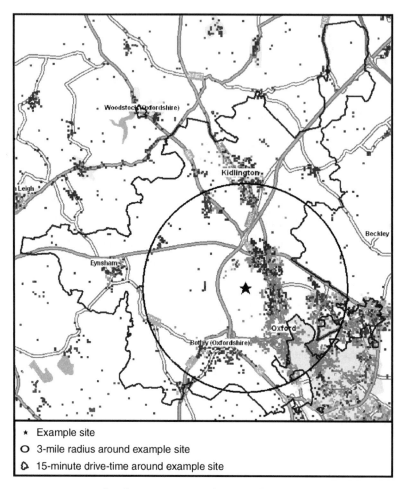

★ Example site
O 3-mile radius around example site
◊ 15-minute drive-time around example site

Figure 4.5 Example of MOSAIC map showing drive-time for a health club in Oxford

Local authorities are organising 'partnerships' with health providers, including the NHS to help tackle this long-term problem. Additionally, the comprehensive performance assessment (CPA) from 2005 to 2008 will assess and measure local authorities' contribution to improving the health of their communities. This is focusing local authorities and their partners on the health of their communities and the role that sports and recreation can play.

Central government has set targets for participation increases; an overall 1 per cent increase in participation year on year.

CONCLUSION

The trends and commercial realities of the health and fitness industry suggest an area of activity which is still maturing and changing. Every year, especially in the private sector, there are mergers, takeovers and new operational practices. No doubt the statistics and figures presented here will change but the aim has been to present an overview and, where trends are evident, to suggest what the future may hold.

The potential for the health and fitness industry has, arguably, yet to be fully realised, with just 11.3 per cent of the population currently members of all facilities across the public and private sector. The UK government's desire to increase activity levels in order to counter major public health issues such as obesity and diabetes presents an opportunity, if harnessed, for driving up the use of health and fitness facilities. The challenge for operators will be to find the best business models to deliver sustainable fitness facilities at reasonable cost to reach out to those not yet participating.

REFERENCES

Fitness Industry Association (FIA)/Leisure Database Company (2006) *State of the UK Fitness Industry Report 2006*, London: FIA.

Hillsdon, M., Panter, J., Foster, C. and Jones, A. (2007) 'Equitable access to exercise facilities', *American Journal of Preventive Medicine*, 32(6), pp. 506–508.

The Leisure Database Company (2006) *The National Audit of Fitness Consumers 2006*, London: The Leisure Database Company, available from: http://www.theleisuredatabase.com/news/news-archive/national-audit-of-fitness-consumers-2006.

Michie, R. (2007) 'Leisure Connection: Centre Operating Costs', letter to J. Stanley, 16 February (personal communication).

CHAPTER 5

WHY DOES GOVERNMENT CARE?
The benefits of sport and physical activity[1]

Department for Culture, Media and Sport and the Strategy Unit

INTRODUCTION

Why should government invest in sport and physical activity? Because they have a major part to play in promoting health and, as part of a basket of measures, can contribute to improved educational outcomes, reduced crime and greater social inclusion.

BENEFITS OF SPORT AND PHYSICAL ACTIVITY: SUMMARY

There is a widely held belief that sport can confer a broad range of economic and social benefits on individuals, communities, and the nation as a whole (Collins *et al*. 1999). As the (then) English Sports Council claimed in its strategy document, *England, the Sporting Nation* (1997): 'the benefits of sport are well rehearsed – national identity and prestige, community development, personal challenge, as well as economic and health benefits. Sport is a central element in the English way of life.'

We consider three ways of engaging in sport and physical activity:

- playing sport and being active recreationally;
- international success;
- hosting events.

In this report we examine the benefits arising from sport and physical activity.

---

[1] Edited from Department of Culture, Media and Sport/Strategy Unit (2002) 'Why do we care: benefits and the role for Government', *Game Plan: A Strategy for Delivering Government's Sport and Physical Activity Objectives*, pp. 42–78, London: Strategy Unit.

Many participants in the sporting world refer to the concept of:

- sport for good – referring to the use of sport to achieve greater social object-ives; and
- sport for sport – referring to participation in sport as an end in itself.

However, as set out in Box 5.1, difficulties in measuring benefits and impacts restrict the quality and quantity of evidence available.

BOX 5.1: DIFFICULTIES IN MEASURING NET BENEFITS OF SPORT

- *Sporting inputs*: it is difficult to obtain a meaningful measure of 'sporting input' which is consistent across all outputs (e.g. the sporting participation input which is relevant to health outcomes is potentially very different to that which is relevant to crime outcomes).
- *Definitions*: there are complex issues of definition and measure-ment: the desired outcomes are often qualitative and rather vague, e.g. better social cohesion, increased national pride.
- *Timing*: many of the impacts of participation are long term, whereas many projects are short term and monitoring does not continue beyond the immediate period of the project.
- *Monitoring and evaluation*: there is a lack of systematic monitoring and evaluation of the presumed outcomes of sports-based projects, with often limited local evaluation expertise and funding.
- *Outcome interdependencies*: There are significant interdependencies between the various benefits: many of the proposed 'final outcomes' (e.g. reduced crime, increased quality of life) are derived from inter-mediate factors like increased self-esteem, increased stake in social relations, etc.

There are a range of possible beneficial outcomes from sport and physical activity:

- personal satisfaction and better social life;
- improved health;
- improved educational outcomes;
- crime reduction;

- social inclusion;
- enhancing the environment.

However, some benefits are easier to achieve than others and sport can also have bad outcomes (e.g. hooliganism).

We conclude in this report that overall:

- the health benefits from physical activity are the most strongly supported by the evidence that is currently available, and the most likely to achieve good outcomes for government;
- there are indications of links between sport and physical activity provision and wider educational benefits;
- some practitioners also report positive results from schemes that use sport to help to reduce crime and social exclusion.

However, systematic evidence is lacking here and we must improve our understanding of the linkages if policy is to be fully effective. We discuss these findings in the six sections that follow.

1. Personal satisfaction and a better social life

Sport provides an opportunity for individuals to express their physicality, and can be a source of personal satisfaction. Pleasure from sport as a leisure activity is derived as a complex mix of physical and psychological benefits: 'They concentrate their attention on a limited stimulus field, forget personal problems, lose their sense of time and of themselves, feel competent and in control, and have a sense of harmony and union with their surroundings' (Csikszentmihalyi, 1975).

In many cases, sport can be the means to providing an individual with a wider social circle.

2. Health

A range of international medical research evidence shows that regular physical activity can yield a number of physiological benefits in adults (see WHO, 2002; Department of Health and Human Services, 1996) (see Box 5.2).

BOX 5.2: PHYSICAL HEALTH BENEFITS OF PHYSICAL ACTIVITY FOR ADULTS

International medical research evidence highlights that regular moderate activity yields physiological benefits in terms of reduced risk of:

- obesity (physical activity helps prevent the development of obesity by ensuring an adequate energy balance);
- cardiovascular diseases, development of high blood pressure and blood pressure for people with hypertension;
- some forms of cancers;
- non-insulin-dependent diabetes mellitus;
- strokes;
- osteoarthritis, as regular physical activity is necessary for maintaining normal muscle strength, joint structure and joint function;
- osteoporosis, as weight-bearing activity is essential for normal skeletal development during childhood, adolescence and for older women.

Research has also found a consistent link between exercise and anxiety reduction; and protection against the development of depression.

For children and adolescents in particular, regular exercise can be an important health maintenance strategy, both now and for the future, helping to prevent obesity and its associated problems. Overweight children are at increased risk of many health problems, including hypertension, hyperlipidemia, type-2 diabetes, growth hormone dysregulation, and respiratory and orthopaedic problems. Further, obesity in adolescence is independently associated with chronic diseases that develop in adulthood.

This is an increasing problem, as Figure 5.1 shows. In 1980, 8 per cent of women and 6 per cent of men were classified as obese in England. In 1998, this had almost trebled to 21 per cent of women and 17 per cent of men (Department of Health Joint Surveys Unit, 1999). There is no sign that this upward trend is moderating: 'the main reason for the rising prevalence [of obesity] is a combination of less active lifestyles and changes in eating patterns' (National Audit Office, 2001).

With these trends in mind, we developed a simple model to estimate the costs of physical inactivity to England. It considered three types of cost:

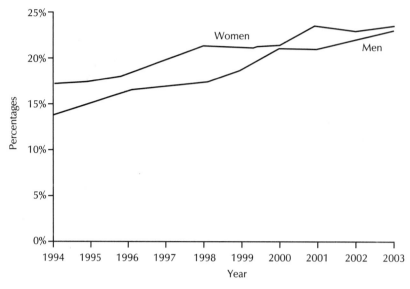

Figure 5.1 Obesity prevalence among adults by sex in the UK

Source: Prescot-Clarke and Primatesta/The Future Foundation

- *Costs to the NHS*: we assessed the contribution of physical inactivity to the costs associated with angina pectoris, myocardial infarction, stroke, colon cancer, type-2 diabetes, hypertension and osteoarthritis.
- *Costs from days off work*: we assessed the contribution of physical inactivity to days off work associated with the diseases above. We then applied an average £75/day income as a measure of lost productivity.
- *Costs of premature death*: there are several ways this calculation might be made. We chose to adopt an earnings lost approach for working age people dying prematurely of causes attributable to physical inactivity.

We considered both the total cost of inactivity and the annual savings from a 10 per cent reduction in inactivity. Figure 5.2 shows that the total cost to England of physical inactivity, according to this basic and conservative model, is in the order of £2 billion a year. This figure comprises indirect costs of about 10,000 working days lost and 54,000 lives lost prematurely (approximately 150/day).

Using this model we also calculated a 10 per cent increase in adult activity would benefit England by around £500 million per annum (6,000 lives/day).

This is a conservative estimate because it assumes relatively low levels of inactivity and a narrow range of diseases:

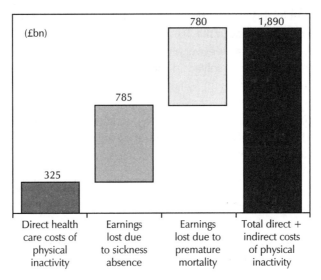

Figure 5.2 Total cost of physical inactivity to England per annum

Source: Strategy Unit analysis.

- *Physical inactivity estimates*: we based our estimates on people doing up to three occasions of moderate or vigorous activity in the last four weeks.
- *Narrow disease range*: no consideration is taken of therapeutic, psychological or secondary preventative effects. Adding depression and back pain attributable to physical inactivity could add 75 per cent to the direct health care costs and approximately 400 per cent to the cost of absence from work.

The costs may therefore be considerably higher. Assuming higher levels of physical inactivity and a wider range of diseases, as described above, a total cost of £8.2 billion (£1.7 billion NHS, £5.4 billion work absence and £1 billion early mortality) can be calculated. This comprises about 5 per cent of the NHS budget.

However, set against this are possible negative impacts of sport and physical activity on health. A national survey conducted in 1991 (Nicholl *et al.*, 1993) found that a large proportion of injury incidents occurred in young men playing vigorous sports, and that most of these cases were new (as opposed to recurrent) injuries:

- Most injury incidents (70 per cent) involve men, with almost half of these (48 per cent) occurring in the 16–25 age group.
- Soccer was responsible for over a quarter (29 per cent) of the incidents, and no other activity was involved in more than 10 per cent of the incidents, although rugby accounts for by far the highest injury rate.

The overall costs of sports injuries were estimated conservatively at up to £996m in 1989/90. This appears to be significant and cannot be ignored. However, it should not deter government from promoting sport and physical activity for health because:

- as current work in schools and improved coaching and refereeing start to have an impact, injury rates should reduce due to improved skill; and
- for those over 45, the balance between health costs saved due to ill health and costs incurred due to sporting injuries is different.

For completeness, another cost associated with increased physical activity which needs accounting for is the increased pension burden on the state from longer-lived pensioners.

The major impact that physical activity has on health is recognised in a number of other countries. Australia, the USA, Canada and New Zealand, amongst others, are currently developing physical activity strategies as part of an approach to sport or health promotion. Increasingly, such strategies focus on physical activity rather than sport in an effort to encourage individuals to have a more active lifestyle. Most recommend a minimum of 30 minutes of moderately intensive physical activity most days supplemented by more vigorous activity to achieve higher health benefits.

Importantly, the physical activity required to achieve the recommended daily target can take many different forms, including brisk walking and cycling, and need not consist of traditional competitive sporting activities.

For many aspects of health, the relationship between activity and health benefits is such that the greatest public health benefit is achieved from sedentary people doing a little more, rather than moderately active people pushing to meet ever higher targets. This is a critical consideration in terms of policy development and who to target.

Figure 5.3 shows the variety of physical activities that can deliver improved health outcomes. In this context, sport will be in a position to make a larger contribution to the health objective when it is seen across a range of organised

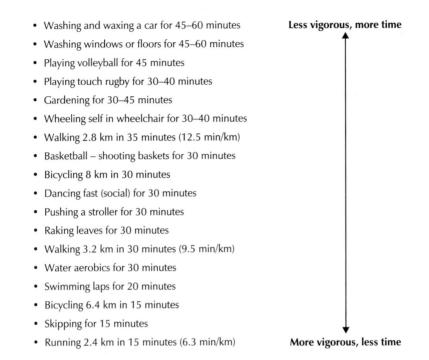

- Washing and waxing a car for 45–60 minutes
- Washing windows or floors for 45–60 minutes
- Playing volleyball for 45 minutes
- Playing touch rugby for 30–40 minutes
- Gardening for 30–45 minutes
- Wheeling self in wheelchair for 30–40 minutes
- Walking 2.8 km in 35 minutes (12.5 min/km)
- Basketball – shooting baskets for 30 minutes
- Bicycling 8 km in 30 minutes
- Dancing fast (social) for 30 minutes
- Pushing a stroller for 30 minutes
- Raking leaves for 30 minutes
- Walking 3.2 km in 30 minutes (9.5 min/km)
- Water aerobics for 30 minutes
- Swimming laps for 20 minutes
- Bicycling 6.4 km in 15 minutes
- Skipping for 15 minutes
- Running 2.4 km in 15 minutes (6.3 min/km)

Less vigorous, more time

More vigorous, less time

Figure 5.3 Alternative ways of meeting moderate physical activity guidelines

Source: New Zealand Health Strategy DHB Toolkit 1 (2001).

and informal activities in both indoor and outdoor settings. This is in contrast to the emphasis of a lot of local authority investment, which has tended to focus on more traditional sporting activities.

Whilst government's interest in increasing physical activity resides primarily in health benefits, many individuals' motivation for taking part in sport is simply because it is fun and provides a means of socialisation. Different sporting and physical activities will be 'fun' to different groups of people. Therefore the over-arching principle in increasing participation should be to offer a wide variety of accessible opportunities, ie. to recognise that different target groups may have different needs and wants, and wherever possible try to cater to them.

The focus on active recreation for health purposes links with a wider health agenda which is interested in any form of physical activity, e.g. walking to work. A key conclusion from a public health perspective, therefore, is that it is increased physical activity (potentially achieved through a range of activities), as much as participation in competitive team sports alone, which delivers improved health benefits to a wider range of individuals.

3. Education

Clearly schools and educational institutions in general are vital places for people to learn sport and physical activity skills. In this section we examine the effect of sport and physical activity on educational outcomes.

There is a range of sociological research (see Stevenson, 1975) looking at the links between sports participation and educational performance, focusing on mechanisms linking sport and educational outcomes, known as developmental theory. Through participation in sports and other extracurricular activities, a student is exposed to social relations such as with school personnel and other achievement-oriented peers who may generate and/or reinforce the individual's academic goals. Participation can also enhance the visibility and popularity of the student and thus have a positive influence on his/her educational motivations (Hanks, 1979). Activities like sports help the students to acquire skills and qualities like organisation, time management, discipline, self-esteem, motivation and inter-personal skills. These skills can lead to future educational success.

There is an absence of large-scale studies in the UK concerning the sports–education linkage. However, a range of case study evidence from the UK lends support to the developmental view of sport, and points to two main conclusions:

- sport may have direct or indirect impacts on cognitive, emotional and motivational development, which may lead to improved academic performance;
- sports can be used to attract under-achieving students to educational programmes.

Typical of such case studies are:

- An investigation by the Qualifications and Curriculum Authority (QCA) into the effectiveness of physical education and school sport. Preliminary results of a three-year investigation (started in 2000) indicate that schools with good records in physical education (PE) reported higher achievement across the curriculum. Schools with high participation in sports also tended to have lower truancy rates and better behaviour.
- The *Fit to Succeed Project* in Exeter, which encouraged students to take part in more regular physical activity and reported fewer behavioural problems. In addition government SAT test scores have been highest in children who say they exercise at least three times a week.

68

- The *Playing for Success* initiative, which uses the environment and medium of sport to raise pupils' educational skills and self-confidence (see Box 5.3).

BOX 5.3: THE PLAYING FOR SUCCESS INITIATIVE

- Leeds United Football Club's Playing for Success Centre provided ten-week programmes for under-achieving pupils from local primary and (some) secondary schools.
- Programmes were held after school hours and on Saturday mornings for pupils from inner-city areas. Just under a third of pupils attending the centres had special educational needs, and under-achievement and low self-esteem were considered major issues.
- Sessions were held at Leeds United's Elland Road football ground.
- Pre- and post-tests in mental arithmetic and reading indicated substantial improvements: there was a 29 per cent recorded increase in Key Stage 2 maths, and a 17.6 per cent increase in reading. At Key Stage 3 the increases were 14.6 per cent and 10.8 per cent in maths and reading, respectively.
- There is clearly a 'value added' in terms of attractiveness to children that results from using the brand of the football club and the location of the study centre at Elland Road. However, the evaluation by the National Foundation for Educational Research suggests that the reasons for the apparent success are largely educational. For example: having access to computers and the internet; high staff–student ratios; an informal, supportive atmosphere and encouragement from staff to allow pupils to develop independent study skills.

Source: Coalter *et al.* (2000).

The fourth of these examples seems to support the view offered by research from the USA that the positive impacts from such projects are more to do with personal attention and support than sport itself. This is an area that would benefit from further research in the UK to establish exactly what factors contribute to improved educational performance.

Another important rationale for investment in school sport is the hypothesis that those who are active in sport throughout their childhood – the 'sports literate' – are more likely to continue to participate throughout their lives. This has been supported by two comparative studies of (European) cross-country participation and a USA-based study.

In England the developmental view of sport is reinforced through the presence of physical education as a statutory requirement in the national curriculum from Key Stages 1 to 4 (ages 5 to 16). A recent paper reiterated the government's commitment that 'all children will be entitled to two hours of high quality PE and sport each week within and beyond the timetabled curriculum' (DfES 2001, p. 12).

Government has put in place a strategy for physical education, school sport and clubs links (PESSCL) to achieve this commitment; to contribute to other objectives such as improved health and socialisation; and to create continuous pathways for participation beyond school. Box 5.4 sets out two of the key elements of this strategy.

BOX 5.4: KEY ELEMENTS OF THE PHYSICAL EDUCATION, SCHOOL SPORT AND CLUBS LINK (PESSCL) STRATEGY

■ *Specialist Sports Colleges*: these are secondary schools with a special focus on physical education and sport, which are funded to provide the lead in innovative practice and to work with partner secondary and primary schools to share good practice and raise standards. The network of specialist sports colleges will be expanded to at least 400 schools. Evidence suggests that they are making progress in raising academic standards, and that they are improving whole-school standards as well as contributing to the development of sport in their neighbouring schools and local community. Ofsted evaluation reports are positive about the wider impact of Sports Colleges on young people's development.

■ *The School Sport Co-ordinators programme*: these are linked with the roll-out of specialist sports colleges, is creating a national infrastructure for the delivery of PE and school sport in England, focusing initially on urban and rural areas of disadvantage. The programme will enhance: strategic planning; primary liaison; school to club links; the quality and quantity of opportunities for out of school hours activities; coaching and leadership; and whole-school improvement. It is a multi-agency initiative, being delivered by DCMS, DfES, Sport England, the Youth Sport Trust and National Lottery funding. By 2006 the number of school sport co-ordinators was set to rise to 2,400.

The success of the schools programme is based on the integration of these elements. Specialist sports colleges provide a 'hub' from which a partnership development manager works with school sports co-ordinators in secondary schools and link teachers in primary or special schools to develop sport and PE in its 'family' of schools.

Other elements of the school PE and sports strategy include:

- lottery investment to improve facilities;
- enhanced PE/sport professional development opportunities for teachers and others.

Overall, there is a range of evidence that supports using sport as part of an approach to improved educational outcomes in the broadest sense (i.e. including attendance, attitude and behaviour). However, such evidence highlights the difficulty of distinguishing between playing sport itself and other factors, such as personal attention, when identifying the key success factors of sport and educational initiatives. To obtain educational benefits, additional inputs such as one to one mentoring or intensive teacher support are required, which increase the cost and risk of failure of the intervention.

The case for physical literacy and the increased likelihood of maintaining participation after school is supported by a range of European and American studies.

There's a need for a 'whole-school' approach to the promotion of physical activity and for schools to encourage their staff and pupils to consider cycling and walking to and from school.

4. Crime reduction

Youth crime is a widespread problem. 25 per cent of males and 15 per cent of females aged 12–17 admitted committing at least one offence in the previous 12 months and approximately 50 per cent of these offenders committed persistent and/or serious offences (Home Office, 1999).

Displacement and therapeutic prevention are the two mechanisms suggested for sport having a positive effect on crime reduction:

- **displacement** – where individuals involved in sport are not available to commit crime;

- **therapeutic prevention** – where sports participation may lead to crime reduction through being:

  - an antidote to boredom (Roberts and Brodie, 1992). To the extent that crime is encouraged by boredom, sports participation might provide a socially acceptable source of excitement;
  - a way of enhancing self-esteem through physical fitness and achievement. Low self-esteem may increase the likelihood of an individual committing a crime. If sporting achievement enhances self-esteem it may reduce crime;
  - a way of improving cognitive skills. Sports participation may improve cognitive skills (e.g. self-discipline and empathy), which can lead to a reduction in the propensity towards criminal behaviour;
  - an alternative to participating in delinquent peer groups. The theory of differential association proposes that adolescents conform to the values and norms of particular social milieu, which may be dysfunctional. Sport offers an alternative social milieu; and
  - a creator of positive relationships with 'significant others' (Schafer, 1969). Sport links participants with a range of individuals (e.g. coaches and teachers) who may act as appropriate role models and espouse conventional values and conformist behaviour.

Evidence from the USA suggests sport and physical exercise, as one of a basket of measures, can have a positive effect on behaviour if it is played with an emphasis on:

- a philosophy of non-violence;
- respect for self and others;
- the importance of fitness and self-control;
- confidence in skills;
- a sense of responsibility.

(Coakley, 1997)

This suggests that simply playing sport is not enough to reduce criminal behaviour.

There are many sports-based schemes operating around the country which are designed to combat juvenile delinquency. Most are aimed at young males.

There is some case study evidence that such schemes can have an impact, as shown in Box 5.5.

BOX 5.5: EVALUATION OF CRIME REDUCTION PROGRAMMES

Positive Futures

This programme is aimed at 10–16-year-olds at risk. It aimed to reduce youth offending, drug use and increase regular participation in sport and physical activity; 24 schemes were operated throughout the country based on offering a sporting programme linked with education.

An evaluation of these 24 schemes concluded that:

- all involved felt that the schemes were valuable in the short term but were less sure about long-term benefits;
- it is difficult to differentiate between the benefits from these schemes and those from other schemes operating in the same areas;
- quantitative evidence showed a decrease in crime in all 24 areas; however, in many cases this evidence did not distinguish between crime reduction amongst young people on the programme and all young people in the local area;
- there was little evidence of the impact on drug use, mainly due to the difficulty in collecting such evidence;
- there was a significant improvement in sporting participation.

Summer Splash

- During summer 2000 and 2001 a number of areas ran Summer Splash schemes providing sport and arts activities for 13–17-year-olds from deprived estates. Evaluation of these schemes was undertaken in both years. Evaluation data from 2000 examined 6 schemes in detail (out of a total of 105) but could only comment on crime statistics in 3 due to a lack of data. Of these 3, 1 experienced a fall in crime, 1 showed no significant change and 1 recorded an increase in crime.
- The 2001 evaluation indicated that crime rates dropped significantly across the board (for example an average 20 per cent reduction in criminal damage) but details were not available to examine the pattern, or causes, of such reductions.

The evaluations in Box 5.5 highlight a number of problems with undertaking such reviews:

- *Establishing a causal relationship*: this is difficult when the intervention is only one of a range of interventions being used at any one time. This difficulty is confirmed by a 1996 Home Office review, which concluded that 'it is difficult to argue that such activities have in themselves a generalisable influence on criminality' (Utting, 1996).
- *Ongoing monitoring*: without adequate monitoring, the nature of the longer-term impacts of programmes is hard to assess.
- *Value for money*: measuring the achievement of value for money is difficult. There is no comparison of the relative cost/benefits of different programmes.

Given the above difficulties, it is unsurprising that the impact of the sporting component of crime reduction programmes has seldom been isolated and measured. There is still, however, a widely held view that sport can have value as part of a package of measures to tackle crime. For example, Sport England states that:

> It would be naïve to think, and unrealistic to claim, that sport alone can reduce the levels of youth crime in society . . . Research evidence to support the effectiveness of sport in reducing criminality among young people is limited by a lack of high-quality systematic evaluation . . . [However,] there is growing experiential evidence that sport can play an influential role. Indirectly sport can have an impact by providing challenge and adventure, and by giving meaning and a sense of purpose to young people's lives where previously there was a vacuum.
>
> (Sport England, 1999, pp. 17/19)

It appears that, like education, playing sport will not lead to a permanent reduction in crime by itself. Successful programmes require a variety of other support mechanisms to be in place.

5. Social inclusion

Broader benefits may accrue when sport is used for community development, for example helping to develop self-esteem and transferable skills. This is particularly beneficial for those who are ordinarily more likely to be excluded from community activities through poverty, disability or ethnicity.

Using sport to promote social inclusion can also help in developing personal skills and enlarging individuals' social networks. Involvement in sport can help to develop other personal attributes such as increased confidence, which can be used beneficially in other areas. (See Long and Sanderson, 1998.)

The issues that communities face can be multi-dimensional and complex. Addressing these issues requires a holistic approach which entails working across traditional departmental and organisational boundaries.

Sport may be able to play an important part in this 'multi-agency' approach to the community, particularly in local authority projects (see Box 5.6). Typically such projects focus on deprived or marginalised groups.

However, it is clear that some competitive sports which have strong identities can lead to social divisions, through religious, geographic or other social rivalries. An example of this is violence arising from inter-club rivalry between certain football club fan groups.

Overall, sport may play a part in achieving social cohesion. But, like education and crime, social cohesion benefits may be derived as much from paying increased attention to previously marginalised groups and helping them with a range of life skills, rather than the use of sport in itself.

BOX 5.6: USING SPORT TO HELP ACHIEVE SOCIAL INCLUSION

The Aneurin Bevan Lodge Children's Home

Run by Kingston-upon-Hull Social Services Department, this was established with the aim of returning to the local community children in care, who were originally from Hull but had been placed out of the area. A wide range of supervised sporting activities was provided, including rock climbing, ice skating, canoeing and horse riding. In the evaluation of the project, the children's home manager concluded: 'It is clear to those involved that this project has had positive outcomes in helping to develop [the young people's] confidence, awareness, self-esteem, trust . . . in a positive way. The recommendation from AB Lodge would be to extend the project with a long-term view to . . . expanding it to encompass other children's homes'.

The Somerset Rural Youth project

This was a partnership project involving a wide range of agencies, including Somerset County Council, Somerset Youth Partnership, the

why does government care?

Community Council for Somerset, the five district councils, the six further education colleges and the (then) Somerset Training and Education Council. The project aimed to reduce the deprivation experienced by young people in the rural areas of Somerset. This was tackled through a wide range of initiatives, including arts and sports projects, access to training and employment opportunities, and involving young people actively in their local communities. Some successful sports projects involved:

- including young people in the planning and development of tracks for mountain biking;
- organising a 'network of contacts' for young people interested in playing football;
- training young people to be effective volunteers in delivering children's play/sporting opportunities leading to 'Junior Sports Leaders Awards'.

6. The environment

Physical infrastructure is an important aspect of community regeneration (Forrest and Kearns, 1999). Through the Lottery and other funding sources, there has been a significant investment in new sports facilities in the UK. Amenities provide the social focal points of the community, and are especially important to those with the least resources and least mobility (e.g. no access to cars) in a neighbourhood. The physical infrastructure also extends to safe access to walking and cycling routes, which offer recreational opportunities and link communities with shops, workplaces and services.

Therefore, the maintenance of otherwise under-used community facilities and wider recreation-related settings (parks, playing fields and walking/cycling routes) may have a significant role to play in the development of the quality of life in communities.

Sport England provides several examples of sports-related projects which have re-claimed derelict land and improved the physical and visual amenity of deprived areas. One is the Reczones project in Bolton that is reclaiming derelict land for playgrounds and general sporting areas.

In terms of impact on the natural environment, sport is purported to have both positive influences (e.g. creation of wildlife habitats on golf courses) and negative influences (e.g. noise pollution) on the natural environment. However, the evidence supporting these effects is largely anecdotal and must be treated with caution.

CONCLUSION

We have examined the various benefits attributed to sport and physical activity. Our conclusion is that much depends on how sporting activities are used and what additional factors are in place. For example, sport can be used as a tool in crime reduction, but expertise in working with 'at risk' youth is the key factor in ensuring the desired outcome.

However, the outstanding message is that the benefits of physical activity on health are clear, well evidenced and widely accepted. Physical activity itself produces these health benefits without additional inputs, whereas for other areas such as education and crime reduction, sport can best be used as part of a package of measures to achieve success.

Therefore, government would most benefit from focusing on increasing levels of physical activity across the population to improve health. In addition, sport and physical activity in schools should remain a priority to improve health and physical literacy and engender lifelong participation.

There is a pressing need to improve our understanding of the links between sport and physical activity, and other policy goals such as crime reduction and combating social exclusion. The evidence base needs to be strengthened to enable policy makers to construct and target effective interventions.

REFERENCES

Coakley, J. (1997) *Sport in Society: Issues and Controversies*, Boston, MA: McGraw-Hill.

Csikszentmihalyi, M. (1975) *Beyond Boredom and Anxiety*, San Francisco: Jossey-Bass.

Department of Health and Human Services (1996) *Physical Activity and Health: A Report of the Surgeon Centers for Disease Control and Prevention*, Washington, DC: Department of Health and Human Services.

Department of Health Joint Surveys Unit (1999), *Health Survey for England*, London: The Stationery Office.

DfES (2001) *Schools: Achieving Success White Paper*, London: DfES.

Forrest, R. and Kearns, A. (1999) *Joined up Places? Social Cohesion and Neighbourhood Regeneration*, London: YPS for Joseph Rowntree Foundation.

Hanks, M. (1979) 'Race, sexual status and athletics in the process of education research', *Social Science Quarterly*, 60, pp. 482–495.

Home Office (1999) *Aspects of Crime: Young Offenders*, London: Home Office.

Long, J. and Sanderson, I. (1998) 'Social benefits of sport: where's the proof?', *Sport in the City: Conference Proceedings*, vol. 2, pp. 295–324, Sheffield, 2–4 July.

National Audit Office (2001) *Tackling Obesity in England*, London: The Stationery Office.

Nicholl, J. *et al.* (1993) *Injury in Sport and Exercise*, London: Sports Council.

Roberts, K. and Brodie, D. A. (1992) *Inner-city Sport: Who Plays and What Are the Benefits?*, Edinburgh: Sportscotland.

Schafer, W. (1969) 'Some social sources and consequences of inter-scholastic athletics: the case of participation and delinquency', *International Review of Sports Sociology*, 4, pp. 63–81.

Stevenson, C. L. (1975) 'Socialization effects of participation in sport: a critical review of the research', *Research Quarterly*, 46, pp. 287–301.

Utting, D. (1996) *Reducing Criminality among Young People: A Sample of Relevant Programmes in the United Kingdom*, London: Home Office.

WHO (2002) 'WHO World Health Day', available from: http://www.who.int/world-health-day/brochure.en.pdf.

CHAPTER 6

PATHWAYS TO SUCCESS

A model for talent development[1]

Geoff Cooke

In the past, I have bemoaned the lack of a co-ordinated system for maximising the potential of thousands of sportspeople throughout the UK. We are arguably the greatest country in the world when it comes to providing participation opportunities in sport across a broad range of ability levels – but in the Atlanta Olympics, Great Britain languished in 36th place in the medals table. Popular theory insists that a broad base is a prerequisite for success but we are not always succeeding at the highest level even though we do have a broad base of participation.

Evidence from the rest of the world suggests that concentration on specific targets is more likely to produce success than competing on a broad front. Is one of the reasons for our success at the Paralympics that we are far ahead of other countries in our care, concern and focus on sportspeople with a disability? Has the concept of *Sport for All* and our egalitarian physical education philosophy in the able-bodied sector actively worked against the production of winners on the world stage? I am inclined to answer Yes to each of these questions.

PYRAMID TOO SIMPLISTIC

The sport development continuum based on foundation, participation, performance and excellence (FPPE) has become widely accepted throughout the UK in recent years. It is usually illustrated graphically in the form of a pyramid (see Figure 6.1). As appreciation and understanding of the sport development process has improved, this model has become too simplistic. Individual development in sport does not flow smoothly from a broad base to a pinnacle of excellence as suggested by the pyramid model.

---

[1] Edited from Cooke, G. (1997) 'Pathways to success: a new model for talent development', *Supercoach*, Vol. 8, 5, 1997, pp. 10–11, The National Coaching Foundation.

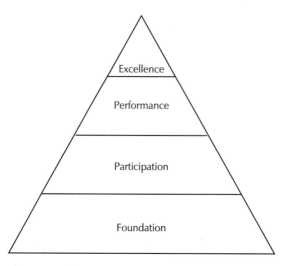

Figure 6.1 The Pyramid Sport Development Continuum

The FPPE sequence is more appropriate to an age-related continuum, more closely aligned to the physical education process than it is to the reality of most adult participation in sport.

THE HOUSE OF SPORT MODEL

The House of Sport Model that I propose (see Figure 6.2) is a more realistic way of depicting the sport development process.

Foundation

A foundation of basic movement literacy is usually gained in the primary and early secondary years at school through the physical education curriculum. For some people this will be a deep foundation but for many youngsters today the foundation will be alarmingly shallow, particularly in view of the lack of specialist PE teachers in the primary sector.

Ground floor

This is the introduction to a sport as a beginner. For most people this is their way in to the sport development process. In the traditional major sports, this

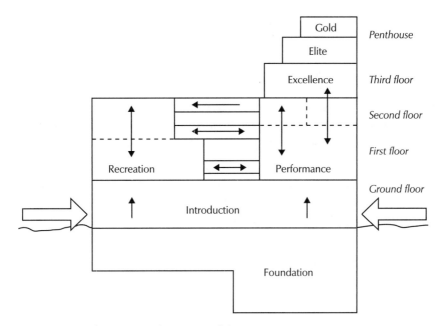

Figure 6.2 The House of Sport Model

introduction usually takes place at school. As the range of sports opportunities widens, increasingly people are being introduced to some sports for the first time in adult life.

First floor

Having been introduced to a sport, many people then become regular participants, though some will decide that sport is not for them and leave. The participants normally take one of two routes:

- *the recreation route*: casual and irregular participation (e.g. occasional games of badminton, squash, tennis)
- *the performance development route*: joining a well-organised club and striving to improve their personal performance and progress through the club's representative system. There is often a two-way flow across a bridge linking these different elements of sports development.

Second floor

The recreation route can develop into more regular and frequent involvement, which might include joining clubs for social participation in competition. The emphasis is still on recreation rather than on committed performance development. On the other side of the bridge, the committed performer has a chance to progress to a higher level of performance through competition, usually by selection for district, county or regional squads.

There can be a two-way flow at the lower levels on this floor but the gap between social participation and quality performance is wide. At the upper level, the flow is usually only one way (i.e. people who have experienced and enjoyed a high level of performance retiring from these demands and returning to sport for recreation).

Many sports performers who reach this level never manage to achieve true excellence and may spend many years at or near the ceiling of their development potential. They never quite make the breakthrough and eventually drop back down through the levels or retire sideways into sport for recreation.

Third floor

On the performance development side, the excellence level is best used to describe those performers who have reached a national representative standard. Here they will be competing or performing alongside the best of their peers in the UK and starting to match themselves against the best in the world. Most will never go beyond this level and many will only reach this level briefly, spending most of their time on the floor below.

There is no third level on the recreation side of the House of Sport.

The penthouse

This is the elite level of sports performance. This describes those who are ranked among the best in the world, measured by their performances and achievements in world competition. Even at this exalted level, only a few are destined to be winners.

NO SHORTCUT TO SUCCESS

The challenge for everyone involved in sports development is clear. How do we help more people progress on the performance side of the House of Sport and reach the elite level? Increasingly the role of the coach is seen to be central in this process, and although this is an encouraging trend, there are other critical factors.

Paramount among these is the attitude and commitment of the performers. They must want to win and be prepared to commit themselves totally to the task, if necessary changing their lifestyles to achieve their objectives.

There are no shortcuts to success. People like the rowers Steve Redgrave and Matthew Pinsent were winners because they had an overwhelming desire to be the best. I do not doubt there are many other performers and coaches with the necessary desire and commitment to produce success in British sport. I do doubt, however, the ability of many people in our sports organisations to identify this talent accurately and to create and manage an environment to nurture and fulfil the potential that exists.

There is still a general lack of understanding by many sports administrators about the amount of quality time needed by performers and coaches working together if they are to prepare adequately to compete against the best in the world.

ACHIEVING CONSISTENT SUCCESS

One of the key messages from Atlanta was the need for full-time athletes and full-time coaches. If we are to have any chance of success in the future, Britain must stop making a religion of volunteerism and start applauding professionalism. This is not to denigrate the invaluable work done by the thousands of volunteers who underpin our sports organisations. In 1995 there were 1.5 million volunteers working for British sport, 80 per cent of them in sports clubs. They will always have an important role but they should be seen as a supporting workforce, not primary deliverers of essential services.

With the National Lottery, shortage of money should never again be a problem but we must ensure that this wealth is applied effectively. That is why we need well-structured National Institutes of Sport (see p. 37) to lead and direct performance planning in a co-ordinated manner. That is why we must think beyond the development of facilities and turn our attention urgently to the delivery of services and human support needed by our top level performers.

PULLING TOGETHER

I hope that the UK and National Sports Councils are able to provide the strong leadership and direction that our sports organisations need. I hope that our sports organisations will work together instead of sometimes pulling in different directions.

I hope the government will facilitate the process that allows the strategic direction of finance to where it is most needed, instead of strangling us in needless bureaucracy.

CHAPTER 7

AN OVERVIEW OF SPORTS PARTICIPATION SURVEY RESULTS[1]

Mike Collins

This chapter examines the 2002 General Household Survey results and asks whether public investment is having any effect on participation levels.

The government's omnibus survey, the General Household Survey (GHS) has included a few questions on sport since 1977, but the questions only settled down to enable strict comparisons after 1987, and trends were able to be measured through results in 1990, 1993 and 1996. Basically these showed very minor increases in participation, with:

- a slow closing of the gender gap that had been evident, probably more due to the popular secular trend for women to take up keep fit and aquarobics rather than anything the state did (see Table 7.1), though equally policies in the 1990s have helped a little;
- a small increase in older people taking part in sport (Table 7.2) though nowhere near to the extent that happens in other parts of Europe like Scandinavia or Flanders (UK Sport *et al.*, 1999);
- a major gap between the high participant professional and managerial social groups AB and the D/E semi and unskilled groups – ironically, a gap even

Table 7.1 Participation by gender, once a month or more often, excluding walking

%	1987	1990	1993	1996	2002	1996–2002 % change
Male	57	58	57	54	50	−4
Female	34	39	39	38	37	−1
Total	*45*	*48*	*47*	*46*	*43*	*−3*

[1] Edited from Collins, M. (2004) 'Sports participation in decline?', *Recreation*, November 2004, pp. 26–28, The Institute for Sport and Recreation Management.

Table 7.2 Participation by age, once a month or more often, excluding walking

% Age	1987	1990	1993	1996	2002	1996–2002 % change
16–19	80	82	81	78	72	−6
20–24	69	72	71	70	61	−9
25–29	63	67	65	63	61	−2
30–44	56	59	58	57	54	−3
45–59	35	42	43	40	39	−4
60–69	23	28	28	30	27	−3
70 & over	10	12	16	13	14	+1
Total	*45*	*48*	*47*	*46*	*43*	*−4*

Table 7.3 Participation by social class, once a month or more often, excluding walking

Socio-economic group	1996 %	Socio-economic class of household head	2002 %
		Large empl/higher management	59
Professionals	63	Higher professional	59
Employers/managers	52	Lower management and professional	51
Intermed/junior non-man	47	Intermediate	43
		Small employer/own account	43
Skilled management self-employed		Lower supervisory/technical	38
non-professionals	45	Semi-routine	31
Semi-skilled/personal service	37	Routine	30
Unskilled manual	23	Never work/unemployed	26
Total	*46*	*Total*	*43*

wider in use of the public temples to sport, sports centres and swimming pools, after price increases above inflation during the period of compulsory competitive tendering (CCT) (Collins, 2003a, and see Table 7.3); and

■ very tiny increases in participation via clubs (see tables) still at a level below several European countries (Collins, 2003a).

So, as Nick Rowe, head of research for Sport England, summarised with restraint: 'The evidence we have points to stagnation in the levels of participation in sport during the 1990s ... [and] evidence on the social class of participants demonstrates that participation is significantly skewed towards the professional groups, and that these social inequalities have not become any less significant over recent years' (Rowe *et al.* 2004, 5, pp. 6).

After a gap of six years, the GHS questions were repeated in 2002. Direct comparisons are difficult because the social categorisation has changed to a scheme that better reflects a service economy. It will be much more helpful as trends develop, but limits immediate interpretation. The questions asked in the survey are limited by space and the resources of the Office of National Statistics, which manages the survey; national sports councils interpret the data for their own nation, with Sport England publishing some UK data. The questions are about participation in 42 sports played in two time periods in the four weeks before the interview and the past year, plus walking, with the option of including others sports in an open box. They also refer to participation as a 'member' of a sports, social or fitness club. Analysis for all questions can be carried out by a few population variables such as age, gender and ethnicity.

1996–2002 TRENDS

The 2002 results showed one striking overall finding: that overall regular participation (once or more in the past month) has decreased by 3 per cent since 1996 from 46 per cent to 43 per cent, excluding walking. For some, this has come as an unforeseen blow. For me, it is not surprising – indeed I predicted that it was likely (Collins, 2003b).

There are several reasons why this might be:

- We spend a modest sum on sport in total, even compared to many European countries.
- This is spread over a larger number of sports than most countries, other than in USA, Russia, Germany and France.
- We are not spending enough to keep our 1970s public infrastructure in good order – Sport England recently updated its 1995 estimates and showed that £110m a year would be needed just to keep existing facilities legal and functioning. To update them would probably double this figure, and together, by my reckoning, Lottery, Exchequer, local authority and private finance initiative (PFI) spending raise a bit more than half of this. So staying level is a real problem, let alone providing the large increases in capacity needed to support the more than doubling of physical activity that Department of Culture, Media and Sport (DCMS) and Sport England aspire to by 2020.

- Everyone says that it is getting more difficult to get voluntary labour, because the jobs are more demanding, involving more training and higher professional and ethical performance standards, and more people want to play longer rather than transferring into coaching, officiating and administration. Even in sport-mad Australia, data shows that while participation once a year went up from 26.5 per cent to 28.9 per cent in 1997–2001, volunteering went down by 9 per cent in the same period, from 11.5 per cent to 9.5 per cent (Cuskelly, 2004).
- The 'new money' from the Lottery and Department for Education and Skills (DfES) is focused on the small numbers of elite performers and school sports. Adults, who would gain the greatest health benefits, have been ignored by DCMS and Sport England in all but rhetorical terms; and the framework (Sport England, 2004b) says nothing to suggest that priorities are shifting or resources increasing.

Against this scenario, is the decline to be wondered at? So, let's look in more detail: how is this change distributed between men and women, younger and older, better and worse off, whites and minorities?

GENDER

Table 7.1 shows that the differential between men and women has continued to fall slowly, but more since 1996, because more men than women have ceased to participate.

AGE

Table 7.2 shows that participation has declined most among the young, the recent school- and college-leavers aged 16–24, traditionally the highest participants; this is hard evidence of reduced interest. It means that DCMS/DfES efforts in schools will, in the short term – even if successful – only make up recently lost ground. If this continues, some qualitative research will be vital to diagnose what is triggering this. It may be other, non-sporting activities like computer games. Interestingly, the tiny group of active septuagenarians increased a little!

SOCIO-ECONOMIC GROUPS

I have described this as the most intransigent of the inequalities in British sport. This is where the changes in classification make only rudimentary comparisons possible. But what is clear from Table 7.3 is that the professional and managerial groups, the bastions of high participation, and the skilled technical workers with good incomes and limited overtime, who had been the spearhead of increased participation in almost every form of out-of-home leisure in the 1980s and 1990s, showed a decrease similar to the total – and, indeed, greater than the lower status, lower paid workers. This is another indication of reduction at the core. Whether this is a result of overall price increases, or of work pressures in the UK's long-hours economy, is open to speculation.

ETHNIC GROUPS

Participation by ethnic minorities, with on average lower incomes, dipped in the 1990–1991 recession and has dipped more than participation by white people since 1996 (see Table 7.4). The gap with certain groups is marked – Indian 26 per cent, Pakistani and Bangladeshi 18 per cent, Black Caribbean 25 per cent, compared to the white majority.

Clearly, for whatever reasons, participation has faltered and, in faltering, has become more unequal rather than more inclusive in gender, class and ethnic terms.

INVOLVEMENT IN CLUBS, COMPETITION AND TUITION

Interestingly, in contrast to this gloomy picture, the data on the more committed participants shows a different scene. There is a marked gender advantage of men in club membership (covering sports, youth and social clubs) and competition,

Table 7.4 Participation by ethnic group, once a month or more, excluding walking

% once a month or more often	1990	1993	1996	2002	% change 1996–2002
White	48	48	46	44	−3
All minority groups	43	38	41	30	−9
Total	48	77	46	43	

Table 7.5 Participation by gender in clubs, competitions and tuition

% who	Male		Female	
	1996	*2002*	*1996*	*2002*
were members of a club in previous 4 weeks	41	44	25	32
competed in last 12 months	32	39	10	14
received tuition in last 12 months	19	30	27	45

but both genders showed a marked increase in the six-to-seven-year period. Those who had enjoyed some tuition from an instructor or a coach increased even more (Table 7.5). Whether these are the first fruits of the greater focus of policy and money on performance sport and more professional coaching is, again, a matter of speculation.

CONCLUSIONS

Coalter (2004) suggested that some trends that seem likely are:

- age becoming a smaller constraint on older people, more of whom will have greater sports 'literacy' from their youth; and
- participation being encouraged if/when more young people pass through higher education with its time and facilities coaching and ethos.

He suggested that, in order to encourage current non-participants (especially young women), there is a need to place greater emphasis on the process of engaging in sport and developing confidence rather than the outcome (winning/ losing) or how good someone is and to increase choice and lessen compulsion (Coalter, 2004, p. 82). 'New', individualistic sports are more attractive to some, for these reasons, than traditional and team games. This is a challenge to sports officers and their development teams and centre managers, whether in direct public provision, extended schools, trusts, contracted-out, voluntary or commercial services.

When the results were published, the then chief executive of Sport England, Roger Draper, stoutly defended the policies in its new Framework (Sport England, 2004). But the stark fact is that they sharpen a major challenge to national and local sports organisations even more. The UK spends much less per head on sport than many other developed countries; all the social marketing in the world cannot overcome a shortage of facilities and trained manpower, much of which has to be through the public purse to attract those older and poorer people who are needed in large numbers if the targets are to be tackled even to half measure. The easy markets have been tapped, and there are no cheap gains to be made from here on.

REFERENCES

Coalter, F. (2004) 'Future sports or future challenges to sport?', in *Driving up Participation: The Challenge for Sport*, London: Sport England.

Collins, M. F. (2003a) *Sport and Social Exclusion*, London: Routledge.

Collins, M. F. (2003b) 'Do we still believe in sport for all?' *Recreation* 62.1, pp. 32–35.

Collins, M. F. (ed.) (2004) *Participating and Performing*: *Sport in Higher Education*, London: Universities UK.

Cuskelly, G. (2004) 'Volunteer retention in community sport organisations', *European Sports Management Quarterly* 4, pp. 59–76.

Rowe, N., Adams, R. and Beasley, N. (2004) 'Driving up participation in sport: the social context, the trends, the prospects and the challenges', in *Driving up Participation: The Challenge for Sport*, London: Sport England.

Sport England (2004) *A Framework for Sport in England*, London: Sport England.

UK Sport et al. (1999) *Compass*: *Sports Participation in Europe*, London: UK Sport.

CHAPTER 8

SOCIAL TRENDS AND SPORTS PARTICIPATION OVER THE NEXT 20 YEARS[1]

Martin Rhys and Indra Sinka

INTRODUCTION

In 2003 a market research company called the Henley Centre was commissioned to investigate the principal trends in society that may have an impact on sports participation in the future. A group of key decision makers were asked to identify the most important issues for their own setting and the results were combined to produce the final shortlist that is outlined below.

This chapter reports nine key trends that 350 key people identified as being the most important for them in trying to develop sport in the future, along with a corresponding summary of what the challenge is for policy makers within each trend. These 'challenge' paragraphs provide a useful summary of the problem that it presents to those making decisions about where and how resources should be spent to get more people physically active. The chapter draws on two sources in particular throughout (Rowe, *et al.*, 2004 and Sport England, 2004).

A wide definition of sport agreed by the Council of Europe is adopted here:

> Sport means all forms of physical activity which, through casual participation, aim at expressing or improving physical fitness and mental well-being, forming social relationships or obtaining results in competition at all levels.
>
> (Council of Europe, 1993)

This definition of sport extends far beyond traditional team games to incorporate individual sports and fitness-related activities such as aerobics and certain dance

---

[1] This chapter is based on information contained in Sport England (2004) *The Framework for Sport in England*, London: Sport England; and Rowe, N., Adams, R., and Beasley, N. (2004) *Driving up Participation in Sport: The Social Context, the Trends, the Prospects and the Challenges*, London: Sport England.

activities, as well as recreational activities such as long walks and cycling. It extends from casual and informal participation to more serious organised club sport. This wide and inclusive definition of sport extends its relevance to the whole population and its value as a significant feature in the broader social agenda.

SOCIAL AND DEMOGRAPHIC FACTORS

Age

It is likely that the biggest influence on the numbers participating in sport will come from the demographic changes that will result in a population which is ageing steadily. By 2020, almost half of adults in the UK will be over 45 (Sport England, 2004). Traditionally older age groups have significantly lower participation rates than the young, and should these differences continue, with all other factors remaining constant, overall sports participation rates will be significantly affected (see Figure 8.1). However, though chronologically older, people are increasingly 'acting young'. Couple this with the higher disposable income of the current over 50s and it suggests a growing demand amongst this age group for sport and leisure-related activities. Sport must be able to respond to the

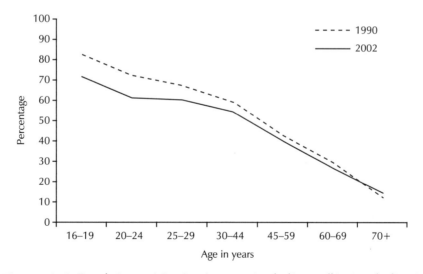

Figure 8.1 Trends in participation in sport (excluding walking) – decline in participation by age (comparing 1990–2002)

Source: Rowe and Moore (2004).

opportunities that this market brings by providing the right mix of activities and quality environments that appeal to this often discerning group.

Sport also needs to address the significant drop-off in participation post-16 (particularly for women) and in the early 30s (particularly for men). Figure 8.2 shows the projected numbers of participants in 2024 based on a continuation of the trends in sports participation seen between 1990 and 1996, taking into account the changes in population structure (Rowe *et al.*, 2004). Based on these assumptions, the number of young participants aged between 6 and 15 years will fall by 250,000 between 1996 and 2024 and the number aged 45 years and over will increase by 1.3 million. Overall, the participation rate will fall from 53 per cent of the population in 1996 to 46 per cent in 2024 (Rowe, *et al.*, 2004).

The challenge

The challenge is to encourage people to stay in sport as they get older, creating a culture of lifelong participation.

Time

The majority of people face time pressures. The reasons for this include working hours and the increasing diversity of family life. Although the average number of

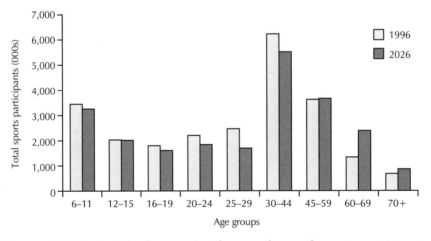

Figure 8.2 Projected changes in the numbers of sports participants (1996–2026), based on trends between 1990 and 1996

Source: Rowe *et al.* (2004).

working hours has stabilised since the 1990s the 'leisure society' (a term from the 1990s which foresaw an imminent increase in leisure time for all mainly due to technological advances) anticipated by many social commentators seems far from becoming a reality. The average weekly working hours in the UK increased from 42.3 in 1983 to 43.6 in 1999. The UK has some of the longest working hours in Europe – for example, the equivalent figure in Germany in 1999 was 40.9 hours, in Italy 38.5 hours and in Belgium 38.4 hours (see Figure 8.3). More people saying they feel exhausted is accompanying this increasing 'time squeeze'. In most surveys asking people why they do not participate in sport, 'I haven't got the time' emerges as a major reason (Rowe *et al.*, 2004). Sport needs to be able to adapt to these time pressures by becoming more flexible and easily accessible to fit into people's busy lifestyles. Trends suggest that pressures of time will continue to have a detrimental impact on the ability of sports organisations to increase participation.

The challenge

The challenge is to develop new ways of connecting sport with everyday life, alleviating time pressure by creating opportunities where people already spend their time – in the workplace, where people shop, alongside other community facilities.

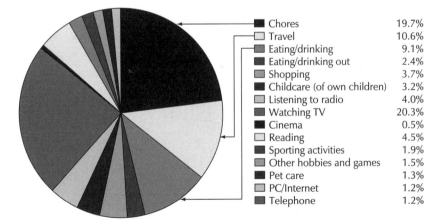

Figure 8.3 Hours per week spent on activities

Source: Office for National Statistics (2003), cited in Sport England (2004).

sports participation over the next 20 years

Health

Data from recent health surveys (see Figure 8.4) showed that the rate of being overweight (a body mass index (BMI) of 25–30 kg/m², calculated as weight in kg divided by height in m²) is similar for men (44 per cent) and women (35 per cent) in England, Scotland (43 per cent and 34 per cent) and Wales (42 per cent and 31 per cent). Sedentary lifestyles and inactivity are resulting in poor health, and increasing health care costs. Trends suggest that the situation is likely to get worse unless action is taken.

For an increasing number of consumers, 'health' no longer refers just to lack of illness. Well-being encompasses feelings about the mind, body and spirituality, environment and relationships. Many see exercise as a 'route to well-being' along with other related lifestyle changes. A 1999–2000 survey carried out by the Henley Centre showed that in England 34 per cent of people would like to change the amount of exercise they do; 25 per cent want to improve the way they look; and 37 per cent want to reduce their weight. This provides an opportunity for sport to promote and align itself to this shift in motivation and expectations (Rowe *et al.*, and Beasley, 2004).

The challenge

The challenge is to create a culture of physical activity that taps into health concerns and thereby engages large numbers of people and motivates them to get involved and stay involved.

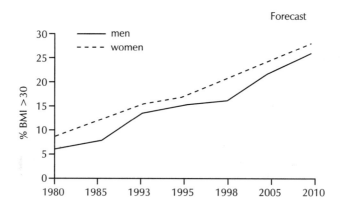

Figure 8.4 Trends in obesity amongst men and women

Source: National Audit Office (2001).

Ethnicity

In 2001 there were 6.4 million people from ethnic minority backgrounds in England, making up 13 per cent of the total population. In Wales the proportion was considerably smaller at 4 per cent. The 2001 census identifies some areas where 'ethnic minorities' are actually 'ethnic majorities', for example in Newham and Brent. Nevertheless, black and ethnic minorities participation rates are 6 per cent below the national average (Sport England, 1997).

The challenge

The challenge, in an increasingly multi-cultural population, is to make sport more sensitive to the barriers that impact on these groups and provide the types of activities that appeal to them within environments that are accessible and welcoming.

OTHER KEY TRENDS

Variations in access

Participation rates in sport display inequality across a range of indicators including those relating to gender, disability and socio-economic status (see Figure 8.5):

- women's participation rates are 13 per cent below those for men (Rowe and Moore, 2004);
- 38 per cent of people with a disability participate in sport, compared with 59 per cent of non-disabled adults (Sport England, 2002);
- people in the 'professional' social class group are three times more likely to participate in sport than those in the 'unskilled manual' group (Office for National Statistics, 1998).

The challenge

The challenge is to widen participation, cater for a diverse population by targeting under represented groups and thus address the inequalities that exist.

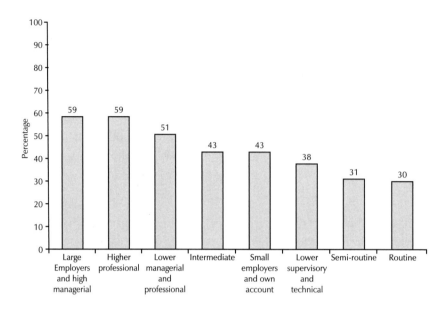

Figure 8.5 Socio-economic classification differences in participation, 2002 (adults 16+ participating on at least one occasion in the previous four weeks, Great Britain)

Source: Rowe and Moore (2004).

Education

Current commitments to create Specialist Sports Colleges in England and a network of School Sports Partnerships, together with the drive to ensure that 75 per cent of pupils aged 5–16 years have access to two hours' PE and school sport a week, will make a tremendous difference, creating the foundation stone for lifelong participation (Sport England, 2004).

In Wales there are no Specialist Colleges of any sort since current Welsh education policy is to ensure that public sector secondary schools are comprehensive and that all schools are firmly based in the community which they serve. However, whilst some schools have an excellent track record in making connections with their community, there is wide variation across the country. Schools can be a major contributor to alleviating time pressure on family life and in creating the bridge to participation after school, reducing the dropout with age.

Facilities in further and higher education can provide similar opportunities. More students are entering higher education than ever before – from 100,000 in the 1950s to 1.7 million in 2000. Research suggests that those who participate in higher education are more likely to participate in sport, both in student life and in adult life (Sport England, 2004).

The challenge

The challenge is to ensure that school facilities are used effectively both during the school day and beyond with appropriate community and club links. Extending current initiatives with primary schools will also help to strengthen sport and PE for children aged 7–11 years, a critical age for developing patterns for lifelong participation.

Volunteers

Sport relies heavily on its volunteers; 26 per cent of all volunteers are involved in sport, making it the single biggest contributor to the voluntary sector (Sport England, 2002). In the UK, some 1.5 million volunteers put an average of 125 hours per person a year into sport according to the Sports Council for Wales (1999). Motivations for getting involved vary, with some people volunteering primarily in order to support their preferred sport and some using sport to support community-based activities. However, there are suggestions that there are increasing burdens on volunteers relating to bureaucracy, concerns around litigation and time pressures from other areas of life (Sports Council for Wales, 1999). In addition, there are relatively few volunteers from ethnic minorities and among people with disabilities.

The challenge

The challenge is to improve the image of volunteering and sporting career structures for young people.

Investment

Expenditure on sport by local authorities has barely kept up with inflation since 1998. In addition, the public sector facilities stock is ageing, with a high pro-portion built in the 1970s (see Figure 8.6). Research commissioned by Sport England and published in 2003 confirms that, for example, £550 million is needed in England from 2003 to 2008 to keep the stock in working order (Davis

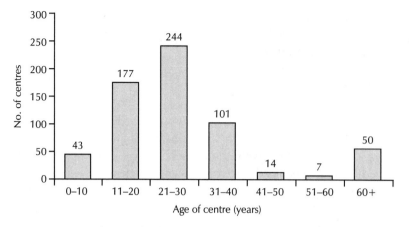

Figure 8.6 Age of sports facilities in England

Source: Davis Langdon Consultancy (2003).

Table 8.1 Stock of sports facilities in Wales at three points over the last 35 years

1972	1997	2007
11 sports halls	180 sports halls	200 sports halls
44 swimming pools	143 swimming pools	141 swimming pools
104 golf courses	182 golf courses	199 golf courses (at 184 locations)
86 squash courts	442 squash courts	377 squash courts (at 157 locations)
0 synthetic athletics tracks	14 synthetic athletics tracks	17 synthetic athletics tracks
0 indoor tennis centres	9 indoor tennis centres	9 indoor tennis centres
0 artificial grass pitches	72 artificial grass pitches	124 artificial grass pitches
0 indoor bowls centres	27 indoor bowls centres	25 indoor bowls centres
0 ice rinks	2 ice rinks	2 ice rinks

Source: Sports Council for Wales (2007).

Langdon Consultancy, 2003). Table 8.1, which shows facility developments in Wales over the last 35 years, gives an idea of the growth achieved and the maintenance task in hand. Furthermore, income for community sport from the National Lottery is, in general, in decline. This is due to how many people play the weekly game (these numbers have dropped off from when it was launched in 1994) and the way that large projects, such as London 2012, divert money away from grassroots sport.

The challenge

The challenge is for community or grassroots sport to make its voice heard among decision makers so that local funding of sport is sustained. Local facilities and coaches are needed to deliver many of the increases in participation hoped for in this chapter.

Family values

From 1971 to 1996 married couple households fell from 11.2 million to 10.2 million, and this number is predicted to continue to decline to 9.4 million by 2011. Single person households will increase from 30 per cent of total households to 33 per cent in 2011. More single person households suggests an increasing demand for out-of-home leisure, creating the potential to drive up sports participation (Rowe *et al.*, 2004). However, although family values are apparently in crisis, there is counter-evidence to suggest that 'family' is still the top goal for many people both emotionally and economically; 94 per cent of people regard their family as 'an important source of pride' (Rowe *et al.*, 2004).

More traffic on the roads, increasing levels of street crime (whether real or perceived) and high profile cases of child abuse are leading to increasing concerns about safety. Over 80 per cent of parents surveyed by MORI in 2000 said that 'children today get less exercise because parents are afraid to let them go out alone'. Unless these trends are reversed there will be fewer opportunities for spontaneous play and an increasing need for alternative environments if children are to remain active. This will place increasing demands on providers and will impact in particular on the voluntary sector, where, for example, individuals working with children will be required to have police checks and will be more accountable than ever for the health and safety of the children in their care (cited in Rowe *et al.*, 2004)

The challenge

The challenge is for sport to tap into this family market by providing more attractive, family-friendly environments which can provide children with the freedom to express themselves and develop their physical and social skills whilst giving parents the reassurance they need that their child is safe.

FACING UP TO THE CHALLENGE

We have already seen that sports participation rates have remained broadly unchanged over the last two decades or so and that sport has continued to be characterised by considerable social inequities. We have seen little change in the social landscape of sport, despite significant investment by local government over this period and continued efforts by government and the UK Sports Councils to increase and widen participation. The 1980s and 1990s saw the development of the recreation management profession, an increase in sports development officers, an expansion of local authority leisure departments, a number of national campaigns, a national junior sports development programme, improved support and training for volunteers and a number of coaching initiatives. Still, participation rates did not go up or inequalities become narrowed.

Even the significant boost in funding provided by the National Lottery in the second half of the 1990s does not appear to have made a significant difference to overall participation rates. These have remained stubbornly static and in some cases even declined (Rowe and Moore, 2004).

Any targets to increase and widen participation must be underpinned by a belief, backed up by a hard-nosed business assessment, that sport can deliver in the future what has not been delivered in the past. Such targets must also take into account the social trends discussed above, which at times are tending to drive participation rates down or at the very least pose challenges for sport to be provided in new ways that meet changing and increasingly demanding consumer expectations.

REFERENCES

Council of Europe (1993) *European Sports Charter*. Recommendation No. R (92) 13. London: Sports Council.

Davis Langdon Consultancy (2003) *Condition and Refurbishment of Public Sector Sports Facilities: Summary*, London: Sport England.

The Henley Centre (2003) *Strategic Framework for Community Sport in England. Meeting the Challenge of Game Plan: Emerging Insights on the Future of Participation in Sport in England*, London: Sport England.

National Audit Office (2001) *Tackling Obesity in England*, London: The Stationery Office.

Office for National Statistics (1998). *Living in Britain: Results from the 1996 General Household Survey*, London: The Stationery Office.

Office for National Statistics (2003) *UK 2000 Time Use Survey Technical Report*, London: The Stationery Office.

Rowe, N. and Moore, S. (2001) *Participation in Sport – Past Trends and Future Prospects*, London: UK Sport/Sport England.

Rowe, N. and Moore, S. (2004) *Participation in Sport – Results from the General Household Survey 2002, Research Briefing Note 2nd July 2004*, London: Sport England.

Rowe, N., Adams, R. and Beasley, N. (2004). *Driving up Participation in Sport: The Social Context, the Trends, the Prospects and the Challenges*, London: Sport England.

Sport England (1997) *National Survey of Sport and Ethnicity*, London: Sport England.

Sport England (2002) *Adults with a Disability and Sport National Survey*, London: Sport England.

Sport England (2003) *Sport Volunteering in England, 2002*, London: Sport England.

Sport England (2004) *The Framework for Sport in England*, London: Sport England.

Sports Council for Wales (1999) *Young People First: A Strategy for Welsh Sport*, Cardiff: Sports Council for Works.

Sports Council for Wales (2007) Internal analysis, personal communication with information officer, March 2007.

CHAPTER 9

MANAGING SPORT AND LEISURE SERVICES[1]

Leigh Robinson

Management is a formal process that occurs within organisations in order to direct and organise resources to meet stated objectives. Mullins regards management as:

- taking place within a structured organisational setting with prescribed roles;
- directed towards the attainment of aims and objectives;
- achieved through the efforts of other people;
- using systems and procedures.

(Mullins, 1996, p. 398)

This chapter introduces the functions of management in the sport and leisure sector. It describes appropriate management styles and considers the skills necessary for effective management. The chapter ends with a discussion of the issues surrounding 'power' and management.

INTRODUCTION

Understanding management and what managers do in organisations has been and remains the focus of intensive research. This is because managers have the ability to fundamentally affect the success of an organisation through their approach to staff, resources and customers. Consideration of the research suggests that there are five approaches to understanding the way that management operates. These are:

---

[1] Edited from Robinson, L. (2004) 'Managing public sport and leisure services', *Managing Public Sport and Leisure Services*, pp. 37–57, London: Routledge.

- *the classical approach*: this approach is based on the premise that there is core knowledge that managers should have in order to carry out their role, such as the ability to plan and organise;
- *the behavioural approach*: this suggests that individuals should be the focus of management, which should address individual needs and wants;
- *the management science approach*: this approach is concerned with rational solving of problems and is based on the premise that there is a 'right' way of doing things;
- *the systems approach*: this suggests that there is a system of management that is made up of a number of parts that all need to come together to achieve organisational objectives;
- *the contingency approach*: this is based on the assumption that there is no single way of managing, rather managers need to be flexible in order to respond to different situations.

(Adapted from Rees and Porter, 2001)

It is this last approach that is the most appropriate for sport and leisure services, as managers need to be able to adopt styles of management that allow them to deal with politicians, funding bodies, different categories of staff, customers and a range of service issues.

The contingency approach to management

The basic premise of contingency theory is that there is no one style of management that is appropriate for all situations. One of the best known contingency theories is the 'best fit' approach (Handy, 1993) that suggests that in any situation there are a number of influencing factors that a manager must take into consideration:

- their operating style as a manager: most managers will have a preferred style of managing which means that they will have a natural way of reacting when under stress. They need to be aware of the strengths and limitations of this style;
- the preferred style of their staff: in order to gain loyalty and respect, a manager needs to be able to manage in a style appropriate for their staff. Staff are likely to have a preferred way of being managed. For example, usually new staff and younger staff will feel more comfortable with strong guidance. Conversely, senior staff or experienced staff are likely to be more

comfortable with participating in decision-making or having work delegated to them;

- the task: the task itself will dictate how a manager should act. If it is a simple task, a discussion about how to undertake the task is inappropriate. The manager should either tell staff what can be done or delegate the task. Alternatively, a complex task that will have a significant impact on staff must be managed through consultation and discussion;
- the environment: the organisation itself will affect style. Some organisations, such as the armed services or emergency services, do not particularly encourage a style of management that emphasises consultation with staff as often decisions need to be made instantaneously. Other organisations will allow a range of styles to be adopted, in order to suit the variety of issues a manager has to deal with.

The need for flexibility in the management of sport and leisure services is reinforced when considering the number of roles that a manager has within an organisation.

The roles of management

The role of a manager is varied and complex. Research carried out by Mintzberg (1979) led him to suggest that managers have ten roles to play within organisations. He further organised these roles into three main sets, as outlined in Table 9.1.

A point worth noting is that Mintzberg, along with other writers, separates management from leadership. He considers leadership to be one aspect of a manager's job, a view supported by Handy (1993), who feels that leading is primarily concerned with the interpersonal activities of a manager's job. Although there are various explanations of the differences between management and leadership, there is a general consensus that leadership is about the ability to influence others in the pursuit of organisational goals. This means that, although all managers should be able to lead, not all leaders will be managers, as leadership is not necessarily related to position in the organisation. This point will be discussed later in this chapter.

Table 9.1 Managerial roles

Interpersonal roles

Figurehead	The manager acts as the representative of the organisation, such as attending industry meetings or giving out staff achievement awards
Leader	The manager is concerned with the relationships between staff, what motivates them and what needs they may have
Liaison	The manager networks/works with others outside the organisation or department

Information roles

Monitor	This requires managers to monitor the internal and external environment in order to stay up to date with changes
Disseminator	The manager has the responsibility to pass on information within the organisation. They have a duty to keep staff informed
Spokesperson	The manager gives information about the organisation to others outside the organisation

Decisional roles

Entrepreneur	This role requires managers to be innovative and to be able to introduce and manage change
Disturbance handler	The manager has to be able to resolve problems and handle conflict
Resource allocator	All managers have to control and distribute resources
Negotiator	All managers will have to negotiate and debate issues in order to successfully allocate resources and meet objectives

Source: Mintzberg (1979).

THE SKILLS OF MANAGEMENT

The management of sport and leisure services requires a number of skills. These skills can be classified into four main categories, which are:

- general management skills, such as communication, decision-making and conflict management;
- personal characteristics, such as leadership, enthusiasm, flexibility and fairness;
- functional management skills, such as marketing or finance;
- industry-specific skills, such as coaching.

Although managers are unlikely to possess all of the skills to be discussed below, they must have abilities in each of the above categories in order to be effective.

General management skills

There are a number of skills that managers need, no matter what their role is in sport and leisure. Those who manage facilities, run outreach programmes or are responsible for the entire operation require the skills outlined below.

Decision-making

Management is all about making decisions. Decisions need to be made regarding the allocation of resources, the future direction of the service or the colour of staff uniforms. To make rational decisions, managers need to be clear about the choices available and the criteria against which the choice should be made. They then need to obtain sufficient information in order to assess the choices against these criteria and use this to come to a decision. Figure 9.1 outlines the rational approach to decision-making, highlighting the process that managers should go through.

However, managerial decision-making rarely follows this process and managers make decisions based on a range of factors such as past experience, judgement, creativity and personal abilities. Decisions are usually made under time constraints and without comprehensive information. Therefore decision-making is rarely rational. In fact, in most cases managers aim to make the best possible or most satisfactory decision under the circumstances. Therefore managers seek solutions that are good enough, rather than being the optimal solution to a problem. This leads to the process of bounded decision-making as outlined in Figure 9.2.

Using this approach, managers try out solutions that have worked in the past, or that they are aware have been successful for other organisations, colleagues or departments. If none of these works, managers either reduce their expectations or will eventually move on to the rational process, where they will seek information and evaluate options. Although bounded decision-making is arguably less effective than rational decision-making, it does allow managers to make the best use of their limited time and to deal with as many issues as possible.

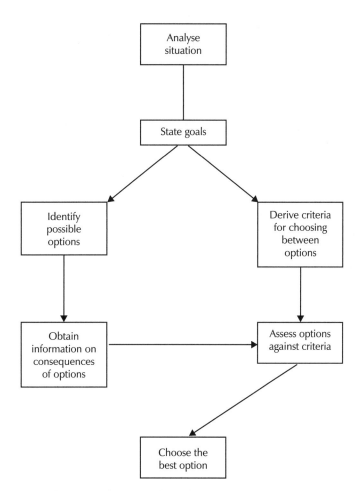

Figure 9.1 The rational approach to decision-making

Source: adapted from Batsleer (1994).

Torkildsen (2005) has suggested a nine-step approach to ensuring that decision-making is as effective as possible. He suggests that managers should:

- define the problem: managers need to be clear about exactly what the problem is. It is often easy to confuse the symptoms of the problem with the problem itself; for example, trying to deal with customer dissatisfaction in general, rather than establishing what has caused it;
- gather and examine information and identify possible causes of the problem;

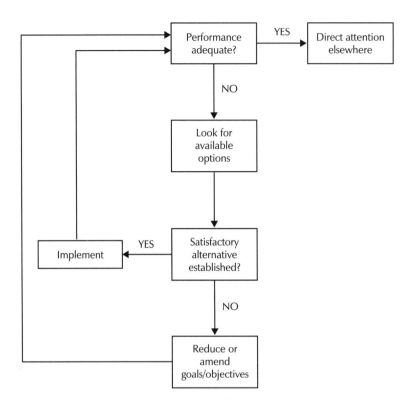

Figure 9.2 The bounded approach to decision-making

Source: adapted from Batsleer (1994).

- consult with others: other people may have a different perspective on an issue and by seeking the opinions of others a better solution may be identified;
- consider choices and alternatives;
- consider the implications of the choices: some decisions may solve the problem, but will cause greater problems. For example, closing a swimming pool will make a significant financial saving, but will lead to a loss of customer goodwill and will increase customer dissatisfaction;
- make the decision;
- communicate the decision: the decision must be unambiguous, communicated clearly and appropriately and managers must be prepared to be able to convince other people that the decision is correct;
- implement and follow up the decision;
- evaluate the impact of the decision and modify the decision if necessary.

This is clearly a lengthy process and is not likely to occur for all decision-making; indeed it is not appropriate for all decisions. It is important, however, that the risk is reduced in decision-making when the decisions are of such significance that they can fundamentally affect the organisation and/or staff working within it.

Communication

The ability to communicate is arguably the most important skill required of managers. Communication aims to influence understanding, attitudes and behaviour and is concerned with the passing on and receiving of information. This allows managers to manage staff, make decisions, carry out planning and solve problems. Communication must be clear, frequent and involve everyone.

There are a number of advantages to good communication:

1   It increases efficiency, since staff make fewer mistakes takes when they are clear about what tasks have to be achieved, why they have to be completed and how to go about these tasks. Not only is this beneficial in terms of motivating staff, it also reduces costs to the organisation as fewer errors are made.
2   Quality is improved by good communication as managers should be able to communicate the meaning and importance of good quality and the routes to obtaining it.
3   Customer responsiveness is dependent on the ability of managers to establish what customers need and pass this on to the organisation.
4   Greater employee motivation and involvement and reduction of mistakes result in better service to the customer.

There are several ways of communicating information and managers are likely to spend most of their time engaged in some form of communication process. The choice of communication method will depend on a range of factors. Information in writing tends to be more formal than that offered verbally. For example, an offer of employment must be made in writing, while an offer of additional training could be made verbally. The target audience also needs to be considered. It is appropriate to carry out staff briefings verbally, for example, whereas customer newsletters will be written. In addition, information needs to be delivered in a language appropriate for the target audience. This may mean that information has to be delivered in large print or even in pictures if trying to communicate with children.

The ability to listen is also an essential communication tool for a manager.

Managers must hear and understand the information that is been passed on, rather than just focusing on the words that are being said. The concept of *active listening* has been developed, a term that covers those characteristics that ensure that managers hear and understand the information that they are being given. Active listening allows managers to demonstrate that they are interested in what is being said and that they have heard and understood the message. Active listening is particularly appropriate for appraisal interviews, or discipline and grievance interviews, or when counselling members of staff.

Aspects of the active listening process included the following:

- the manager must listen for the feelings of the speaker and try and perceive what is actually being said through the way the message is being delivered;
- these feelings need a response and managers need to demonstrate that they recognise and understand how the speaker is feeling;
- the manager must note the verbal and non-verbal cues that are being given off to check for mixed messages;
- finally, the manager must reflect on what has been said, by paraphrasing the information back to the speaker to show that they have understood.

Managing conflict

Conflict between individuals and teams is a part of every organisation. Individuals and teams compete for financial resources, time from managers, equipment and even customers and this competition will, on occasions, result in conflict within the organisation. Conflict within organisations is not always a bad thing and constructive conflict can serve a variety of functions. First, it can encourage people to work together to fight a common enemy. Second, it can help to define roles and increase understanding of the feelings of others in the team. Finally, constructive conflict can increase understanding of the issues involved, as conflict usually arises when individuals are not aware of the concerns of all involved. Alternatively, destructive conflict is usually detrimental to the organisation as it tends to be based on personality differences or is concerned with the preservation of power. Managers need to be able to identify destructive conflict and have a strategy for dealing with it.

Much the same as the contingency style of management, there is no correct way of handling conflict and managers should be able to adopt a range of styles. Managers must have the personality characteristics and communication skills to be able to deal with the conflict in a calm, rational and fair manner. If they lack these skills, it is often better that someone else deals with the situation. The timing of the intervention is important. Managers must intervene at a time when they can actually be of use, rather than too early or too late, when intervention may escalate the conflict or inflame it.

Although handling conflict is often an unpleasant task, if it is ignored there are likely to be negative consequences for the organisation. The best strategy is to be aware of where conflict may arise and to set in place plans to prevent it from arising. This is not, however, always possible and, once identified, conflict needs to be managed in an efficient and effective manner.

Delegation

Delegation is the process of giving a subordinate additional responsibility for a certain task *and* the authority to get the job done, whilst retaining overall control. As an important part of staff development it gives staff the opportunity to learn new skills and take on extra responsibilities with the guidance of their manager.

Delegation of work has many benefits. It is often necessary to ensure that the range of work for which managers have responsibility is carried out. It enables managers to concentrate on the key aspects of their job as defined by their personal objectives and, as outlined above, provides an opportunity to extend the skills and experience of other staff. As a result, it acts as a motivating factor and increases morale. More importantly, it ensures that the work is done.

Despite these benefits, many managers are poor at delegating work and Rees and Porter (2001) identified two main reasons for this. First, some managers think that they are the only person who can do the work, and, second, managers often feel that they do not have the time to train the staff member who could be doing the work. Delegation is initially time-consuming as staff need to be shown or trained to be able to carry out the additional work. Staff need to be clear about what has to be done, why it has to be done and when by. In addition, as they first tackle the task they will invariably be slower at it than a competent person. However, after this initial slowness, with appropriate support, staff will be as effective as the manager at the delegated task.

In addition, delegation requires some relinquishing of control and many managers find this difficult, particularly as they still remain ultimately accountable for the work. However, managers who are effective delegators demonstrate confidence in the abilities of the staff member and let them know that they are available for advice and guidance. Finally, it is important to let other people know what responsibility and authority have been given. If these principles are followed, delegation will become an important technique for managing the workload of managers.

Time management

Managing time is one of the problems of being a successful manager. Managers often find it difficult to say 'no' to additional work, particularly if it appears of value to their team or themselves. However, if time is not managed properly, managers run the risk of being unable to complete their work to the standards they would like. Alternatively, they may become so overburdened that not all work can be completed. The pressure of time is exacerbated for sport and leisure managers as some of their work takes place during anti-social hours, such as evenings and weekends. This is because these periods of time are leisure time for most individuals and therefore organisations that provide sport and leisure services need to be managed during these hours. This creates more time pressure for managers, as evening and weekend work will conflict with the demands of their own home life, social activities and sport pursuits. The management of time becomes even more important as time lost in normal working hours cannot be caught up. Managers therefore need to be skilled at time management.

In order to have the time to do the work required, managers must have a time-management strategy. First, however, they need to be aware of the activities that cause time to be lost. These activities include:

- a lack of preparation: not spending enough time prioritising tasks or being clear about what has to be achieved;
- procrastination: putting off tasks that have to be achieved because they are too difficult or boring;
- poor prioritisation: working on tasks that are simple rather than important;
- confusing what is urgent with what is important: responding to the person who 'shouts the loudest' rather than doing the most important task;
- poor delegation: trying to do everything, rather than getting someone to assist, or delegating so poorly that the staff member has to continuously ask for help;
- poor communication: giving out incorrect or poorly expressed information so that time is wasted by having to provide more information or correcting errors that have come about as a result of poor information;
- lengthy phone calls, meetings or conversations: these often take longer than is required because the purpose is not clear or information is missing;
- taking work home after a full day: this is inefficient because of tiredness or conflicts with other demands.

(Adapted from Rees and Porter, 2001)

Once time-wasting activities have been identified, a time-management strategy should be formed, based on four principles. First, managers must record all commitments, including meetings, tasks to be completed and deadlines. They must carry out regular work planning and record this to ensure that plans are followed. Second, managers need to be clear about what it is that they have to achieve. It is not possible to do everything, so managers need to assess the tasks that are required of them in terms of what is necessary to achieve the objectives of their job. This will allow them to prioritise the tasks they have been asked to complete. It is easy to get sidetracked and to waste time on things that are interesting, but not essential. Third, managers need to structure their time. Time needs to be divided into blocks and allocated to certain activities. Tasks requiring concentration and research should be allocated to the time when the manager feels at his or her most alert. Alternatively, responding to phone calls, paperwork and e-mail can be left for times when concentrated work is less possible. In addition, it is important to identify time periods when managers can and cannot be disturbed by those who work with them. Finally, and most important, managers need to learn to say 'no'. Rather than making a manager appear lazy, the ability to turn down requests for work when overloaded or faced with other priorities is an indication of efficiency.

Managers will, over time, develop time-management strategies that work best for them. Different techniques, such as delegation, using a 'To do' list or working from home, will suit different occupations, management styles and organisations.

All of the skills outlined above are necessary for the effective management of sport and leisure services. The ability to make decisions and communicate these and to organise and complete a full work load is required of all managers. Fortunately, all of these skills can be developed or improved by personal development activities, such as training courses. Therefore it is important for managers to evaluate their level of skill in the above areas and then improve on this if necessary.

Personal characteristics

The issue of personality traits and management has always been contentious as it implies that some people will be better managers simply because of their personality, rather than because of any learned knowledge or abilities. The contingency approach to management suggests that style is more important than personality; however, there are personal characteristics that can be considered to be essential for effective management. These are:

- consistency: the ability to be consistent in decision-making and in the management of staff;
- decisiveness: the ability to make a decision;
- diplomacy: the ability to be subtle and tactful when dealing with others;
- enthusiasm: demonstrating keenness and eagerness about the work to be done;
- fairness: the possession of a sense of fair play and the ability not to 'take sides';
- flexibility: the ability to adapt and respond to change;
- honesty: being trustworthy, truthful and ethical;
- leadership: the ability to influence and guide others;
- self-confidence: being confident of decisions and actions;
- self-control: the ability to be calm and controlled in all situations.

The level at which these characteristics naturally occur will vary: indeed, some may appear to be absent. However, like general management skills, it is possible to learn to adopt these characteristics. It is therefore, once again, important that managers are aware of their level of ability with respect to these characteristics and, if necessary, that they seek personal development activities to ensure they are making the best use of their individual characteristics.

Functional management skills

Most larger organisations, are split into separate business functions, or departments. This allows staff within these departments to become experts within their chosen function, the premise being that they will then be in a position to advise other staff and departments on their particular function. The main functional areas are typically:

- finance
- strategic planning
- legal
- human resources
- marketing.

Organisations will have departments that deal with these functions of management.

Despite this, managers must have skills and knowledge in these areas. There are two reasons for this. First, these functions need to be applied to the sport and leisure context in order for them to be most effective. Some organisations such as local authority departments are unlikely to have as detailed a knowledge of the context as a sport and leisure manager. Second, in order to manage the performance of the service, managers need to understand all of the operations and activities affecting their service. This requires them to know how the service is financed, how it is performing, how to recruit appropriate personnel and how to manage the quality of the service. Indeed, at a minimum, they need skills in the functions outlined in the following section of the book.

Industry-specific skills

This category of skills is needed to integrate and apply the above skills to the context of sport and leisure provision. Managers may have technical knowledge of how to operate and maintain facilities and equipment and the ability to coach.

The technical skills associated with the industry are, however, less important than the abilities outlined above. It is not particularly necessary for a manager to be able to take a 'Learn to Swim' session or to set up equipment, although this may bestow credibility with staff. It is the ability to apply good management principles to the sport and leisure industry, alongside an awareness of how public organisations operate, that is important, as these are required for sport and leisure managers to be effective.

POWER AND MANAGEMENT IN SPORT AND LEISURE

The possession of the skills discussed above will improve the effectiveness of managers within sport and leisure. There are, however, factors that will affect the way that managers can operate. This section looks at the impact of power on management.

Despite the vast body of academic literature considering power in organisations, there is no generally accepted definition of power. One definition of power that has been offered defines it as the ability of one person or group A to get another person or group B to do what A wants. This implies that power is not possessed, but manifests itself in terms of relationships with others and, as a result, power within organisations is not fixed.

Organisational power is considered to come from a number of sources, which are outlined below:

- *physical power*: power comes from physical characteristics such as size, intelligence or looks. Strong people have physical power over weaker people as they are able to use their physical power to force the weaker person to do what is wanted. From an individual perspective, the exertion of physical power is inappropriate within organisations, although harassment and bullying unfortunately occur within sport and leisure services, as in any other field;
- *position*: people are powerful in organisations because of the position that they hold within the organisation; managers are more powerful than front-line staff. In addition, some less obvious positions can be considered powerful. For example, the Personal Assistant to the Chief Executive is likely to be powerful as he or she controls access to the Chief Executive;
- *resource power*: people who control access to resources within an organisation are powerful, particularly in times of resource constraint. So not only is a budget holder powerful, but the staff member who controls the allocation of staff car parks may be powerful if there is a shortage of parking facilities;
- *expert power*: power comes from having knowledge or abilities that are limited within an organisation. For example, the person who knows how to set up a new piece of equipment has expert power. This source of power is different from those outlined above, as it only exists for as long as there is a need for the expertise, or if no one else can develop the knowledge and skills that the expert has;
- *personal power*: some people are powerful in organisations simply because of who they are. It is often difficult to determine what brings about personal power, but it is likely to be linked to personal characteristics such as charisma. People with personal power will be leaders within the organisation, although they may not be managers. This is because they are able to use their personal power to motivate, influence or bring about change;
- *negative power*: this is the power of individuals to prevent decisions from being implemented in organisations. Much organisational decision-making relies on the goodwill of staff to follow decisions and to work within the organisation's guidelines. Staff can, however, exert power over managers or the organisation by refusing to do what is being asked.

Having considered the above sources of power, it would appear that power in sport and leisure should be based on organisational position. However, the power of politicians within sport and leisure services is often not as great as expected. Policy changes have increased the complexity and amount of decision-making required of politicians involved with these services. This has led to an increasing reliance upon the information and advice offered by sports professionals in order to deal with the growing number of the issues that affect sport and leisure services. This expert power, which comes about because of industry-specific knowledge, makes professionals increasingly powerful within the delivery of their services.

SUMMARY AND CONCLUSIONS

This chapter has considered the roles and functions of management in the sport and leisure sector. It discussed the need for managers to have general management skills, outlined desirable personality characteristics and highlighted the desirability of functional management skills. The main set of skills, however, relate to industry knowledge. The ability to provide advice and guidance on sport and leisure and to be able to respond to the wide range of factors that impact on the delivery of services is the key to successful management.

Without knowledge of the way that services can be delivered, of the impact of legislation and the expectations and desires of customers, managers will have little opportunity to shape the direction of their services. The opportunity to shape that direction is enhanced by an understanding of expert, positional and personal power.

REFERENCES

Batsleer, J. (1994) *Block One: People*, Foundations of Senior Management Series, Milton Keynes: The Open University.

Handy, C. (1993) *Understanding Organisations*, 4th edn, Harmondsworth: Penguin.

Mintzberg, H. (1979) *The Nature of Managerial Work*, Englewood Cliffs, NJ: Prentice Hall.

Mullins, L. J. (1996) *Management and Organisational Behaviour*, London: Pitman.

Rees, W. D. and Porter, C. (2001) *Skills of Management*, 5th edn, London: Thomson Learning.

Torkildsen, G. (2005) *Leisure and Recreation Management*, 5th edn, London: E&FN Spon.

SECTION 2

REGULATION AND LEGAL RESPONSIBILITIES

INTRODUCTION

This section aims to provide a greater understanding of the different stimuli which give rise to regulation and to raise readers' awareness of the way in which legal and safety matters influence working practice. A variety of authorial voices provide a selection of pertinent narratives in a way which we hope will increase the accessibility of the material. The section starts with an introductory reading that gives some consideration to historical aspects in the development of public health and shows how these have evolved into current concerns about issues such as smoking. The focus then shifts slightly to consider different means of regulating the quality of sport/fitness provision, through statutory and voluntary means. Later readings outline the legal background to health, safety and welfare, before a manager's perspective provides two practical illustrations of how this legal background influences workplace practice.

Chapter 10 is a written record of a speech made by **Tony Blair** when he was prime minister. This provides a useful introduction to how the state has acted on health issues in the recent and more distant past. It addresses the question of whether healthy living is an individual or state responsibility.

Chapters 11 and 12 consider two different scenarios which required regulation but where the issues were resolved in different ways. In Chapter 11, a representative of the Adventurous Activity Licensing Authority (AALA), **Jan Bradford** (former senior inspector with the AALA), explains how a canoeing tragedy led eventually to an act of Parliament which introduced statutory regulation to improve safety. Chapter 12 is written by **Mark Talley**, former Group Health & Fitness Manager for the premium health and racquets club chain Esporta and now employed by the leisure trust Fusion as a Regional Operations Manager, and as an independent consultant to The Open University. He examines the rise of voluntary regulation within the fitness industry and assesses the progress and impact of the Register of Exercise Professionals, formed in 2002.

Jane Goodey, lecturer in law at in the Open University Business School and a keen long distance runner, outlines in Chapter 13 the legal framework that underpins several important aspects of sport and fitness. She explains the interpretation of key concepts such as the duty of care owed by those working in sport and fitness to those who use their services, and 'occupiers liability', which is connected with providing safe facilities. Some fascinating case studies are used throughout the chapter to illustrate how the law applies to real-life events and incidents.

Chapters 14 and 15 contain a manager's perspective of safety issues. **Neil Wright** is the former Senior General Manager of the Broadgate Health Club, in London, having spent 24 years within the health and fitness industry. Now he is the Operations and Sales Director for SmartSpa, he also runs his own consultancy, NW Management Consultancy. Neil uses a diary format in Chapter 14 to describe the surprising amount of hidden work of a facility manager in keeping the facility, its staff and customers safe. Chapter 15, also by **Neil Wright**, then considers lessons from his personal experience of dealing with a fatality at a sport and fitness facility and suggests appropriate strategies for responding to such a 'monumental crisis'.

CHAPTER 10

HEALTHY LIVING
Whose responsibility?[1]

Tony Blair

INTRODUCTION

This chapter is a transcript of a lecture that addresses a topic that the former prime minister believes will dominate the public and political debate in the time to come: healthy living. It provides a useful introduction to how the state has acted in the recent and more distant past. The chapter starts by looking back at how government has helped develop the health of the nation from the nineteenth century. Mr Blair then discusses the challenges the issue of healthy living poses: in respect of the increasing strain unhealthy living will put on the NHS; and in relation to how the state needs to provide information to help people make their own individual choices about healthy living; and in some cases where, he feels, the state is morally obliged to act and regulate, e.g. smoking. This transcript has been heavily edited but Mr Blair's words have not been changed. When words or sentences have been cut it is shown by an ellipsis [. . .]. Amendments or additions appear in square brackets.

THE PRIME MINISTER'S SPEECH

[. . .] In the future, health care cannot be just about treating the sick but must be about helping us to live healthily; this requires more from all of us, individuals, companies and government and for government it has to encourage, it has to inform, but, if necessary, in a tougher way than ever before, it has to be prepared to act. [. . .]

---

[1] Edited from Blair, A. (2006) *Healthy Living: Whose Responsibility*, http://www.number-10.gov.uk/output/Page9921.asp, London: HMSO.

It is the questions thrust upon you that define you as a politician. The questions thrust upon a politician of the early nineteenth century were stark and bleak. Britain was industrialising and urbanising. The population almost doubled in the 50 years from 1801. The poor crowded into the big cities, usually into desperate slums that became hothouses for the sharing of disease. In the late 1840s the cities of northern England received thousands of starving Irish, fleeing the potato famine. [. . .]

And yet the very basics of a public health infrastructure were lacking. Housing was crowded – in 1847 a typical street in the East End of London had 1,095 people living in only 27 houses. Sanitation was poor – an outside water privy might have to serve 20 households. Water, usually drawn from sources infected with untreated sewage, was impure. Infectious diseases, once they took hold, were deadly; there were no vaccination programmes, few effective drug treatments. [. . .]

The [cholera] epidemics of 1832 and 1848 killed 140,000 people. Cleansing action by no one individual could ever be certain to be enough. The role for government was clear. This required collective action. [. . .]

The Victorians took up the challenge by legislation, then accompanied by the great feats of Victorian engineering [in building a sewer network]. [. . .]

The state gradually began to assume responsibility for problems that had once been considered individual or voluntary affairs. [. . .]

We are now in a new era, the time of conditions of affluence, of degenerative and man-made diseases. Today, our main killers are circulatory and cardio-vascular conditions which very few people in the Victorian and Edwardian eras would ever survive long enough to contract.

The problems of nineteenth century public health were colossal. But [the] collective solutions were easy to identify – to improve slum dwellings; to construct a disposal system; to purify the water; to make the fruits of medical research available to the poor. Of course these were great accomplishments and a testament to the will of many great reformers. [. . .]

In the first decade of the twentieth century life expectancy for men was a mere 49 years. By the final decade of the century male life expectancy had risen to 73. Average infant mortality was 150 per 1,000 births. Now, even in the poorest sectors of society, it is no more than 10 per 1,000.

It was an era of great policy success. Perhaps no era can claim such a clear boost to human well-being. It is very different from today. Our public health problems are not, strictly speaking, public health questions at all. They are questions of individual lifestyle – obesity, smoking, alcohol abuse, diabetes, sexually transmitted disease.

These are not epidemics. They are the result of millions of individual decisions, at millions of points in time. For example, 20 per cent of all children in the UK eat no fruit or vegetables in a week. 65 per cent of adults and half of all children do not take the recommended amount of exercise.

Obesity is rising rapidly: 1 in 4 adults and children in the UK is obese, and rising. The social effects of alcohol abuse are widespread and worsening. [. . .] Three-quarters of diabetics are type-2 diabetics and two-thirds of them have a disease that could be preventable with exercise, diet and more healthy choices.

These individual actions lead to collective [health] costs. [. . .]

But the question still hangs in the air [. . .]: Whose responsibility is it? The individual? The state? The company? Should it be a proper area for government intervention at all? [. . .]

In formulating policy, I have undergone my own personal journey of change in this respect. A few years back, I would have hesitated long and hard over issues like the smoking ban. Now, and particularly where children are concerned, I have come to the conclusion we need to be tougher, more active in setting standards and enforcing them.

Indeed this is part of a pattern that has developed hugely in the past few years. Now, we have legislation on a host of matters pertaining to public health: food, air, water quality, drinking and driving, drug classification, seatbelts, childproof medicine bottles, speed restrictions and so on.

In 2002 we banned most tobacco adverts and sponsorship. [. . .]

We are banning poor meat, fizzy drinks, crisps and chocolate in school meals. Pupils should get regular good meat, poultry and fish along with two options of vegetable and fruit every meal. The Education Bill will also ban the sale of junk food and fizzy drinks in vending machines and schools will have to meet tough new standards for school meals [. . .].

We are working on a code with the food industry on limiting the advertising of junk food to children. But if [. . .] the voluntary code [doesn't work], we will make it mandatory. [. . .]

Legislation can, itself, help to change a culture. To outlaw an activity is, of course a strong signal that such behaviour is unacceptable. But we need, at the same time, a more subtle approach.

This is partly about providing good information. The consumption of cigarettes declined 50 per cent over 50 years when the true nature of the risks were exposed. The facts changed and so people changed their minds.

But in many cases government is not the organisation to persuade us to change some of our most personal behaviour.

So government needs to work with others – with industry, with the media, with civil society – to have an impact on persuading more people to make more healthy choices. [. . .]

We are forming a new partnership with industry and the voluntary sector to prevent obesity in children under 11. Forty stakeholders from food manufacturing, food retailing [and the] physical activity sector have been developing this approach. This will now extend to encompass broadcasters, the video game industry and leading employers with large occupational health programmes. [. . .]

But weight is a combination of calories in and calories out. We need to ensure that we are doing all we can to enable people to take enough exercise. It is disputed whether the calorific intake of the nation has actually increased at all over the last 50 years. But our lifestyles certainly have. Manual, physically demanding occupations have declined to be replaced by sedentary, office-bound work. Labour-saving devices have made work in the home more convenient and less taxing. The time we devoted to physical activities has been squeezed. The municipal facilities we used were neglected, in many cases sold off entirely. At the same time, car use has grown extensively. We drive short journeys that, once, we would have walked. We are more wary of walking or cycling now. The numbers of children walking to school declined from 61 per cent to 53 per cent between 1994 and 2004.

We have already developed some very effective partnerships. [In] 2007 the NHS will be employing 1,200 health trainers [to] help people to make and sustain good lifestyles. Already, some big organisations, like the army and the prison service, are involved. [. . .]

But I think we can be even more ambitious. Already, nearly 400,000 people take part in a Great Run event each year. This is the biggest sporting participation programme in the world. We have the Olympics in London in 2012.

There is surely a partnership to be arranged, between voluntary, private and public sectors, to encourage mass sporting participation of this sort, as those like Brendan Foster have been arguing. We can join up all the activities that are going on at the moment, engage the private leisure sector, get schools involved and sports clubs. 400,000 could become 2 million; 400,000 should become 2 million.

In the private sector, Tesco have committed to get 2 million people running, cycling or walking in events that they will sponsor as we approach 2012. [. . .]

All of this is good. All of it indicates a big change of approach. But I still think there is a vast untapped potential out there for still greater partnership between public, private and voluntary sectors. There is an industry out there in health and fitness, in improving lifestyle choices whose ideas and experience we could harness; there are huge amounts of community facilities, not least in schools, that are often under-used; and there is a public that, though it may not always know what to do, knows it should be doing something. [. . .]

SUMMARY

This lecture provides a useful historical perspective to how regulation has impacted on public health in the past and the huge improvements made. Mr Blair, in response to the question 'Whose responsibility is it?' concludes that a combination of approaches is needed to tackle many healthy living issues. This might involve legislation, investment, information, voluntary codes and partnerships.

Certainly government cannot solve these problems alone and a lot of the second part of the speech talks about collaboration and the need for the different sectors to work together. He also argues that if you provide people with accurate information and clear messages, individuals are more likely to make better lifestyle choices.

CHAPTER 11

FROM LYME BAY TO LICENSING

The development of current regulation of outdoor adventure activities[1]

Jan Bradford

The deaths of the four teenagers in the Lyme Bay canoeing tragedy in March 1993 will be remembered for a very long time by many people, not only family and friends, but also those involved in the outdoor activity community.

The canoeing tragedy itself was the result of a series of errors and circumstances, which the Devon County Council report states, 'quite simply, should not have happened'. This report goes on to say that 'the immediate cause of the tragedy was, however, the lamentable failure of the St Alban's Centre to organise and supervise the canoeing activity, to employ suitable staff and to have prepared and operated sensible and pre-determined procedures when difficulties arose'. The successful prosecution of the parent company, OLL, and the managing director, Peter Kite, was based around these issues.

THE 1993 TRAGEDY

The canoeing party set out from Lyme Regis at about 10 a.m. on 22 March 1993. The party of eight pupils and their teacher were accompanied by two instructors from the St Alban's Centre. The intention of the trip was to cross to Charmouth and return to Lyme Regis by lunchtime. Almost as soon as the trip got underway, the teacher experienced difficulties, and whilst one instructor attended to him the other instructor rafted the pupils together. The raft rapidly drifted away from the teacher and instructor, and lost sight of them. The pupils were wearing life jackets, the instructors buoyancy aids. No flares were carried, and the pupils

---

[1] Edited from Adventurous Activities Licensing Authority (2001) *From Lyme Bay to Licensing: Past, Present and Future – the Development of Current Regulation of Outdoor Adventure Activities,* Cardiff: Adventurous Activities Licensing Authority.

did not have spray decks (essential safety covers to stop water entering the canoe in rough weather).

As the raft of kayaks drifted away from the coast, the wave height increased and gradually, one by one, the kayaks were swamped, until all nine individuals were in the water. Although the group had been due back for lunch at 12 noon, the emergency services were not asked to help until 15.30. The teacher and one instructor had remained in their kayaks, and were rescued by the inshore lifeboat at 17.31. The rest of the group were picked up by rescue helicopter between 17.40 and 18.40.

The events that surrounded and led to the loss of these four young people reinvigorated the campaign to better regulate the safety of outdoor activity providers, particularly those providing activities for schoolchildren.

BACKGROUND

By the early 1990s, outdoor education was increasingly offered by a range of providers, not only Local Education Authorities (LEAs) and charitable organisations, but also commercial organisations. There was concern that the reduction in local authority monitoring and control would lead to a reduction in standards of both quality and safety.

Indeed, moves towards a national system of registration or code of practice to ensure satisfactory standards of safety in the outdoor activity sector had already started before Lyme Bay. The Health and Safety Executive (HSE) had started to plan a programme of visits to outdoor activity centres to assess the situation in late 1992 and early 1993. This programme of visits was given further impetus in March 1993 after the deaths in Lyme Bay.

Also, prior to the Lyme Bay accident, providers of adventure activities could, if they chose, opt into voluntary codes of practice with a variety of organisations. For example national governing bodies such as the British Canoe Union and Royal Yachting Association, which focused on the delivery of their activities only; centre accreditation under the British Activity Holiday Association (BAHA) schemes; approval through membership of the Association of Heads of Outdoor Education Centres; or accreditation through a regional body, such as the Cumbria Association of Residential Providers. All these approval systems were voluntary, limited in scope, and any one centre could have approval from different bodies. There was not universal acceptance of any one scheme.

In 1993, the English Tourist Board brought together a group representing most of the voluntary approval bodies and other interested parties, known as the Activity Centres Advisory Committee (ACAC). In April 1994 the ACAC published a code of practice, which 'is a statement of principles and expectation for the responsible provision of organised outdoor adventure activities'. The ACAC played a significant role in the development initially of a voluntary code of practice, and in the eventual government support of a statutory scheme.

The ACAC Code of Practice was widely accepted within the outdoor industry as a major step towards a credible national scheme, and many providers stated in their literature that they operated within its framework. The voluntary scheme was welcomed by the campaigners for a statutory scheme as 'a step in the right direction' but they considered that it 'did not go far enough' (Devon County Council, December 1994). However, the inspection system was superseded before it started by the new Activity Centres (Young Persons Safety) Act 1995.

WHAT TYPE OF SAFETY REGULATION?

Between the Lyme Bay deaths in March 1993 and the introduction of the Act in January 1995, opinion had been sharply divided between those demanding statutory regulation and those maintaining that self-regulation on a voluntary basis was adequate.

In November 1993, the then Secretary of State for Education, John Patten, introduced a four-point plan as 'government action to safeguard pupils and others in outdoor activity centres'. This plan consisted of:

- an immediate survey, already in hand, of outdoor activity centres followed by a special programme of inspection visits by the HSE looking at standards of health and safety in them, over the next two years;
- making publicly available factual information about the inspections and any enforcement action arising from them;
- new comprehensive and detailed guidance by the then Department for Education (DFE) with the assistance of the HSE, to provide information to schools and local authorities on the lessons which they should draw from the Lyme Bay incident;
- changes in the documents concerning schools' articles of government to make explicit the legal duty of care concerning health and safety.

Those campaigning for statutory regulation greeted this four-point plan with widespread dismay. The Chief Education Officer of Devon County Council, Simon Jenkin, issued a statement saying the plan 'places Education Authorities across the country in an invidious and untenable position' and 'unless some formalised national system exists to record and monitor the qualifications and provide reports of accidents and near misses, then parents, teachers and pupils must have serious doubts about safety standards at outdoor activity centres'.

The parents of the teenagers who died in Lyme Bay were campaigning hard for statutory regulation, lobbying MPs and Secretary of State for Education John Patten, and were aided by a national press almost universally in support of their aims. The *Daily Mirror*, on 9 December 1993, stated that 'Thousands of children are facing appalling physical dangers because of the Government's refusal to bring in laws controlling holiday activity centres'. This article went on to quote John Patten as claiming that the Lyme Regis tragedy was an 'isolated incident', and the paper detailed several other deaths and near misses in recent months in activity centres.

Throughout this period the government maintained its position that it believed statutory accreditation was unnecessary, and this was also the opinion of the HSE. In a statement issued on 8 December 1994, a DFE spokesman said:

> Since the Lyme Bay tragedy, the Government has taken wide-ranging action on the safety of outdoor centres. This includes a special two year programme of inspections, and publication of guidance to centres was issued in September. It is the opinion of the Health and Safety Executive, on the evidence available, that further regulation or statutory accreditation is not necessary. The Government's view remains that there is no advantage to be gained from adding to the existing legislation and supports the voluntary accreditation scheme.

THE 1994 TRIAL

However, at the trial in December 1994 of the company and its managers who ran the activity centre in Lyme Regis responsible for the ill-fated canoeing trip, the Judge, Mr Justice Ognall, made a powerful call for an immediate and thorough appraisal of the running of activity centres. He said the potential for injury or death was too obvious for safety procedures to be left 'to the inadequate vagaries of self regulation'. He added that authoritative control, supervision and, if necessary, intervention were essential, and arranged that his observations be passed to the then Secretary of State for Education.

Clearly the opinion of the trial judge, that self-regulation is inadequate, and the stated position of the government, that further regulation or statutory accreditation is not necessary, were greatly at odds.

MOVES TOWARDS LEGAL REGULATION

The campaign for regulation was gaining momentum, supported by the Association of County Councils, the National Union of Teachers, Holiday Which? The Townswoman's Guild, other elements of the media, parents and teachers. The opinion of the Health and Safety Executive, that further regulation was not necessary, was challenged by the campaigners, on the basis that children were entitled to a greater measure of care than the general public. The campaigners considered that the level of risk that parents accept when allowing their children to participate in school or similar activities is much lower than that considered acceptable on a more general basis by the HSE.

HSE published an interim report in January 1995 on their survey of activity centres. This report noted that 31 per cent of centres were accredited by an existing voluntary scheme, and that 84 per cent of providers had made a satisfactory assessment of the risks and had adequate control measures in place. It also noted that 'there was no room for complacency' and that there was 'a real need for improvement in a significant minority of centres'. David Jamieson MP used these figures and statements to support his push for regulation, focusing his concerns on the 69 per cent not participating in voluntary inspection and approval. He pointed out that the figures showed that 16 per cent of providers did not have a satisfactory risk assessment, and asked if these were safe.

Additional pressure was brought to bear on the government by the conclusions of ACAC, who significantly had been brought together with a remit to examine the feasibility of viable self-regulation for the industry, but concluded that a statutory scheme would be the best option.

David Jamieson tabled a Private Member's Bill, which was accepted and supported by the government, gaining Royal Assent in June 1995, as the Activity Centres (Young Persons Safety) Act 1995.

The final form of the regulations which informed the Act took effect from 16 April 1996.

HOW REGULATION WAS HANDLED

An independent licensing authority was designated by Parliament. This organisation, the Adventure Activities Licensing Authority, is funded by the Department of Education and Employment (DFE) and operates under the guidance of the HSE.

An inspectorate was appointed, drawing on skilled and experienced individuals from within the outdoor community. The aim was to provide an interface between the outdoor community and government officials. The statutory function of inspecting providers of adventure activities and issuing licences could be achieved, under the guidance of HSE, using many of the existing ethics and structures of the outdoor community.

The Licensing Authority commenced inspections of activity providers in the autumn of 1996, visiting the majority during the summer of 1997, and by September 1997 had made decisions on the issuing of licences to all providers who had applied for a licence.

The initial number of licence holders was 875. The Licensing Authority refused to issue a licence to 13 of the original applicants, and a further 49 withdrew their application. By February 2000 the total number of licence holders had increased to 911 and total refusals to 29.

Inevitably, the implementation of the Regulations required the Licensing Authority to interpret the guidance and make decisions about 'grey areas', endeavouring to remain within the letter of the law and the spirit of the overall intentions of the Regulations. Areas that caused most difficulty, and led licence holders to query the Licensing Authority, included: the cost of obtaining a licence; the difficulty of deciding if an activity was licensable or not; the fact that voluntary groups and schools taking young people on identical activities do not require a licence; and the lack of overall publicity and public awareness of the scheme.

A triennial review was envisaged at the outset of the scheme, and this took place in 1999. The review was undertaken by DfEE, and a consultation document circulated widely.

Overall, the majority of respondents to the review were of the opinion that the scheme 'was doing its job' and three-quarters said it should continue, with further reviews.

FINAL THOUGHTS

It is clear that the scheme exists not only to promote safety in the provision of outdoor activities to children, but also to 'provide an assurance' to the public that the activity provider has been inspected and is operating to acceptable safety standards. This latter point, of 'providing an assurance', will be key to the credibility and acceptability, from the public's point of view, of any scheme that supersedes the existing regulations.

The final conclusion of the Select Committee in 1995 stated:

> It should be possible to implement legislation which reduces the level of risk in such activities to a minimum without reducing the opportunities for young people to participate in them. Above all, we hope that the passage of legislation will help entrench among providers – and users – of activity centres the culture of safety which is ultimately the best defence against tragedies like that at Lyme Bay.

FUTURE

Changes to the scheme are focused on reducing 'red tape' and the financial burden on smaller providers. The challenge to all involved will be to develop a credible, acceptable scheme, which continues to 'provide an assurance' to the public that their children are in safe hands, and which does not reduce the opportunities for young people to participate.

CHAPTER 12

THE VOLUNTARY REGULATION OF THE FITNESS INDUSTRY

Mark Talley

One of the options available between, on the one hand, non-regulation (the absence of any rules governing operation) and, on the other, statutory regulation (i.e. by legal means) is voluntary or self-regulation. Many traditional professions have opted for this route. For instance, medicine, the law and accountancy have elements of voluntary regulation to enhance the status of the profession and provide assurance to consumers. This chapter considers how the fitness industry came to adopt voluntary regulation in late 2001 and assesses its impact. The author's close contact with the industry over the last two decades is drawn upon to supplement existing information that is referenced in the text.

INTRODUCTION

The UK health and fitness industry has grown rapidly over the last 15 years, providing a proliferation of employment opportunities. Employment in the sector brings with it an expectation from both the employer and the consumer that staff should be approachable, have good communication skills and be appropriately qualified in the area in which they work. Specifically, exercise professionals must provide guidance on the safe and effective use of equipment and the design of exercise programmes. Exercise professionals are the main employee group within the sector and arguably have the most contact with and subsequent impact on the customer.

In general terms, the industry is perceived as having a relatively young and low paid workforce, although interestingly the current average age of members of the Register of Exercise Professionals (REPs) is almost 34 years. A glance at recruitment websites and employment journals shows that it is not uncommon for instructors to be paid modestly, with little differentiation accorded to either qualification level or experience. Staff turnover is fairly high and there is still no legal requirement to hold a qualification. High staff turnover does not mean staff are lost to the industry – promotion prospects into junior management positions are good as the industry continues to grow rapidly, and some will move to other employers.

THE REGISTER OF EXERCISE PROFESSIONALS

Within this context of relatively low pay and high staff turnover, the Register of Exercise Professionals was established in late 2001 as a system of self-regulation with the aim of ensuring standards of training and qualifications for exercise professionals working in the exercise and fitness industry. REPs is a not-for-profit company whose only aim is to raise standards in the health and fitness industry.

The mission statement of the Register of Exercise Professionals is simple:

> To ensure that all exercise professionals are suitably knowledgeable and qualified to help safeguard and to promote the health and interests of the people who use their services.
>
> (REPs, 2007)

Registration is voluntary and is achieved and maintained through the gaining of qualifications and completion of training which are nationally recognised and linked to the National Occupational Standards for exercise and fitness. Registration allows transferability of qualifications throughout the UK, across Europe and around the world as REPs continues to expand its partnerships with similar organisations in other countries.

Inclusion on the Register ensures the following:

1   The member has a recognised and approved qualification. To gain entry to the Register a qualification must be nationally recognised and linked to the National Occupational Standards for exercise and fitness.
2   The member has demonstrated competence in their working environment. All qualifications defined above require the candidate to demonstrate practical competence.
3   The member has demonstrated a commitment to continuing professional development (CPD). Members are required to complete CPD in order to maintain their registration.

4   The member is appropriately insured. Members must provide evidence of
     adequate and appropriate civil liability insurance incorporating professional
     indemnity.
5   The member has demonstrated a commitment to the REPs Code of Ethical
     Practice. Further details of the code are available from the website of the
     Register of Exercise Professionals.

Registration is available to all exercise professionals working in areas such as
gym instruction, group exercise, circuit training, keep fit, personal training, yoga,
aqua, advanced instruction disciplines, working with special population groups
and exercise referral. There are four levels of entry to the Register depending on
prior qualifications and training. Members receive a certificate of registration
and a membership card which lists their full status of registration and which
should be produced on demand. This status is replicated on the public register
on the REPs website. There are a number of other benefits, including a quarterly
journal. The registration fee in 2007 was £25 per year.

Once on the Register, members must complete appropriate CPD training.
Evidence of this training must be maintained and made available for inspection
at the time of annual re-registration. Currently the level of re-registrations is
70 per cent per year.

BACKGROUND TO THE REGISTER

A number of reasons are identified by Lloyd (2005) for the formation of REPs,
the chief amongst which was to reduce concerns about possible user and
member litigation in an unregulated marketplace. A formal register would also
provide guidance for instructors in evaluating and progressing through the
multitude of qualifications and training available in the sector. In turn it was
hoped that recorded professional and developing standards would provide a
benchmark to help increase pay and reduce staff turnover.

In addition, many health professionals do have statutory protection of their title
as distinct occupations – and some have overarching legal protection of
title through the Health Professionals Council (e.g. physiotherapists). There was
general consensus within the fitness industry and training providers not to wait
for Parliament to define what an exercise professional was but to self-regulate.

Two other factors were influential at the time. Highly critical reports of industry
practices by the media and the consumer organisation *Which?* highlighted that

there was no regulation within the industry. Second, the expansion of the NHS Exercise Referral Scheme required a register to provide a framework within which the scheme could operate, raising the industry's credibility and professional status with the medical profession.

In an unregulated industry, with a fast growing customer base motivated by the proven and well-publicised benefits of improved health and fitness, the REPs was an initiative to improve the image of the industry and raise the quality of both individuals and organisations operating within it.

ASSESSING ITS IMPACT

Formation of the Register has met with unprecedented levels of success in the registration of members. Key achievements have been as follows:

- The Register has a current active membership in excess of 24,500 members, making it the largest qualification-based fitness organisation in the world. It has also recorded over 47,000 first-time registrations since its launch.
- There are over 900 endorsed training programmes and conferences accredited by REPs offering both members and prospective members guidance concerning the suitability of qualifications and CPD training. The level of interest in the organisation is high, evidenced by over 2 million annual hits on the REPs website.
- The level of qualifications held by REPs members increased progressively between 2001 and 2007:
  - Level 3 members now account for over 60 per cent of all members.
  - 26 per cent of members are qualified as personal trainers, a 50 per cent increase between 2005 and 2007.
  - The number of members qualified to work in exercise referral has increased to 6 per cent, an increase of 50 per cent between 2005 and 2007.

(REPs, 2007, p. 17)

In addition, most large health and fitness operators/employers are committed to compliance with the Register. In a 2006 stakeholder consultation with members, employers, awarding bodies, training providers and the Fitness Industry Association, it was clear that REPs is viewed as a vital support to the industry (Leisure-net Solutions independent Customer Survey for REPs, October 2006).

These achievements are extremely impressive and seem to provide a clear indication that the quality and qualifications of registered fitness professionals have improved since 2002. There are, however, a number of areas that require further examination.

AREAS FOR IMPROVEMENT

Technical competency vs social skills

As previously mentioned, employment in the sector brings an expectation of being approachable and having good communication skills as well as having technical competence.

As the health and fitness marketplace becomes increasingly competitive and operators seek ways to differentiate themselves in order to attract new customers and retain existing ones, more and more are focusing on the quality of service they provide. Every exercise professional makes a direct impact on service with every customer interaction, a point made in considerably more detail in Chapters 18, 19 and 22.

In the author's experience, one frequent criticism made of REPs is that registration and CPD are focused predominantly on technical competence. Whilst this may be the priority for most fitness professionals, employers are looking for employees who can help make a real service difference in addition to giving advice and guidance on the technical aspects of health and fitness.

Although customer service, communication and exercise adherence skills are mentioned in the National Occupational Standards, technical skills prevail in all qualifications, both in time spent and in student interest. Similarly, there are noticeable gaps in the customer service areas of REPs-endorsed CPD training. There is a skills gap between the technical-based training that most instructors seem to prefer and the service-based focus that many employers desire. To combat this, a number of employers have now developed extensive recruitment and induction procedures designed to identify instructors with the skills and attitude required to interact effectively with members; employers then train staff in organisation-specific procedures and protocols.

According to Lloyd (2005), it was an orientation towards customer care that was continually cited as being what a manager looked for in a fitness employee. The technical expertise of exercise instructors was only mentioned by 3 out of 12 companies as being a measure of the quality of a club.

However, this criticism, when directed at REPs, is unfair. REPs is solely concerned with professional practice and competency, registering members based on their conformity to National Occupational Standards. The issues relating to customer care will only be addressed through continued development of the National Occupational Standards for Exercise and Fitness through consultation with employers.

Raising the level of qualification

Another comment sometimes made is that, despite REPs success in terms of the number of registrations, the increased percentage of higher level 3+ registrations and raising the profile of the industry, the minimum qualification level (level 2) to be an exercise professional remains modest. Although this minimum guideline qualification level existed before the formation of REPs, subsequent CPD requirements only partially up-skill the level of the instructor.

However, we have seen that the level of qualifications held by members of the Register has generally increased. Undoubtedly more prospective exercise professionals are choosing to complete more advanced qualifications when first becoming qualified, which is good news for the industry as a whole.

The suggestion that level 2 is set and has remained at too modest a level to effectively up-skill the workforce is a question for the industry to debate. The minimum qualification level is set as part of the UK National Qualification Framework and is therefore not a REPs issue. In order to genuinely raise the technical quality of instructors, consideration could perhaps be given to making the minimum licence to practice a level 3 advanced instructor qualification. However, this change would require considerable industry consensus.

Continuing professional development

In a young and fast-paced industry it is essential that fitness professionals refresh and develop skills to continue to do their job effectively. Failure to do so will at best make the role repetitive and at worst possibly lead to out-of-date practices.

REPs ensure that CPD is completed on a regular basis. REPs members currently spend on average £300 and five days per year on the completion of CPD, though the extent to which that CPD leads to increased quality and better qualified fitness professionals is open to discussion.

For example, current CPD opportunities are both extensive and diverse in their requirements of both time and intellectual investment. This diversity, whilst positively intentioned to assist members gain CPD requirements at a relatively low cost, does raise questions about the suitability of some CPD. In addition to technically based educational workshops and courses, CPD credits can also be gained by attendance at tradeshows and conventions, along with the reading of approved articles and completion of certain self-development courses. Whilst there are limits to the accumulation of this type of CPD points, a member can still gain a significant proportion of the points required for re-registration in this way.

The appropriate balance in making sound CPD requirements between accessibility, cost and level is one that is difficult to achieve and will always be subject to different opinions.

CONCLUSION

The Register of Exercise Professionals has been extremely successful in gaining acceptance and credibility within a relatively young employment sector. Registrations are in excess of 24,500 and continue to grow, and the level of qualifications held by the members has increased. Less than 16 per cent of members now hold provisional status as a result of the REPs conversion programme compared with 40 per cent in 2003, another indicator that qualification levels are increasing.

Technical competence, however, does not always translate into successful practice. The emphasis on the softer instructor skills focusing on interaction and motivation needs to be developed further through continued consultation with the industry and further evolution and development of the National Occupational Standards for exercise and fitness. But, to be clear, this is not solely the job of REPs, which should continue to focus on professional competence and adapt to any changes as and when they may be introduced.

Since REPs was established the entry level of qualification for exercise professionals in the industry has remained unchanged at level 2. Although the level of qualifications of REPs members has increased, to raise quality consideration might be given to raising the future entry level qualification. This would require a change in the UK's National Qualification Framework and the full support of the industry.

Continuing professional development training is an essential requirement of registration and should be a compulsory element of any professional occupation. REPs members currently invest significant time and money in CPD, but getting the balance right in terms of guaranteeing genuine enhancement and development of skills is an area which will generate ongoing debate.

Finally, the Register does not have 100 per cent compliance from all exercise professionals and associated professions working within the sector. Whilst massive strides have been made, some individuals and employers continue to ignore the Register and benefit from the naivety and ignorance of many consumers. The Register cannot be blamed for this. It has invested heavily in employee, employer and consumer awareness. Over 1,000 members of the public check out the qualification and registration status of members each day, a direct result of the successful awareness campaigns run by REPs; 100 per cent sector compliance will ultimately only be achieved by government legislation leading to compulsory regulation of the industry.

The Register has had many successes and has undoubtedly contributed to both the credibility and development of the sector (and instructors) in recent years. It fulfils a vital function as the need to increase professionalism and credibility is as important as ever. The Register must continue to be supported and all of us who have an interest in the sector should support its work and champion its cause. This support and subsequent sheer momentum will force the non-compliant elements of the sector to work to and buy into the standards demanded by the Register or to fail to survive. The alternative is unthinkable – a sector that reverts to complete non-regulation, wasting the hard work and credibility that have been established and that both the sector and the consumer demand.

REFERENCES

Lloyd, C. (2005) Training standards as a policy option? The regulation of the fitness industry, *Industrial Relations Journal*, 36(5), pp. 367–385.
Register of Exercise Professionals (REPs) (2007) *Health Club Management*, REPs Update, May.
SkillsActive (2006) *Working in Fitness, 2006*, available from: www.skillsactive .com/resources/research, accessed August 2007.

CHAPTER 13

LEGAL FRAMEWORKS OF HEALTH AND SAFETY

Jane Goodey

INTRODUCTION

This chapter explores the subject of the law of tort which underpins the regulation of health and safety in sport and fitness settings. 'Tort' is an old French word meaning 'a wrong'. The law of tort aims to protect individuals from harm by defining the circumstances in which individuals have a duty to think about other people. The duty is fixed by law and affects everybody. When a tort is committed and the duty is breached or broken, then a claim for damages may result. Tort is a wide area of law covering the law of negligence, occupiers' liability, nuisance and trespass. This chapter will only consider negligence and occupiers' liability. First, though, some examples might help to explain the importance of tort:

- All road users have a duty not to drive negligently, so the car driver who opens his car door without checking and knocks a cyclist off her bike causing her injuries may be liable to compensate the cyclist for her injuries.
- The swimming teacher who is negligent in ensuring that his lesson on learning how to dive is conducted safely may be liable for accidents that occur during the lesson.
- The gym manager who fails to check that the gym equipment is checked and maintained according to the manufacturer's guidelines may be liable to a club member who is injured whilst using a faulty piece of equipment.

Having established that a tort is a civil wrong, we can explore the importance of the law of tort as underpinning health and safety requirements by looking in more detail at the particular torts of negligence and occupiers' liability.

NEGLIGENCE

Negligence concerns situations where the claimant (the person who is injured) suffers those injuries as a result of another person breaching their legal duty to take care.

In its everyday use the word negligence means, for example, carelessness, forgetfulness or thoughtlessness. However, as these are somewhat vague and subjective, the courts have to be more precise and objective. Therefore in order to pursue a claim of negligence the law of negligence says that the claimant must prove:

1 that the defendant (the person alleged to have caused the injury) owed the claimant a duty of care;
2 that the defendant broke that duty of care; and
3 that the claimant suffered injuries as a result of the breach of duty of care.

Going back to our earlier example of the gym member injured by the faulty equipment, the claimant will have to prove that the gym manager owed them a duty of care in being the person responsible for the gym, that the manager breached that duty by failing to check the equipment properly and that the injuries the member suffered were as a result of that failure. The gym member must realise that all three elements have to be proved, otherwise the claim will fail. Each of these elements is considered in turn below.

The duty of care owed to the claimant

The duty of care owed by those working in sport and fitness to those who use their services underpins the regulation of the sector. Typical examples of services supplied are instructional activities and/or use of facilities. For example, in the fitness industry it is embedded in the code of practice of the Fitness Industry Association.

> The Code of Practice represents an important Statement to Government and other regulatory bodies that we are a professional industry that is capable of self-regulation and takes its operation and duty of care seriously.
>
> (Fitness Industry Association, 2007)

The duty of care is a legal concept which determines the circumstances in which one person is liable to another in negligence. The concept originated in the famous case of *Donoghue v. Stevenson* ([1932]S.C.(H.L.)31 AllER Rep1) (see Box 13.1).

BOX 13.1: DONOGHUE v. STEVENSON

One August evening in 1928 Mrs May Donoghue and her friend went to an Italian café in Paisley near Glasgow. Mrs Donoghue's friend bought her a bottle of ginger beer. The bottle (as was usual in the 1920s) was made of opaque glass. As Mrs Donoghue poured out the ginger beer, a decomposing snail fell out of the bottle. Mrs Donoghue became ill and wanted to sue the manufacturer for her illness/injury. In considering her claim, the House of Lords had to decide whether or not the manufacturer of a drink was under any legal duty to the ultimate consumer to ensure that the drink did not contain any defect that might cause an injury. The decision of the House of Lords that the manufacturer did owe a duty of care to Mrs Donoghue went on to form the basis of the law of negligence and to determine the extent of the duty of care that we each owe to other people. Lord Atkin defined those to whom we owe a duty of care in the neighbour principle. He said:

> You must take reasonable care to avoid acts or omissions which you can reasonably foresee would be likely to injure your neighbour.

He went on to define neighbours as

> persons who are so directly affected by my act that I ought reasonably to have them in contemplation.

In our earlier examples, then, the swimming teacher owes a duty of care to those under his supervision, and the gym manager owes a duty of care to the club members using the gym.

The phrase 'reasonably foresee' is important, and needs further examination. 'Reasonably foresee' means quite simply that the defendant could reasonably envisage a person being injured as a result of the defendant's actions. The case of *Bourhill v. Young* ([1943] AC92) illustrates this clearly. John Young, a motorcyclist who was riding negligently, collided with a car and was killed.

Mrs Euphemia Bourhill, the claimant, was getting off a tram when she heard the sound of the collision some 50 feet away and saw the blood on the road. She was pregnant at the time and was so shocked by what she saw that she suffered a miscarriage. The House of Lords decided that John Young did not owe her a duty of care, as he could not have reasonably foreseen that the accident caused by his negligence would cause her to suffer such injuries, i.e. the miscarriage.

A breach of duty

Having proved that the defendant owed the claimant a duty of care, the claimant must then prove that the defendant went on to break or breach that duty of care owed to him or her. This means that the court must look at the evidence and decide whether or not the defendant did something they ought not to have done, or failed to do something that they ought to have done. Our gym facility manager would appear to have failed to have done something that he should have done. In making this decision the courts are looking to see if the defendant has fallen below the standard of behaviour expected of someone undertaking the activity concerned. So, with our example, the court would need to consider whether the facility manager fell below the standard expected of managers in those positions. In this consideration, the standard is an objective one. It does not matter if the facility manager considers that his conduct is fine; the standard is that which could be expected of a reasonable person in that role. The standard of care in negligence does not amount to an absolute duty to prevent injury. Instead, the duty amounts to what a reasonable person would do to prevent harm occurring.

THE REASONABLENESS TEST

In deciding on what would be reasonable behaviour in each circumstance, the courts consider a number of factors. These may include special characteristics of the defendant; special characteristics of the claimant; the magnitude of the risk; and how far it is practical to prevent the risk.

In considering the defendant, the court considers such factors as whether the defendant has a special skill or profession. If the defendant has a profession or a special skill (such as our facility manager) the law will expect that person to exhibit the standard of competence usually to be expected of an ordinary skilled person when doing their job properly. That would amount to reasonable behaviour.

The same standard is applied whether the defendant is experienced or inexperienced. In the case of *Wilsher v. Essex Area Health Authority* ([1988] 1 AllER 871) a very inexperienced junior doctor mistakenly inserted a catheter into a vein. The Court of Appeal said that he could not escape liability because of his lack of experience. The reasonable behaviour/standard was that expected of any doctor rather than the particular doctor who made the mistake. In *Nettleship v. Weston* ((1971) CA 2 QB691) it was decided that a learner driver is judged against the standard of a reasonably competent driver. Mrs Lavinia Weston's inexperience as a driver could not excuse the fact that her driving fell below the standard expected of a competent driver. The gym manager who fails to check the equipment properly cannot escape liability by saying that he was only appointed a month ago. He would be expected to carry out his duties to the standard expected of a competent gym manager.

In considering the claimant, the court expects the reasonable person to take account of any special characteristic or incapacity which increases the risk of harm. This would, for example, be of particular importance to those responsible for weights rooms and gyms. In *Paris v. Stepney Borough Council* (1951), Mr Paris, who was blind in one eye, was employed as a garage mechanic. One day when he was welding without wearing goggles, a piece of metal flew up and damaged his good eye. The court decided that knowing of his disability his employer should have taken extra care to provide him with goggles, because of the potentially serious consequences of such an accident as he only had sight in one eye.

The courts will also consider the magnitude of the risk, i.e. the chance of damage occurring and the seriousness of that damage. This is illustrated clearly in the case of *Bolton v. Stone* (1951). The claimant, Miss Stone, sued Cheetham Cricket Club when she was hit by a cricket ball whilst standing on a road adjoining the cricket ground. The court decided that, given the circumstances in which this occurred, the cricket club was not negligent. The ball had travelled over a 17 foot fence and a distance of some 100 yards. The ball had only been hit out of the ground six times in the past 30 years. The court will also consider how far it is practical to prevent the risk. So, in the *Bolton v. Stone* case the court decided that the cost and complexity of building such a high fence or even constructing a dome over the whole cricket ground were completely out of proportion to the degree of risk.

The standard of care expected is that which a reasonable person would undertake to prevent harm occurring. The idea of the 'reasonable man' as described by Baron Alderson in *Blyth v. Birmingham Waterworks* (1856 11EXCHG 781) is central to an understanding of whether an act or omission has amounted to a breach of the duty of care. In this case, Mr Blyth sued Birmingham Waterworks for negligence when his house was flooded during a severe frost when the plug failed on a hydrant. The court decided that it was not reasonable to have expected the Waterworks to have anticipated such a severe frost. Baron Alderson said:

> Negligence is the omission to do something which a reasonable man, guided upon those considerations which ordinarily regulate the conduct of human affairs, would do, or doing something which a prudent and reasonable man would not do.

Causation

Having proved that the defendant breached the duty of care owed to the claimant, the claimant must now prove that the injuries suffered were caused by the breach of duty. The claimant cannot sue in negligence just because the defendant has acted negligently. The negligent act or omission must have resulted in injuries to the claimant. The law does not make us liable ad infinitum, but applies tests to decide what losses/injuries were actually caused by the defendant. The first test to be applied is called the 'but for' test. This simply means asking would the claimant not have suffered the injuries 'but for' the negligent act or omission of the defendant. The test can be seen clearly in action in the case of *Barnett v. Chelsea and Kensington Hospital Management Committee* ([1968]2 WLR 422 High Court). William Patrick Barnett was a night watchman on duty with two colleagues at the Chelsea College of Science and Technology. At about 5 a.m. the three men drank some tea. Immediately after drinking the tea Mr Barnett and the other men began to feel ill. At 8.00 a.m. when the day workers arrived the three men, who were still ill, drove to the casualty department of St Stephen's Hospital. The men told the nurse on duty that they had been vomiting continuously since drinking the tea three hours earlier. The nurse (thinking that the men had been drinking alcohol) was hesitant as to what to do. She then phoned the medical casualty officer and explained what the men had told her. The doctor advised that the men should go home and go to bed and contact their own doctors. Mr Barnett returned to the College, where by 1 p.m., when he was still unwell, he was taken back to the hospital in an ambulance, but he was found to be dead on arrival. He had died of arsenic poisoning. His widow Mrs Bessie Barnett sued the hospital for negligence for failing to investigate and diagnose his condition when he first went to the hospital. The defendants denied negligence, specifically denying that any negligence on their part caused Mr Barnett's death. The court decided that the casualty doctor did owe a duty of care to Mr Barnett and did breach that duty by failing to examine him. However, the court then decided that the breach did not cause Mr Barnett's death. There was medical evidence that even if he had been examined it would have been too late for any treatment that would have saved his life. It therefore could not be said that 'but for' the hospital's negligence he would not have died.

Causation becomes more difficult to establish when there may be more than one cause of injury, with the defendant's act or omission being among the causes. The courts then have to determine the operative cause (this is illustrated in Box 13.2).

BOX 13.2: WILSHER v. ESSEX AREA HEALTH AUTHORITY

In the case of *Wilsher v. Essex Area Health Authority* ([1988]2 WLR557) the court had to decide whether the negligence of a doctor in administering too much oxygen to a premature baby resulted in his blindness, or whether the blindness was caused by any one of five other medical conditions from which baby Martin Wilsher suffered at birth. The court decided that the negligence of the doctor in administering the excess oxygen was no more likely than any of the other medical conditions to have caused the blindness. Therefore causation was not proved.

Further problems arise in establishing causation when an intervening event occurs after the breach of duty which contributes to the claimant's injuries. This intervening event is then said to have broken the chain of causation. When this happens, the defendant will only be liable for such injuries as occur up to the intervening event. This is known as *novus actus interveniens*, which means a new act intervenes. This can be illustrated by the case of *Wright v. Lodge and Shepherd, Kerek v. Lodge and Others CA* ([1993] A11 ER299) (see Box 13.3).

BOX 13.3: WRIGHT v. LODGE AND SHEPHERD, KEREK v. LODGE AND OTHERS

The defendant Miss Shepherd's Mini broke down on a foggy night on an unlit stretch of the A45 dual carriageway outside Cambridge. Instead of asking her passengers to help her push the car off the road, she negligently left it on the road. An articulated lorry being driven recklessly by Mr Lodge collided with the car, injuring Miss Duncan, one of Miss Shepherd's passengers. Mr Lodge then lost control of his lorry, which crossed the central reservation, where it crashed into several other cars, injuring Mr Wright and killing Mr Kerek.

The court decided that Miss Shepherd was negligent in failing to get her passengers to help her push the car off the road. However, the reckless driving of Mr Lodge had broken the chain of causation, so Miss Shepherd could not be held liable for the injuries suffered by Mr Wright and the death of Mr Kerek.

Having satisfied the 'but for' test, the claimant must also prove that the injuries suffered were not too remote from the defendant's breach. So, the court applies the remoteness test to decide for how much of the claimant's loss the defendant will be liable. The test states that a defendant will only be liable for the injuries that could be reasonably foreseen at the time of the breach. Injuries are too remote if a reasonable man would not have foreseen them. This test has become known as the *Wagon Mound No. 1* test. The *Wagon Mound* case involved a ship loading oil in Sydney Harbour. Through the negligence of some workers, oil leaked into the water and spread to a neighbouring wharf. The oil damaged the slipway, but a few days later, ignited by sparks from welding work, the oil ignited, causing far more serious damage. The court decided that the damage to the slipway was reasonably foreseeable, but given that oil needed to be heated to a very high temperature before it would catch fire, the fire damage was not foreseeable.

For a claimant to succeed in a claim for negligence they must satisfy the court that the defendant owed them a duty of care, that the defendant breached that duty and that the claimant's injuries occurred as a result of that breach.

OCCUPIERS' LIABILITY

One area of the law of tort that is particularly important for those managing sports and fitness facilities is occupiers' liability. This concerns the duty that those who occupy land and the buildings on the land have for the safety of others who come onto the land. For example, it would cover the possible danger from slippery floors in changing rooms, rubbish littering football pitches or the lack of adequate signs warning of danger near a boiler room.

The law concerning occupiers' liability is found in the Occupiers' Liability Act 1957, which is concerned with people coming onto land with permission, and the Occupiers' Liability Act 1984, which deals with people coming onto land without permission, i.e. as trespassers.

An occupier is the person who controls the premises, i.e. the person who has enough control to allow or prevent other people entering the premises. This is illustrated by the case of *Harris v. Birkenhead Corporation* ([1976] 1 W.L.R. 279). Birkenhead Corporation had served a compulsory purchase order on a house, which allowed the council to take over the premises. The council knew that once houses in that area were empty they were targets for vandals but they failed to board up the house. This house was subsequently vandalised. A 4-year-old child went into the house through an unsecured door and was injured when he fell from a second-floor window. The Court of Appeal decided that the local authority was the occupier of the premises as it had the legal right to control the premises, and was in the best position to secure the property to prevent accidents.

Premises are defined in the 1957 Act in section 1(3) as including land, buildings and 'any fixed or moveable structure, including any vessel, vehicle or aircraft'.

The duty of care expected of occupiers

This is defined in section 2(2) of the 1957 Act, which says that 'The common duty of care is a duty to take such care as in all the circumstances of the case is reasonable to see that the visitor will be reasonably safe in using the premises for the purposes for which he is invited or permitted by the occupier to be there'. An interesting illustration of the duty of care is found in the case of *Cunningham and others v. Reading Football Club* ([1991] P1QR 141). In this case the football club was found liable as the occupier of Elm Park ground for the injuries suffered by a number of police officers on duty at a match because those injuries had resulted from the club's failure to carry out repairs to ensure that the ground was safe. Due to the 'appalling dilapidated' state of the football ground, the fans had been able to break off lumps of concrete, which they had thrown at the police officers, causing a number of injuries. In his judgment Judge Drake said, 'my conclusion is that the defendants are liable to the plaintiffs for breach of duty under the Occupiers' Liability Act 1957'. He went on to confirm that 'those who control football grounds remain under the clear duty to take such steps as are reasonable in all the circumstances to see that lawful visitors to their grounds – spectators and others alike – will be reasonably safe at those premises'.

It is important to note that an occupier must provide a higher standard of care for children. Section 2(3)(a) of the 1957 Act states: 'An occupier must be prepared for children to be less careful than adults. If the occupier allows a child to enter the premises then the premises must be reasonably safe for a child of that age' In *Moloney v. Lambeth LBC* ([1966] WL 23259) a 4-year-old child was injured when he fell through the balustrade on the stairs of some council flats. The court decided that the railings protecting the stairwell did not provide enough protection for a child even though an adult could not have fallen through the balustrade, so the council was liable in that it had not complied with the standard of care required for children by the Occupiers' Liability Act 1957.

The courts recognise that children are less able than adults to recognise danger and may not be able to read warning signs. In particular, due to their natural curiosity they may actually be lured or attracted by potential dangers. In the case of *Glasgow Corporation v. Taylor* ([1922]) a 7-year old child died after eating poisonous berries he had picked from a bush in a park controlled by Glasgow Corporation. The court decided that the council had breached its duty of care to the child by leaving the berries on the bush. The berries, which looked like cherries, had been an allurement to the child.

An occupier may not be liable for injuries to a very young child if it would be expected that such a young child would be accompanied by someone looking after them. In those circumstances, the duty of care would amount to a warning that someone competent to look a young child would understand. In *Phipps v. Rochester Corporation* ([1955] IQ.B. 450) a 5-year-old boy fell and broke his leg whilst out blackberrying with his 7-year-old sister. The boy had fallen into a trench that had been dug for laying a sewer. The court decided that the defendants were not liable because, although they had failed to try to keep children away from the trench, they could presume that the responsibility for such a young child rested primarily with his parents, whose duty it was to ensure that their children did not wander about unaccompanied.

Occupiers can protect themselves from liability by the use of warnings. Section 2(4)(a) of the Occupiers' Liability Act sets out the requirements for warnings. It says that an occupier cannot escape liability by just giving a warning. The warning will only be considered adequate if it is sufficient to enable the visitor to be reasonably safe. Whether or not a warning does so will be determined by the circumstances in which the warning is given. So, for example, a warning sign on the newly washed floor of a changing room saying 'Danger' would be less likely to be adequate compared to a sign saying 'Danger – wet slippery floor – take care'. As discussed earlier, warnings where children may be involved may need to be different in nature to those for just adults.

It is important to note that, under the 1984 Occupiers' Liability Act, if certain conditions are met, the occupier has a duty of care to people who are not invited or given permission to enter onto the land. This can include not only burglars and trespassers, but also someone who wanders onto land when they are lost. It is possible to enter a building as a whole as a visitor, but then become a trespasser in specific parts of the building. For example, a member of the public may go into the sports hall at their local leisure centre as a lawful visitor to play a game of badminton. They may then become a trespasser if they go into the sports hall storage room marked 'Authorised sports hall staff only'. The occupier, the council, may then be liable if the person is injured when some poorly stacked weights fall on top of them.

Occupiers' liability is, then, a crucial area of tort for those managing sports and fitness facilities.

Damages

If a claimant succeeds in proving liability he or she will expect to be compensated for any injuries. The aim of compensation here is to restore the claimant to the position he or she would have been in had the tort not been committed. In many cases this also involves insurance.

DEFENCES

As has been explained, to pursue a claim of negligence the claimant must prove that the defendant owed him or her a duty of care, the duty was breached and the claimant suffered harm that was a foreseeable consequence of that breach. Even if the claimant succeeds in doing all of this there are some defences that the defendant can raise. Of particular interest to those working in the sports and fitness industry will be the defences of contributory negligence and *volenti non fit injuria* (no cause of action arises to someone who voluntarily accepted the risk).

Contributory negligence

Contributory negligence occurs when the claimant's own negligence contributed to his or her injuries. The Law Reform (Contributory Negligence) Act 1945 determined that where the claimant is found to have been partly at fault, the judge can reduce the damages to be awarded to the claimant by a proportion that takes into account the claimant's own negligence. The case of *Sayers v. Harlow Urban District Council* ([1958] 1W.L.R.623) illustrates this very clearly. On the morning of 14 January 1956 Mrs Eileen Sayers was with her husband waiting to catch a bus to London. She went to visit the public toilets owned and operated by Harlow Urban District Council. Unfortunately, due to a faulty lock, the door jammed and Mrs Sayers could not get out. She became anxious as she didn't want to miss her bus and shouted for help, but no one came. She then tried to climb over the top of the cubicle's door. In doing so, Mrs Sayers stepped on the toilet roll, the roll span around and she slipped, lost her balance and fell, injuring her leg. Mrs Sayers sued Harlow Urban District Council. The Court of Appeal decided that, although the Council was negligent, Mrs Sayers was also negligent in trying to balance on a revolving toilet roll. She had contributed to her injuries, so her damages were reduced by 25 per cent to take account of her own carelessness. So, the person who is injured when slipping on the wet changing room floor may succeed in his claim against the leisure centre for negligence in not keeping the floor dry. However, he may find his damages reduced if the court decides that the bottle of wine he had consumed at lunchtime contributed to him being rather unsteady on his feet.

It is important to note that where young children are concerned the courts recognise that they cannot be expected to have sufficient awareness and experience to be aware of potential danger, and so are unlikely to be found contributorily negligent.

Volenti non fit injuria

The Latin phrase *volenti non fit injuria*, or *volenti* for short, can be raised as a defence in situations where the defendant says that the claimant was voluntarily taking the risk of harm. Its meaning can be clearly explained in sport; for example, if you play rugby, or take up boxing, simply by taking part in the match, or entering the boxing ring, you have voluntarily accepted the risk of possible injury. *Volenti* can only apply when the player is injured during a game or sport played according to the rules. This is illustrated in two incidents occurring in rugby matches. In *Simms v. Leigh Rugby Football Club Ltd* ([1969] 2 All E.R.923), Mr Simms broke his leg when he was tackled and thrown towards a concrete wall running along the touchline. The court decided that the rugby club could raise the defence of *volenti* as the injury occurred during a tackle which was within the rules of rugby league, and that he had willingly accepted the risks involved in playing on that particular pitch. The wall, which was 7 foot 3 inches away from the touchline, met with the requirements of rugby league's by-laws.

In contrast, where the game has not been played according to the rules the defence is much less likely to succeed. *Smoldon v. Whitworth & Nolans* ([1997] P.I.Q.R.133) involved a colts rugby match. The claimant, Ben Smoldon, who was playing hooker, suffered a broken neck when a scrum collapsed. He sued Mr Nolan, the match referee. When Mr Nolan tried to raise the defence of *volenti* saying that Mr Smoldon had consented to the ordinary incident of a game of rugby, the defence failed. The Court of Appeal refused to accept his defence. This was because there were special rules for colts games, including a provision that there should be no collapsed scrums. In allowing the scrum to collapse, the referee had breached his duty to apply the rules. Therefore the match had not been played according to the rules applicable to a colts match.

The defence of *volenti* can also apply to spectators. In the case of *Wooldridge v. Sumner* ([1961] WL20448) a photographer, Edmund Testocq Woolridge, was knocked down and severely injured at the National Horse Show by a horse named Work of Art ridden by Ronald Holladay, an experienced horseman, when the horse left the arena. When he sued Hugh Sumner, the owner of the horse, the court said that spectators at sporting events have voluntarily assumed the risk of harm caused by a participant in the sport as long as the participant's action is not undertaken with reckless disregard for the safety of the spectators.

The law recognises that individuals must take some responsibility for their own actions.

CONCLUSION

The law of tort and in particular the concept of duty of care, which lies at the heart of tort law, clearly underpin the health and safety regulations that govern the operation of the sports and fitness sector in each and every one of the wide range of activities covered within the sector.

Those managing and working in everything from a local council swimming pool, through a private racket and fitness centre, to a football club or an outdoor adventure centre should have an appreciation of the law of tort which underpins the health and safety regulations that they work with every day.

REFERENCES

Cracknell, D. G. (2004) *Obligations: The Law of Tort*, 3rd edn, London: Old Bailey Press.

Elliott, C. and Quinn, F. (2003) *Tort Law*, 4th edn, Essex: Pearson Educational Limited.

Fitness Industry Association (FIA) (2007) FIA Code of Practice, available from: http://www.fia.org.uk/, accessed August 2007.

Hepple, B. A., Howarth, D. A. and Matthews, M. H. (2003) *Tort Cases and Materials*, 5th edn, London: LexisNexis Butterworths.

CHAPTER 14

THE HIDDEN WORK OF A FACILITY MANAGER

Neil Wright

Francesca has managed a medium sized fitness club (with 30 employees and 2,000 members) for three years. The club is part of a multi-site branded health and fitness chain. She kept a diary of her health, safety and welfare activities for two months.

1 DECEMBER

First job today is to review the previous month's health and safety records. The aim is to ensure that all statutory checks have been carried out and that we are compliant with company policies and procedures.

The raft of checks requiring scrutiny includes:

- the duty manager's 'building open' checklist (this is the checklist that the duty manager uses to ensure that the club is safe and prepared for opening to members) and 'building close' checklist;
- accident reports (staff, contractors and members);
- fire alarm and extinguisher checks.

I have arranged to spend two hours today with my deputy club manager to ensure that everything is complete. We will also carry out spot checks on random aspects of the checklists to ensure that we are actively taking part in the process. Once complete, the records will be filed and kept for future reference. I will sign off my paperwork and send a copy to head office where a master report for the whole company will be compiled.

A key aspect of the two hours is to identify any emerging issues (either repeated failures or reoccurrence of similar issues, or any noticeable patterns) and then agree and implement an action plan to deal with these. The action plan needs to clearly identify the issues, what actions are required, the timescale within which the actions should be completed and who is responsible.

2 DECEMBER

I will have to carry out our annual risk assessments in January. We must assess risks and identify measures that we need to have in place to comply with health and safety law. As December is a quieter month, it will give me plenty of time to review and plan with the team to ensure that the process is carried out effectively. Our club's approach to health and safety is important on a number of levels, which are explained further in Box 14.1.

BOX 14.1: THE IMPORTANCE OF HEALTH AND SAFETY

Q: Why do you need to ensure that health and safety works in your club?

Francesca: I want everyone who enters my club to enjoy a healthy, safe environment, but I also have a legal and moral responsibility to all the staff and guests, to ensure that they are not exposed to preventable risks.

Poor health and safety can affect 'the bottom line'. If you operate a business that is perceived not to offer a healthy, safe environment, your customers will go elsewhere. If successful claims are made against you, your systems and procedures may be judged to be inadequate and insurance costs will increase.

Failing to ensure that health and safety lives and breathes within your club can have serious consequences, including:

- preventable accidents
- financial fines and penalties
- loss of your job
- potential imprisonment.

The plan will have two review stages.

I will review the current policy and procedures with the national health and safety manager to ensure that there have not been any fundamental changes.

There will be on occasions times when changes are made to existing statutory requirements or new regulations are introduced, or the company adapts its own systems to comply. It is the company's standard procedure to update all managers during the year as required. However, it is always worthwhile ensuring that nothing has been missed. I will also review the skill base for the staff carrying out the assessments. It is essential that as many staff as possible are involved, for the following reasons:

- share the work load;
- if directly involved staff will have more ownership and understanding;
- health and safety becomes part of the culture and not just one person's job.

We need to review the skill base, as it's a requirement that. 'Any member of staff who carries out risk assessments should be suitably trained and competent'. There are certain specialist risk assessments that do require specialist knowledge or training, such as that for display screens.

4 DECEMBER

I've organised for all of my management team to attend a two-hour meeting to review the existing risk assessments. We need to see which ones can be rolled over and used again, which assessments require rewriting and if we have introduced any new activities that require new risk assessments to be carried out.

Each department manager will have to nominate a staff member to carry out the assessments from within their team. They will also need to identify any training requirements; we've booked a training session on 8 December.

5 DECEMBER

A piece of gym equipment is out of action. Fortunately the team member who found the fault has removed it from the gym. I have ensured that my maintenance team is aware and that the unit is repaired. I am keen that the unit is back in operation as soon as possible since with January looming it is essential that we do not have any equipment out of action.

I'm pleased my staff got it off the gym floor immediately – I know of another club where a weights bench was damaged and reported, but the staff member concerned only placed an 'out of order' sign on it. The note fell off of the bench, which subsequently collapsed under one of their members, resulting in an injury. This led to a legal claim for compensation.

7 DECEMBER

I want to 'walk' the building with my maintenance manager to carry out our weekly checks. I missed last month and I am concerned that we seem to have more issues around the club than I would expect. The number of lamps out and minor issues seem to have escalated over recent weeks. I want to look at everything in detail to understand whether we have a simple staffing issue or something more serious.

Having had the meeting with my maintenance manager I believe it is a human resource issue; I need to address it with the facility's management team.

8 DECEMBER

I arrived at work today to a report that a member had abused one of the staff team the previous night. As well as safety issues I am also responsible for the welfare of all users and staff; hence my interest. It would appear that a member spent 10 minutes at reception verbally abusing one of the reception team for what initially would seem a fairly minor issue. Fortunately, a full report has been made using the company's incident report form. I now have to carry out a full investigation, which means I need to:

- obtain full written statements from all staff either involved in the incident or witnesses to it;
- obtain statements from any independent witnesses;
- invite the member concerned to come to the club to hear their point of view.

9 DECEMBER

I have concluded my meeting with the member, who has reluctantly accepted that their behaviour was unreasonable. I have informed them that if there is ever a repeat of the behaviour, their membership will be terminated. It is essential that staff feel confident that management will support them during such instances and that you are seen to be fair and consistent in your decisions.

Head office have notified me that our six-month health and safety (H&S) audit will be taking place in seven days' time. That means a full day reviewing all of the files (see Box 14.2) in detail to ensure that I am complying with all of the company's requirements and that I am operating a safe club. There will also be spot check interviews with staff to check their understanding of policy and practice.

BOX 14.2: A LIST OF HEALTH AND SAFETY FILES

- accident book
- audits (health and safety)
- CCTV system
- contractors
- Control of Substances Hazardous to Health (COSHH)
- daily building open & close checks
- display screens
- fire extinguisher/sprinkler system
- emergency action plans (EAP)
- emergency lighting
- fire alarm system
- first aid
- maintenance building checklists
- health and safety policy/health and safety reports/minutes/letters
- insurance and licenses
- intruder alarm
- lifts and hoists
- working at heights
- lightning protection
- manual handling
- new and expectant mothers
- normal operating procedures (wet)
- normal operating procedures (dry)
- normal operating procedures (children)
- panic alarms
- pest control
- portable appliance testing (PATS)

- personal protective equipment (PPE)
- preventative maintenance
- residual current device testing
- reporting of injury, disease or dangerous occurrence (RIDDOR) (F2508)
- risk assessments
- sunbeds
- training records
- waste transfer
- water hygiene and testing

Now obviously this could lead to a frenzy of activity trying to prepare for the visit, but fortunately I have a very effective and diligent deputy general manager so I'm confident that we'll be okay. We have come out reasonably well on previous visits and normally genuinely learn something from them.

16 DECEMBER

The H&S audit was long and stressful, but we scored well, with a 10 per cent improvement on our last one. As with so many of the present company practices, all the audit scores are entered onto a league table. The great news is that our ranking has moved up, making us one of the top ten clubs within the company. I'm treating my deputy club manager (DCM) to a meal out with her partner for all the hard work she has put in.

Companies often use competition and comparative scores of other clubs to motivate staff and highlight areas of concern. Each section of the safety audit is scored out of 2 points. If we achieve full compliance for each section we score 2 points. A compliance of 75–99 per cent scores 1 point. Less than 75 per cent scores 0 points. In the final section scores are added up and set against a maximum possible score.

18 DECEMBER

Today is our in-house induction session for new staff. It lasts two hours and I again cover the fundamentals that were delivered in the company induction day they recently attended. It's vitally important that the staff that have just joined us genuinely understand that health and safety is not just an exercise carried out off-site but is actively practised within the club. (See Box 14.3 for ways in which the right health and safety culture can be developed.)

BOX 14.3: THE RIGHT CULTURE

Francesca: I have found the single most effective way of developing a health and safety conscious culture within my facility is through effective induction of new staff.

Each new member of staff should receive a formal induction at the start of their employment. It's important that from day one new staff understand the company's requirements and how health and safety practices are integrated into our working day.

The health and safety induction should cover all the basics, including:

- company health and safety policy
- manual handling
- COSHH
- fire evacuation
- daily building checks
- emergency action plan (EAP)
- personal protective equipment (PPE)
- risk assessments.

This is going to be one of the first experiences that new staff will have of a company and first impressions count, so the induction should be interesting, informative and, wherever possible, fun.

If existing staff have been working for the business for quite a while, then there's never any harm in a bit of revision and they can be great ambassadors for health and safety with new recruits.

---

19 DECEMBER

It is Friday and we have carried out our weekly fire call point test (commonly referred to as break glass points). Each week we test a different call point, which ensures that all call points are tested over a period of time. We allow the alarms to sound so that we know that everything is functional.

We are required by law to carry out an unannounced full evacuation of the building every six months. This is useful as it tests both the staff's and members' reactions to as near to a real-life situation as possible, identifying any gaps in training or procedures that we have to address.

Once complete, all results need to be logged. Any failure needs to be identified and an action plan developed if required.

In relation to firefighting there are some great videos available on the market that enable staff to view how to safely use fire safety equipment without the need to actually discharge a unit. These are used in the induction sessions and I require each member of staff to view the tapes every six months.

20 JANUARY

It's my monthly induction and review training session today. Many suppliers of cleaning chemicals now provide all the training for your staff that you will require, satisfying your legal requirements for the control of substances hazardous to health (COSHH). This is due to the fact that they also have a responsibility to ensure that the regulations concerning COSHH are comprehensively complied with and the easiest and effective way for them to do so is to provide the training themselves. Therefore I have organised for all operational staff to attend the training in two one-hour sessions. As always, the training will be fully documented and recorded. The training has been organised to take place at the early/late shift change over. The late shift arrives an hour earlier to cover the club whilst the early shift receive the training. I also require those staff that are 'off shift' to come and attend one of the one-hour training sessions.

23 JANUARY

Today we have a contractor on site to service our boilers. My deputy had to explain the building evacuation procedures to the contractors, keeping a record of the training to prove it had been undertaken.

25 JANUARY

We have received back our monthly swimming pool bacteriological tests report today from the independent testing laboratory that we employ to monitor our pool water chemistry, in addition to the tests we do ourselves. Fortunately, at the time of testing our free chlorine, combined chlorine and pH tests were within acceptable parameters. These tests and the tests we carry out every two hours daily ensure that we effectively manage our pools and that the records demonstrate that we do so. This is paramount as pool water is one of the most common areas for complaint and the area where the most claims for the receipt of illness and communicable disease can be made by members against you.

31 JANUARY: CONCLUSION

Part of my responsibility as a general manager is to act as a mentor and coach to my team. It is critical that every manager has a succession plan in place to ensure the longevity of their club and organisation. On a personal level I can only be promoted if there is a replacement, so what better than having a replacement that has been trained by me and is immediately available. In addition, there is nothing more rewarding than when a member of my team whom I have developed and had involvement with is promoted to a new and more challenging role.

With this in mind I meet monthly with Emma, my deputy club manager, to discuss her training and development needs. Today a key aspect of the review was the achievements we had made in relation to health and safety over the last few months. She asked me what drove me to embrace a subject that some would label dry and boring. My response was that as general manager I have the final responsibility for all aspects of the club. When I am away from the club this responsibility does not diminish.

By encouraging and ensuring we have a proactive health and safety culture I know that I do not have to worry for the welfare of my staff, members or any other person using the club. I know that if we were to have an incident we could know that we had carried out everything within our powers to have tried to prevent the situation occurring. If we were inspected by an outside body such as the Health and Safety Executive (HSE) we would not be found wanting. That if I had to answer to a coroner, I could do so with a clear conscience. This knowledge enables me to sleep at night and not worry about what 'might' happen within the club that I am responsible for. The key is to not let the activities become dry or mundane but to make them interesting, fresh and vital. By doing so, staff will happily be involved in the clubs operations and carry that enthusiasm with them into all their tasks.

CHAPTER 15

MANAGING A MONUMENTAL CRISIS[1]

Neil Wright

INTRODUCTION

The monumental crisis that I will be describing is the death of a member while using a health club. The chapter's purpose is to provide an insight into the impact the death of a member may have on your business and your customers and staff. I have drawn on personal experience and suggest ways that you may manage this crisis and potentially achieve some positive outcomes from what is a very distressing and traumatic event.

There is no doubt that the death of a member while using a health club is one of the few events that can affect your business on such a myriad of levels. It will affect your emotions, your team, the family of the deceased and members. It can affect your revenue if you have to close facilities or obtain a bad reputation. Ultimately, it can result in your business being remembered for the wrong reasons. Additionally, the death of a member may challenge you in completely unique ways.

The advice that I am offering should not detract from any systems, procedures or processes that may exist within your organisation to deal with such eventualities. However, it does come from my personal experience in having to deal with deaths and the issues that I have encountered.

GROUPS INVOLVED

You have chosen a career that by default will expose you to greater potential for having to deal directly with a fatality. It is a common belief that it will always

[1] Edited from Wright, N. (2006) 'Managing a monumental crisis' in Algar, R. (ed.) *Mastering Health Club Management*, pp. 172–187, Brighton: Oxygen Consulting.

happen to someone else and that emergency action planning is therefore not a priority. Adhering to this belief may leave you poorly prepared in an emergency and exposes the club to potentially disastrous consequences.

If you are unfortunate enough to have to deal with a member's death, there will be six key groups (to a greater or lesser degree for each individual case) that you will have to deal with:

1   Health and Safety Executive
2   your line manager/board of directors
3   your staff team
4   members
5   family of the deceased
6   the media.

HEALTH AND SAFETY EXECUTIVE (HSE)

First, remember that the HSE are only doing their job and are duty bound to investigate if it is deemed necessary. It is not their intention to catch you out. However, they will be thorough and challenging in their approach.

The key objectives for the HSE to establish during their investigation are:

1   Was the death preventable?
2   Were the actions taken during the incident correct and proper?
3   Is any individual or group of persons responsible in either causing or contributing to the death?
4   Were all those involved trained to a suitable and appropriate level?
5   Were their qualifications valid?
6   Had the necessary risk assessments been carried out and any corrective actions undertaken?
7   Is there documented evidence in relation to points 2, 4, 5 and 6?

The sport and fitness industry places a significant demand on a facility general manager. It is very easy to ignore issues that are less pressing and focus on immediate priorities. This sometimes results in issues such as staff training, accurate record-keeping and risk assessments being deferred. From experience, you will wish that time had been spent ensuring that all bases were covered if you find yourself being inspected. My advice is to ensure that you make time.

If you are confident that you can meet the objectives listed, then you and your team should not be concerned by an HSE investigation.

RESPONSIBILITY TO YOUR ORGANISATION

A general manager is the key person ultimately responsible for all aspects of the club. Given the potential for corporate manslaughter charges, the company places a significant responsibility on the manager. During a major incident this sense of focus on the manager is heightened. The organisation will be relying on you to ensure that the business is not exposed to unnecessary commercial risk.

The staff team

An effective general manager leads and guides the staff team and is a leader, mentor and figurehead for the club. A manager is responsible for staff welfare, training, performance and development. During an incident the staff will look to you as the pivotal person in all the issues that will arise during and after the incident.

Should you immediately take control of the team?

If possible you should assist your staff in dealing with the incident. This does not mean charging in and taking control. If your staff are trained correctly and are competent, then they should already have the situation under control. You should slot into the team and assist as necessary. This achieves several things:

1   You will be able to empathise with your staff as you have a shared experience.
2   They will have a greater respect for you as you provided support when things became difficult.
3   You will develop a greater sense of team unity.
4   You will have seen first-hand how effective the emergency action plan was, the effectiveness of training and can speak from a position of genuine authority when suggesting possible improvements.

Following the incident, all the staff (even those not directly involved) will look to you for leadership. This is a difficult time, as you must initially suppress your own emotions and ensure that your team is supported and that all necessary actions are being taken. However, the defining moments of how your staff team view you and your performance will be condensed into the hours and days following the incident. I have therefore produced a time-related plan that covers the aspects that need to be taken into account after a critical incident, before going on to discuss the other groups involved (members, family of the deceased, the media) in Box 15.1.

BOX 15.1: CRITICAL INCIDENT ACTION PLAN

The first few hours

- The incident takes place.
- Ensure that the emergency services are called as per your Emergency Action Plan (EAP).
- Visit the incident scene and assist as required.
- Ensure that someone is posted to meet and direct the emergency services.
- Gather as much information from the emergency services as possible, including the hospital the casualty will be taken to.
- Gather all those staff directly involved and move them to a private area away from external contact.
- Reassure the team that they have done a good job. If there were errors, now is not the time to apportion any blame. Allow staff the opportunity to express their emotions and to discuss what they have experienced.
- Brief the team on what will happen over the next 24 hours and reassure them of your full support.
- Tour the club and meet with each member of the team. Brief them on the incident. Advise them that if anyone, including the media, requires further information they must contact you.
- Establish if team members are in a position to carry out their duties. It is surprising the effect that a death can have on people, even those not directly involved. If they are not in a position to continue, delegate to a trusted member of staff the task of recruiting additional staff to assist.
- Contact your organisation's health and safety officer (or person designated by the organisation) to inform them of the incident and be directed by them.

- Establish the psychological condition of team members and if they wish to continue working. Let them make the decision unless you categorically feel that they are unable to. If they wish to leave the club, ensure that someone is available to take them home and that they can be cared for over the next 24 hours.
- Team members who wish to continue working must be constantly monitored and not put in a position where they could compromise the safety of members or themselves.
- Before they leave the club, request that all staff involved provide a written statement of their account. If they feel that they are unable to, then this should be submitted within 24 hours.
- Contact your line manager, if you have one, and brief them on the incident. Be directed by them. If possible request that either they or the designated person/organisation assist with responding to possible enquiries from the press.
- If there has been a breach in health and safety, ensure that no further breach can occur. This may require closing the incident area, pending investigation.
- If it appears that the fatality is an unavoidable accident such as a heart attack, I would suggest trying to return the club to normal operation as quickly as possible. This ensures that a sense of normality returns and reduces the number of questions that may arise. It also means that staff do not have to explain the reason for the closure to a growing number of people and reinforces the fact to staff and members that there is nothing to worry about. However, be guided by your own organisation.

24–48 hours

- Continue following up the welfare of the staff team.
- Contact the hospital to understand more about the background to the incident.
- On two occasions I have invited the paramedics who attended the incident to come to the club and meet with the staff who directly worked on the casualty. Again, you should be guided by your organisation's policy and only do this if natural causes were the probable cause of death. Meeting with the paramedics helped my staff to recognise that they had acted professionally and had done everything that was expected of them. This reassured the team and helped reduce the feelings of guilt.

- Speak to your human resources (HR) team and organise formal counselling for those staff who feel that this would be worthwhile. One way of structuring this is by having a counsellor attend the club. They should be sited in a private area and then staff can meet the counsellor more informally. This removes any possible embarrassment that they may feel having to book in via a third party. However, there are other ways of offering this service so be guided by your own organisation.
- Check that the necessary reports have been filed with the Royal Society for the Prevention of Accidents (RoSPA) and the HSE.
- Start reviewing internal records and procedures in preparation for an investigation.
- Prepare to respond to questions from staff and members. Decide how much information you wish to disclose and how you will meet staff and members. You may still be answering questions weeks after the incident. Two of the main reasons why members will want to know about the incident is for personal reassurance and to find out the truth, given that there will be a number of rumours circulating.
- Collate all the information that has been generated in relation to the incident and create a case file. It helps to have all the information in one place (including training files, safety checks, risk assessments, copies of the emergency action plan and witness statements).
- Decide ahead of time whether you are prepared to meet with the family/friends of the deceased and how you wish that meeting to take place, but, again, be guided by your organisation.
- Meet with your management team and ensure that they are fully briefed on the incident and what you expect of them.
- If any team members have been signed off from work due to the incident, ensure that your HR team is aware and that cover is provided.

BOX 15.2: BE PREPARED TO ADAPT TO CIRCUMSTANCES

On one occasion, a member suffered a massive heart attack and was not expected to survive. Police delays meant that no contact was made with next of kin for over 20 hours. During this time, members of the family began to contact my club as they knew he had been swimming. Should I disclose information to the family or delay until the police made contact?

What if I passed on information and they were at home alone? What if the partner rushed to the hospital and crashed their car. Would I share some of the responsibility? On the family's third call to the club, I decided to inform them of the incident and arranged for a taxi to take them to the hospital. The family later thanked me for breaking with protocol.

The legacy

The death of a member at the club can have a very strange effect. It is quite common for a member of staff who appears to have dealt well with the emotional and physiological effects of the incident to have a relapse several weeks or months later. Therefore, it is important to be aware and to monitor your team's behaviour. Possible manifestations can be:

- changes in their normal behaviour pattern;
- unusual sickness patterns;
- a drop in their performance;
- changes in their personal relationships with other team members;
- a sudden desire not to work in or around the area where the incident took place;
- flashbacks.

These are only some of the potential symptoms. If you encounter such a situation, the best course of action is to discuss it with your HR department and be guided by their advice.

MEMBERS

It always amazes me how much interest members take in their club. They will regularly comment on staff changes, pick up on the latest club news and react to any major changes or incidents. Therefore, if a fatality occurs at your club and it was dealt with in a professional and sensitive manner, this will soon spread among the members. On one occasion, I had a family at a club comment that they always wondered what would happen if there was a major incident. Having actually witnessed how well my team dealt with an incident they now felt very reassured. They now knew just how safe the club was. They subsequently recommended some friends to join the club who had experienced a negative situation years before at another facility. However, if it is perceived that you and your team performed poorly, then the negative legacy can take a long time to change. Therefore, again I would recommend that the best way to prevent poor performance is to prepare now.

BOX 15.3: PUTTING A MEMBER'S NEEDS FIRST

I was directly involved in attempting to resuscitate a member. Resuscitation took place while his distraught wife looked on. The ambulance arrived and she pleaded with me to accompany her to the hospital, although as the General Manager I was extremely reluctant to leave the club and my team. I decided to travel to the hospital and support the partner although I was contravening guidelines.

What would you do?

Open door policy

I would advocate an open door policy with members. If someone wishes to discuss the incident with you, then make time to meet. This way you can ensure that accurate information is provided and the members do not feel that you are trying to conceal anything. You will also remain aware of any misinformation that may be circulating.

MEETING FRIENDS AND FAMILY OF THE DECEASED

This is a very difficult and personal issue. There is always the possibility that the family or friends of the deceased may wish to visit the incident scene and meet with you or your staff. This can be a valuable experience for them:

- It helps them to achieve a greater understanding of the circumstances surrounding the death.
- It assists with 'closure'.
- It gives them the opportunity to discuss the incident with the people who dealt with it.

- It provides them with the opportunity to pay their respects where the incident took place.

You will need to decide on the merits of such a meeting, unless a protocol is already outlined in your organisation's guidelines. If you are intending to meet, I would suggest that:

- you establish a clear agenda beforehand;
- you establish in advance of the meeting the particular questions that you are prepared to answer;
- you establish who will be attending the meeting;
- you seek legal advice to ensure that you do not compromise yourself or a team member;
- you are accompanied by an independent person from your organisation or a recognised representative who was not involved in the incident.
- you do not meet during peak times. For example, if they wish to visit the poolside where the incident took place, do so when the pool is closed to members. Also meet at a time when you can guarantee them your full attention;
- you may choose to meet in a neutral location so as to minimise the potential emotional trauma of meeting at the club.

HANDLING THE MEDIA

In my experience if you have a good working relationship with the media, the three main reasons why they are likely to want to cover the story of a death at your club are:

1 They have column inches to fill and no other stories.
2 There is something unusual or suspicious about the death.
3 They feel that there is something you are trying to hide from them.

In the initial period after the incident ensure that you alone deal with any enquiries from the media. Make sure that you brief your team. If you have to take an enquiry, do not be pressed into releasing information until you are ready to do so. Therefore, prepare a short holding statement such as:

> I can confirm that there has been an unfortunate incident at the club. As you would expect, our immediate concerns are the welfare of the

family, staff and members. Therefore we will be releasing more information shortly.

Ensure that a specific individual is responsible for dealing with media enquiries. This could be a public relations company retained by your organisation, your HR department or your line manager. They should have the relevant experience to be able to communicate with the media in a professional manner that gives everyone what they need without compromising the organisation. Once then are appointed, it is essential that all enquiries from newspapers (local and national), radio and television are referred to this individual.

SUMMARY AND KEY ACTIONS

Working in sport or fitness means that you are more likely to experience a fatality during your career. The purpose of this chapter has been to share my experience when this catastrophic event occurs. I have outlined the six different types of people or organisation that you will interact with and advice on how to deal with each, but always be guided by your organisation's procedures. A strong manager will ensure that their team is thoroughly prepared for a major incident and is not of the mindset that it only happens to others. Should a major incident occur, then trust your team to conduct themselves in a calm and professional way. Remember, they are well trained and prepared for such an incident.

1   Do not fall into the trap of assuming that it will happen to someone else. Are you ready?
2   Check to see if your organisation has clear guidelines that regulate for a major incident.
3   Time invested now in checking systems, training your team and keeping correct records will ensure that your team is ready to deal with a major incident.
4   Never assume that all your plans will automatically go according to expectation during a crisis. Test your systems repeatedly.

SECTION 3

VALUING CUSTOMERS OF SPORT AND FITNESS FACILITIES

INTRODUCTION

The purpose of this section is to stimulate understanding and thinking about the issues, concepts and working practices surrounding customer care well beyond basic principles. A variety of authors provide a range of perspectives from academic, managerial and consultancy backgrounds. The section starts by defining terms and coming to a clearer understanding about the nature of customer relationships and decision making. The following chapters develop the recurring section themes of understanding customers, the role of customer expectations and the elements that contribute to customer satisfaction. The importance of strategies that support customer retention is emphasised in further chapters before an outline of staff training and development issues is discussed. Later chapters consider industry perspectives of customer profiling and the development of consistent branded customer experiences through appropriate staff interaction and management processes. Throughout there is recognition of the vital role that staff play in the delivery of sport and fitness services.

Chapters 16, 17 and 20 adapt existing material from the Open University Business School management courses in order to help the reader focus on crucial issues of customer care. Chapter 16, edited by **Indra Sinka** of The Open University, considers the question 'What is a customer?'. It explains the essential differences between products and services and explores what might be involved in the decision making process of consumers. Chapter 17, edited by **Martin Rhys** of The Open University, explores different ways of understanding customer needs and wants, including the concepts of the marketing mix, brand value, customer expectations and market research in a wide-ranging reading.

Chapter 18 is written by **Glynis Young**, a Senior Lecturer in undergraduate programmes in Health, Fitness and Personal Training at Southampton Solent

University, and **Ben Oakley** of The Open University. It discusses the ingredients of customer satisfaction in relation to customer expectations and explains the concept of 'quality gaps'.

Chapter 19 is written by **Leigh Robinson** (a water-polo player and former manager of the Great Britain and England women's water-polo teams). She now works at Loughborough University (School of Sport and Exercise Sciences) as a lecturer in sports management. In this chapter she reviews the literature concerning the essential aspects of good customer care and outlines five main 'rules' which emerge.

Chapter 20 is edited by **Tom Power**, a lecturer in education at The Open University and, in his earlier years, a health and fitness instructor. It concerns the vital objective of customer retention, first discussing the characteristics of loyal customers before moving on to consider the nature and causes of customers' changing expectations.

Chapter 21 is written by **Mark Talley**, former Operations Manager for the multi-site branded fitness operator Esporta and now employed in consultancy and training solutions. In this chapter he gives a manager's perspective of customer retention in a fitness club environment, drawing on research, best practice and his own management experience. He presents a four-part model of retention management that follows the member journey from pre-joining to leaving.

Chapter 22 is written by **Debbie Lawrence**, a freelance lecturer and author of several books on fitness and exercise. Here she explores the value of staff training and development for promoting customer service and discusses different types of activity, including induction and socialisation. A model of practice is proposed that identifies training and development needs and recognises a range of training methods.

Chapter 23 is written by **David Minton** of the Leisure Database Company. He outlines the principles and benefits of customer profiling, which contributes to organisations being able to better understand their customers and the potential local market.

Chapter 24 is written by **Duncan Green**, who is Chief Executive of Momentum Business Development and has experience of more than 230 health and fitness facilities over a 20-year career. In the chapter he discusses the importance of delivering a consistent branded experience to customers and the ways in which staff can contribute towards this by considering members' previous health club experience.

CHAPTER 16

WHAT IS A CUSTOMER?[1]

Indra Sinka (editor)

INTRODUCTION

As someone interested in sport and fitness, you will have used, and at some stage paid for, a product or service linked to the sport you are involved in. The term 'customer' can be used to describe anyone, or any organisation, that benefits from such a product or service.

Subsumed under the umbrella of the rather general term 'customer' are *consumers* and *stakeholders*, and each of these has different wishes and needs. In addition, it is vital for any organisation to be able to categorise and identify different groups of customers. Consider, for example, the needs of teenage sport and fitness participants in comparison to those aged over 50: would they demand the same services or value the same products?

This chapter explores how you can understand what a customer is, and the main differences between products and services, and discusses the factors that influence the choices that customers make. It then goes on to consider the way in which organisations can break down the total spectrum of customers into groups, known as segmentation, so as to target their efforts and better understand customer needs.

THE EXCHANGE PROCESS

In the exchange process an organisation offers a product or service and the customer offers a sum of money in return. The amount of money is nearly always

[1] This chapter is an edited and adapted version of OU Business School Certificate in Management Programme, B630 *Managing Customers and Quality*, Book 1 *Understanding your Customers* (2001), Milton Keynes: The Open University.

determined by the organisation, and the customer must decide whether they think the product or service is worth what is being asked.

The assumption is that both the customer and the organisation value what the other has to offer. If they did not, then one or other would go elsewhere, if they could. The essence of the exchange is mutual value; there must be a belief on both sides that the exchange is fair and equitable. If the customer does not perceive it as such, they are unlikely to take part in the exchange. It is also possible that a customer will take part in the exchange but decide later that it was not fair or of mutual value, in which case they will be unlikely to come back to the organisation in the future.

There is inevitably a tension in this exchange. The organisation will try to provide what the customer wants and values at the lowest cost to itself. It will not try to provide more than it needs to, as this will be likely to cost it more for no greater return. If the customer will buy something without any extra features, there is little point in the organisation adding them. However, the customer often looks for better value, and if another organisation offers it the customer may be encouraged to change supplier. So an organisation must always try to keep the exchange balanced, but also make sure that the exchange it offers is better value than any offered elsewhere. This idea of mutual value, or balance and equity, in the exchange is likely to lead to customer satisfaction and possible repeat purchases. However, many organisations recognise that they may need to do more to encourage customers to buy from them on a regular basis.

This idea of exchange also operates within organisations. How often have you heard people at work complaining about the service offered by another department? Often these conversations end with someone saying, 'We'd be better off doing it ourselves'. The same principle of exchange is at work here, so that within organisations there are 'internal' customers. If you are not providing something of value, and your customers do not perceive that there is a fair exchange, they may look elsewhere.

If you work in a public sector or non-profit organisation (e.g. a Leisure Trust or a sports club), you may think that customers will continue to come to you and your organisation because they have no choice. However, the local authority, or whoever funds your service, may decide that you are not delivering what they want. They could choose to stop funding your service or pay some other organisation to provide it. Thus the principle of an exchange process remains valid: in this case it is between those who hold the resources and those who provide services that meet the needs the resource providers identify.

CUSTOMERS, CONSUMERS AND STAKEHOLDERS

We have already established that it is not just the people who buy a product who need to be considered as customers. This chapter will use the general term 'customer' to include two kinds of people:

- customers, who buy or pay for the products and services an organisation provides, although they may not use them themselves;
- consumers, who use an organisation's products and services, but do not buy them.

Most commercial organisations tend not to make a distinction between customers and consumers. This is because they have to satisfy the needs of both groups with their products or services. Those providing swimming lessons for children, for instance, have to make sure that their lessons are fun and effective for children, and they also have to package and present them in a way that is attractive to parents. The distinction is still important as it is the parent (the customer) who has to be encouraged to complete the exchange process with the organisation, and they may want something different out of the exchange from the child (the consumer). In this case the parent would perhaps be particularly concerned about safety.

It is worth mentioning that any organisation will have a number of different customer groups. Finding a way to categorise and identify different groups of customers is very important. However, for some organisations it is very simple. Consider a small business, managed by the owner, providing physiotherapy for sports injuries. Her customers are sport participants, to whom she provides her services. She does not have any employees, and only works with individuals in her treatment room, which is at the front of her family home, so she deals directly with the end-customers, with no one between her and them. Situations are not always this straightforward.

Consider a leisure centre and ask yourself who the customers are. In broad terms, the customers are the people from the local area who come to use the facilities; however, these people can be divided into those who come for team games and those who come as individuals, for example to use the gym. The leisure centre could also identify the children who come with their parents and need to be kept occupied, and the parents who come to watch their children play. Another group might be the babies and toddlers for whom a crèche is provided so that their parents can take part in sports. Each of these groups of customers needs to be identified and what they want from the exchange process worked out, so that products and services can be developed which will suit them.

So, organisations will have several different groups of customers and consumers, who all expect different things from their relationships with organisations.

We can take this even further and introduce other parties who neither buy nor directly use an organisation's services. We use the term 'stakeholder' to mean those who have an interest in an organisation because they can affect, or be affected by, what is done by the organisation.

Doyle (1998) argued that the survival of an organisation depends on its effective management of a broad range of stakeholder interests. He pointed out that satisfying the multiple and often conflicting stakeholder expectations is the role of every manager within an organisation. He identified stakeholders and their expectations in the model shown in Figure 16.1. Note that compensation covers salary, wages and other remunerative benefits. As you can see from Figure 16.1, stakeholders include a number of groups of people whom we would not call customers in the sense we have been using. In other words, 'stakeholders' is a much broader term, which encompasses, but is not limited to, customers.

Stakeholders can also be defined as those who have a stake in and/or an influence over the organisation's performance or development. For instance, two important stakeholders for an organisation wishing to develop a town's sport or fitness facilities are the local community and local/national government, since they both can strongly influence local planning and design consent.

GOODS AND SERVICES

We are now going to explore the differences between goods and services and look at the idea of delivering value to the customer since it has important implications for customer care.

If asked, we could all list tangible goods: running shoes, a car, a tennis racket, a book, soap. We could also quite easily list intangible services: public transport, fitness advice, golf or tennis lessons, medical treatment, entertainment. However, the distinction is not quite as straightforward as this would imply. In general, most products are accompanied by services, while services tend to have products that support them. The distinction between goods and services is not clear cut. This was recognised as long ago as 1977 by Shostack, who put forward

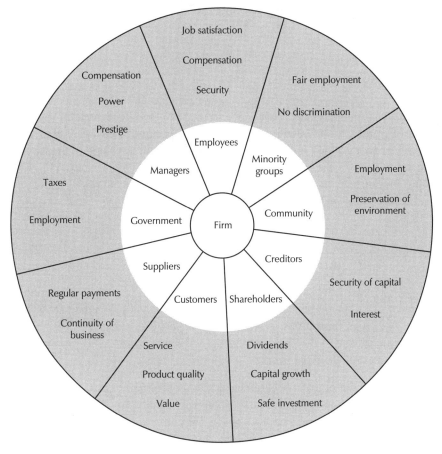

Figure 16.1 Stakeholders and their expectations

Source: Doyle (1998, p. 12).

the idea of the product–service continuum. This proposes that there are no pure products or services, but that each product will have an element of service within it, and each service will have some products.

THE CHARACTERISTICS OF SERVICES

The special nature of services derives from four distinctive characteristics, which we discuss next. These characteristics help shape the internal and external customers' perception of what the organisation has to offer them. The extent to which these different characteristics apply will also affect the way you manage the service.

Intangibility

Your customers cannot see, touch or experience a service before they buy it, so word of mouth and recommendation are important. This means that your customers need to look for other clues about the quality or value of the service you offer, such as the physical environment, the cleanliness of the changing rooms, the dress of the staff, their politeness or their qualifications as shown by certificates on the wall.

Inseparability

Services are normally sold, produced and consumed at the same time, unlike goods, which are manufactured, stored, sold later and consumed later still. Obviously, if you have a fitness session with a personal trainer you have to be present to 'consume' the session. The trainer is the person who provides the service and is therefore part of it.

A further consequence of inseparability is that, unlike most goods, which can be checked before they leave the factory, services cannot be checked so easily. Often the service cannot be separated from the personality of the seller. Consequently, the provider's reputation is frequently a key factor in the decision to buy a particular service. Inseparability means, therefore, that the firm producing a service needs to establish high-quality and reliable recruitment and selection processes as well as training programmes for its employees, as it is the employees who will be delivering the service.

Heterogeneity

Inseparability produces a further characteristic: the heterogeneity or diversity or variety of a service. By this we mean that it is difficult to standardise services in the way products can be standardised. Each particular pair of running shoes should conform to the same specifications; each edition of a particular book should have the same cover, the same number of pages and the same words on those pages. Most services are delivered by people to people, and because people are all very different in their personalities and ways of dealing with others, it is difficult for service companies to ensure that each customer's experience is the same as the previous customer's.

Service companies spend a lot of time trying to guarantee homogeneity or consistency in the provision of their services by means of an effective human resources policy of staff selection, training and motivation.

Fluctuating demand

A further feature of service industries is that demand can fluctuate, depending on, for example, the season or even the time of day. A fitness club may see a huge boost in membership after the New Year as guilt-ridden customers try to lose some weight, but the initial enthusiasm soon wears off in the majority of cases. Use of the gym generally hits a peak at around 6 p.m., which is when many people use it on the way home from work, but the gym can be more than half empty from mid-morning to mid-afternoon.

Service firms have to try to maintain an operational capacity which can meet peak demands but which may lie idle for some of the time and therefore incur extra costs. Firms may consider pricing their services differently to encourage use at off-peak times, or they may find other uses for idle equipment; for example, some ski resorts turn themselves into resorts for golf and walking holidays during the summer.

THE DECISION-MAKING PROCESS

How do customers decide which goods and services to use? Economic theory argues that decisions about what to buy are based on price. However, this is only one of the factors people take into account when choosing products. Sometimes no money changes hands, yet decisions still need to be made.

In reality the decision-making process is often confused. A wide range of factors influence customers during this process. Figure 16.2 shows a framework which we will use to discuss how decisions are made and the various influences on the decision-making process. As you work through this section you should remember that this is a simplification of what can be a very complex process.

In the left-hand box in Figure 16.2 are the four main spheres of influence on the customer. Customers could be influenced to make certain choices by their own

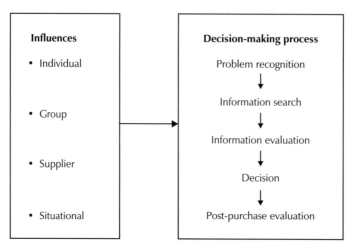

Figure 16.2 Influences on the decision-making process

Source: Open University Business School (2001).

perceptions and motivations and their own personalities – individual influences. They may be influenced by groups of people, such as their families, friends and colleagues. In some situations the supplier may be the greatest influence on a decision because of effective marketing and promotion. Changes in the environment may also have an influence on the customer; for example, lack of snow could lead to the cancellation of a skiing trip. We call these situational influences.

The right-hand box shows the stages in what we call the decision-making process: a logical sequence of steps people may go through to make a decision. We will look at each step in the process and consider the various influences on the decision.

Problem recognition

The first step in the decision-making process is to recognise that there is a problem or need. The recognition process can happen in many ways, from a requirement to fulfil a basic need to a logical thought process that arises from trying to carry out a task. The process may be internally generated (e.g. an individual's desire for new running kit since the existing clothing is ineffective) or externally influenced by situational factors or by suppliers' information and advertising. Thus, the recognition might be something as simple as 'I haven't got anything to run in', or a more complex stimulus such as a desire to run in an event in support of a charitable organisation. Usually, there is not much an organisation can do about its customers' internal processes, except recognise them. Any influence on them is likely to be indirect and difficult to control.

Information search

The next step is to find out how the problem can be solved. Buying an expensive item such as a rowing machine will probably involve gathering a lot of information, whereas suddenly deciding that you need a T-shirt for training does not require much information gathering. At this point an organisation trying to influence customers needs to ensure that information is available to them.

Information evaluation

Once customers have enough information they will try to evaluate it in order to distinguish one product from another. For example, one possible fitness facility choice might be reasonably priced and close to work. Another facility might be more expensive, but it might have a good reputation for food and a larger swimming pool; however, the walk from work takes an extra ten minutes. A third facility choice might be attractive because a friend has already been there and given good reports of its equipment and staff. We can think of this process as a series of filters, each of which corresponds to a particular requirement of the product or service sought. The product that emerges from this filtering process should satisfy the criteria.

Decision

This step may be easy or difficult depending on the outcomes of the previous stage. If only one product or supplier emerges, the decision may be easy. If, after filtering and matching products against criteria, the choice is between two or more products, then other criteria for selection may need to be generated. Again, a supplier can influence the decision, perhaps by offering superior after-sales service or a finance package. How often have you looked at similar alternatives and then purchased from a supplier who could offer immediate delivery, or from one who offered better advice and help?

Post-purchase evaluation

One of our characteristics as humans is that we review any decision we have made and try to convince ourselves that we made the right one. An organisation can also influence this process by ensuring that its product or service lives up to the expectations of its customers. If it does not, then repeat purchasing is threatened, and the opportunity for a lasting relationship can be forfeited. Organisations increasingly use brand image to help reinforce the decision that a customer has made, e.g. that a product is reliable or offers superior benefits (for brands, see Chapter 17).

INFLUENCES ON THE DECISION-MAKING PROCESS

The four influences on the decision-making process are individual, group, supplier and situational. We will look at each in turn.

Individual influences

A number of psychological factors are thought to influence customers' decision-making, such as perception, motivation and attitude. Perception is the process by which an individual selects, organises and interprets information inputs to create a meaningful picture of the world (Dibb *et al.*, 1997).

Our perceptions can be linked with our attitudes. Once someone has formed an attitude, it can be difficult to change. For example, some people believe that public sector organisations are not as efficient as private sector companies. This belief may be unfounded and may adversely affect people's responses to services provided by public sector organisations.

Group influences

Each of us will interact with a number of different groups. We may have colleagues with whom we spend time, and we may belong to a club of like-minded people, such as a tennis club or hiking group. Within each group there is a powerful force at work which encourages its members to conform to the values of their 'reference group'. A group can exert peer pressure, which can modify expectations, opinions, needs and purchasing patterns.

Supplier influences

It is in this area that organisations seek to influence their customers and potential customers by offering products that meet their needs at an appropriate cost, and in places which are convenient to them. This is supported by providing accurate, interesting and appropriate communication in places and environments that will guarantee it is noticed and remembered by customers.

Situational influences

Decisions are usually made in the context of the external environment that surrounds and influences us, consciously or unconsciously. For example, our behaviour may be affected by, on one level, something as simple as the weather; or something less tangible such as society's changing attitudes to the ideal body shape. Both these examples may influence everything from the food we buy and the clothes we wear to the exercise we take.

SEGMENTATION

In the previous section of this chapter we discussed the many influences on people which affect the choices they make. We implied that if they all behaved in the same way, or had certain characteristics in common, this might lead to their having similar needs for particular products. Some examples may help:

- People of similar ages might want similar products. For example, people in their 30s with young children might be interested in sport or fitness facilities that provide some form of children's play area or crèche.
- Young people may purchase the same brands of designer trainers.
- People with a high level of disposable income and an interest in slightly adventurous activities may purchase skiing holidays.

Segmentation thus involves breaking down the total spectrum of customers into groups. It can be defined as:

> the process of splitting customers, or potential customers, within a market into different groups, or segments, within which customers have the same, or similar requirements satisfied by a distinct marketing mix.
>
> (McDonald and Dunbar, 1998, p. 15)

It is worth highlighting three important aspects of this definition. First, it identifies that customers can be grouped together in various ways so as to help organisations meet their common needs. This focus can save money and time and increase effectiveness. Second, the definition suggests that managers can use the information about their customers to design a marketing mix (see Chapter 17 for a fuller treatment) which will attract a particular group of customers more than the marketing mix of their competitors. Finally, it implies that customers' needs can be explained by and even predicted from information about what they have in common with others.

Organisations are likely to use a combination of characteristics or segmentation variables to develop easily identifiable segments or groups of customers. Using a range of segmentation variables makes it possible to identify the types of people who will seek particular benefits from a product. The extract from an article from *Marketing Week* in Box 16.1 is a good example of how markets can be segmented by lifestyle.

BOX 16.1: RECOGNISING GREY MATTERS

There is a fundamental change occurring in the structure of the UK population. By 2020, nearly half the population will be over 45, while the proportion of under 25s will drop to just 25 per cent.

Studies of the over 55s – commonly referred to as the 'grey' market – conclude that this group is experiencing a new sense of emotional and financial freedom . . .

Despite [the impressive size of this market] the commercial opportunities presented by the grey market remain largely untapped. Marketing and advertising tends to focus on younger markets, while the over-55s, who constitute one-third of the total UK population, are largely ignored.

Understanding the mind-sets and motivations of target markets lies at the heart of successful marketing and advertising. The reason the grey market has so far been ignored suggests a lack of willingness rather than a lack of ability on behalf of marketers. Misconceptions about their lifestyles, ranging from bus passes and bingo cards to dentures and dementia, perpetuate the problem.

The reality is somewhat different. Carat Insight concludes that for many over-55s approaching retirement, an important personal objective is to

---

indra sinha

secure good physical and mental wellbeing by engaging in active life-styles. This can involve sports and leisure activities, as well as community issues and local affairs. Contrary to the belief that many older people are couch potatoes, the Carat Foretel Attention Study observed that only 30 per cent of over-55s watch TV for the sake of 'wanting something to do'.

A 'young at heart' attitude is a key trait of the grey market and this is not only reflected in active lifestyles, but also in the desire to experiment and to continually learn. For example, Carat states that few older consumers are truly 'fearful' of technology and constitute almost 10 per cent of all UK Internet users . . .

Despite their propensity to experiment, greys are more experienced and wiser in their purchasing behaviour. Being 'time rich' allows them greater freedom to inspect the market and they prefer more informed purchases rather than impulse buys. Saga Services has found that over-55s view the information gathering process as an enjoyable activity.

[. . .] Overall, the over-55s exhibit a vast disparity in health, wealth and social circumstances. Consequently, classifying all 19 million greys as a single audience ignores the rich diversity in personality, character and psychological make-up.

Source: Rakhia (1999, pp. 28–29).

We can see from Box 16.1 that the main segmentation variable used here is age, but it is linked to lifestyle. The over-55s are seen as an exciting group of customers who need to be further analysed and divided into smaller groups, depending on the activities they like, and their attitudes and motivations.

In most cases a combination of different segmentation variables is used, for example of age and lifestyle, as in Box 16.1, or of age and attitude. Organisations need to find meaningful ways of dividing up potential and existing customers for their products so that they can develop products which will appeal to a particular group. For instance, large public sector leisure centres try to appeal to a very wide range of segments but they try and target certain groups to help generate off-peak usage. Typically, this might be the over-55s, the unemployed and, where possible, school groups.

SUMMARY

This chapter has introduced the importance of identifying both who customers are and the exchange relationship that exists between them and an organisation. The essential differences between products and services was then discussed, and the influence on people in services was emphasised. Following on from this the influences on customer decision-making were outlined, among which people's perception, attitudes and values were considered. Finally, the idea of segmenting those with similar aspirations and needs was introduced, with a particular case study focused on the over-55 group, who represent an increasingly important customer group.

References

Dibb, S., Simkin, L., Pride, W. M. and Ferrell, O. C. (1997) *Marketing Concepts and Strategies*, Boston, MA: Houghton Mifflin.

Doyle, P. (1998) *Marketing Management Strategy*, 2nd edn, Hemel Hempstead: Prentice Hall Europe.

McDonald, M. and Dunbar, I. (1998) *Market Segmentation: How to Do It, How to Profit From It*, 2nd edn, London: Macmillan.

Open University Business School (2001) 'Book I: Understanding your customers', *Managing Customers and Quality*, Milton Keynes: The Open University.

Rakhia, R. (1999) 'Recognising grey matters', *Marketing Week*, 22(27), pp. 28–29.

Shockstack, G. L. (1977) 'Breaking free from product marketing', *Journal of Marketing*, 51, January, pp. 34–43.

CHAPTER 17

UNDERSTANDING CUSTOMERS IN SPORT AND FITNESS[1]

Martin Rhys (editor)

INTRODUCTION

You will know from your own experience that understanding any individual is a complex process. Once you have achieved that understanding you are able to adapt your behaviour in order to produce a particular effect on that individual – to please them or annoy them. Even when you think you have the measure of someone, they may still be capable of surprising you with a change of behaviour or attitude even after several years of relative predictability. The more important the relationship, the more important the understanding in order to sustain it.

There can be no more important relationship for an organisation than with its customers. Without them, it would cease to exist. To get them, and more importantly to keep them, it has to understand them – their needs, their expectations, their attitudes, their behaviours, their tolerances. Once this understanding is achieved, it has to be the driving force behind everything the organisation does.

This chapter examines some of the ways in which understanding the customer is pursued in the hope of meeting customer expectation. It is structured in five distinct sections covering different but interrelated concepts; the first section presents a framework that provides a useful foundation for what follows.

---

[1] This chapter is an edited and adapted version of OU Business School Certificate in Management Programme, B630 *Managing Customers and Quality*, Book 1 *Understanding your Customers*, and Book 2 *Meeting Customer Needs* (2001), Milton Keynes: The Open University.

THE MARKETING MIX FRAMEWORK

The idea of matching the expectations and needs of one party in the exchange process (see Chapter 16) to the goods and services provided by the other is what marketing is all about. Defined as such, it is as relevant to a firm trying to sell its products as to a local authority leisure centre trying to ensure it provides the services its customers want and need.

No single organisation can produce everything for everyone. Each organisation has particular skills and strengths developed over the years. To be successful, it has to match what it is capable of doing with what specific customers want. Providing a product which fulfils the customer's needs is important throughout an organisation, but to satisfy external customers all the internal customer relationships must be working well first. For this reason, everyone in an organisation needs to be involved in marketing.

One of the challenges faced by an organisation is how to design its products to satisfy its customers' needs. A framework has been developed and used for a number of years which can help managers to consider all the relevant factors they can control when seeking to satisfy or communicate with customers. It is commonly known as 'the marketing mix' and was developed in the 1960s by writers and researchers such as Borden (1964) and McCarthy (1960), who identified which interrelated factors marketers found important. These were then popularised as the 'four Ps': product, price, place, promotion.

It is fairly obvious that potential customers cannot or will not purchase or obtain a product unless:

- they know of its existence (promotion);
- it will fulfil their needs (product);
- it is affordable (price);
- it is made available (place/distribution).

However, the four Ps framework has been criticised for being too inward-looking. In other words, the mix concentrates on an organisation's operations rather than on its customers' requirements, and for this reason a number of alternative mixes have been proposed. One of these is the four Cs:

- *Customer needs and wants*: designing all the elements of a product or service so that the final offer will satisfy the customer.
- *Cost*: the customer will consider many factors when deciding if a product or service is value for money. For example, they will think about the time taken

to purchase it, the psychological 'cost' of owning it, and other resources which may be needed. For example, an amateur motor racing enthusiast may buy some well-known branded roll bars from a local store where the price includes delivery and fitting the roll bars into his car. Another local store may offer almost identical non-branded roll bars but will not include fitting. The cost to the enthusiast in this case therefore includes his time, effort and energy to build and fit, and there may be some doubt in the reliability and quality of the non-branded item. He may also not feel confident of his skill in this area and so be happy to pay the higher price.

- *Convenience*: the delivery of products and services to customers involves factors such as quality, access and availability, reliability and the need to develop good customer relationships. For example, the amateur racing enthusiast might find that it is more convenient to use a well-known brand since it is widely available and that they 'trust' what they know about the product rather than research the technicalities in depth.
- *Communication*: organisations need to ensure that customers know about the benefits of products and services and where to obtain them. They need to communicate with customers and let customers communicate with them so that what they offer can be refined in light of feedback.

As you can see, this mix looks outwards to customers, concentrating on their viewpoint.

Zeithaml and Bitner (2003) consider that, whilst the four Cs above are essential for the marketing of products, some modifications are required when applied to services. Since sport and fitness facilities offer a number of services their approach is particularly appropriate for this setting. Their modifications take the form of an expanded marketing mix which includes a further three Cs. (Zeithaml and Bitner actually use the earlier four Ps framework and add three Ps – their terminology has been adapted here in line with the rest of the chapter.)

- *Contact*: all the people who play a part in service delivery – how they are dressed, their personal appearance, their attitudes and behaviours – influence the buyer's perceptions of the service itself. The service provider or contact person can be very important – in fact, for some services, such as personal training, the provider *is* the service. Research suggests, however, that all potential front-line staff personnel – from receptionist to maintenance – can at different times be the focal point of 'service encounters' that can prove critical for the organisation.
- *Context*: the physical environment in which the service is delivered and where the organisation and customer interact. The physical evidence of

service includes all of the tangible representations of the service such as equipment, décor, changing facilities, brochures, signage, reception area. The physical context can provide excellent opportunities to send consistent and strong messages regarding the focus and nature of the service.

- *Conducting the process*: the actual procedures, mechanisms and flow of activities by which the service is delivered; the service delivery and operating systems. A distinguishing characteristic of the process, which can provide evidence to the customer, is whether the service follows a production line/standardised or personalised/customised process. An induction session which is timetabled once per week for a duration of some twenty minutes and includes up to ten new members is hardly likely to feel personalised and will inevitably lead to an initial impression of regimentation.

These three additional marketing mix elements are all within the control of the organisation and any or all of them may influence the customer's initial decision to purchase a service as well as the customer's level of satisfaction and repurchase decisions.

Therefore, the above seven point marketing mix (the seven Cs) is a very useful framework that can be used to link together the different customer care themes that are presented elsewhere in this chapter and this book since it concentrates on the customer's perspective rather than the organisation's. You may find different terms used in other sources but the basic ideas are often very similar. An idea that is often raised in other sources is the concept of customer orientation, which is discussed next.

CUSTOMER ORIENTATION

The ideal

At its extreme, customer orientation means that everything a manager does is driven by a concern to meet customers' needs, whether those customers are external, internal or in a private, public or non-profit context. It would mean, for example, that when you are working out management priorities, making decisions, participating in meetings or appraising a member of staff, your customers' needs would influence you. The theory behind customer orientation is that it should be the dominant orientation in any organisation; after all, serving its customers is surely why any organisation, or a part of it, exists.

Customer orientation means responding promptly to customers to ensure their satisfaction. You may care to consider what makes you respond with urgency, either at work or in some other context. It may be your manager, or someone in authority, telling you to do something, or a colleague or friend presenting a problem that needs attention. It may be your own sense of responsibility when you are faced with a task or a deadline. Perhaps you respond with urgency when you find out something new or significant that a competitor, a similar organisation or another section in your organisation is doing. Perhaps you respond with urgency when a customer or family member says or demands something that makes you drop everything else.

The reality is probably a mixture of several causes, and the issues you respond to cannot be as clearly categorised as implied here. The reality of customer orientation is more problematic than the rhetoric.

The reality

In order to fulfil the promises made to their customers, organisations and their staff need to become customer-focused and customer-responsive. It is common sense that organisations that do so will be better able to survive in hard times and thrive in good times, but there is more than simple common sense to support this contention. For example, a UK study by the Strategic Planning Institute (Finkelman and Goland, 1990) shows that companies that were rated highly on customer service increased their market share faster and achieved significantly higher profits than their lower-rated competitors.

Furthermore, the same study suggested that two-thirds of the customers lost by industrial companies were lost as the result of the companies' indifference in one form or another, and only 9 per cent as the result of lower prices elsewhere.

Poor responsiveness to customers is also costly: services may have to be repeated without any extra revenue. Dealing with complaints can absorb much expensive staff time, and the morale of those spending that time often suffers, thus damaging an organisation's important main asset, i.e. its staff. When an organisation acquires the image of being unreliable or providing poor service or poor aftercare, customers adopt negative attitudes, and front-line staff often bear the brunt of them. Excessive and expensive employee stress and turnover can result.

In reality, organisations and their staff tend to follow practices and policies that have been dictated by past conditions, by internal politics and/or by organisational and personal goals, many of which may have developed independently of customers' interests. These are discussed here because it is necessary to understand *why* staff are not responsive to their customers before there can be hope of changing their behaviour. Customer orientation is often difficult for individual managers to bring about because of other pressures that seem to dominate their organisations. These can be considered competing orientations, and the most significant ones are shown in Table 17.1, which provides examples from a variety of business sectors.

CUSTOMER EXPECTATIONS: THE ZONE OF TOLERANCE

Customers have expectations of services and the task of organisations is to make sure that they meet, or even exceed, those expectations. If they do this, we assume that the customers will be satisfied, and that if the expectations are not met the customers will be dissatisfied. There are three elements which contribute to a customer's expectations, and we show them in Figure 17.1.

This model shows how a customer's expectations and perceptions of the various aspects of a service will affect their final quality assessment. In fact, the same process will be used by customers when assessing all products, whether tangible or intangible. The model suggests that a customer forms expectations before purchase. These arise from word-of-mouth recommendation, past experience, external communications and the customer's own needs. The customer will then assess these expectations in the light of their experience of the purchase. They will assess both the process and the output. In other words, they will consider the way the product has been delivered to them: the intangible service part of the product and the quality of the tangible good itself. The relative importance of each of these elements will depend on the product and on what

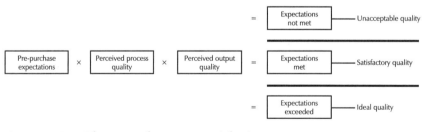

Figure 17.1 The roots of customer satisfaction

Source: Based on Berry *et al.* (1985, p. 47).

Table 17.1 Competitors of customer orientations

Orientation	Features	Example
Technology orientation	When the excitement of what can be done comes before the requirements of customers	The car sound system so technically advanced that it was too complicated to operate and the cost of designing it exceeded the value of any benefit the customer received (or *thought* they would receive)
Product orientation	When organisations think they know that what they produce or provide is what customers want	The clothes retailer that put so much effort into getting fashions that had sold well in the past to its customers that it failed to notice what they currently wanted to wear
Producer orientation	When what the staff want (or do not want) comes before customers' interests	The post office or government office that closed at lunchtimes and weekends, when it would have been convenient for customers, because staff did not want to work then
Financial orientation	When making profits or cutting costs in the short term comes before longer-term customers' interests	The holiday company that was so keen to show its shareholders annual increases in profitability that it failed to design and invest in new e-mail and internet enquiry facilities for its customers until it was too late
Sales orientation	When selling (or delivering) higher volumes becomes an end in itself at the expense of customer satisfaction	The new specialist radio station that used the best advertising and public relations firms to generate opening audience figures that far exceeded its expectations, and promptly lost 85 per cent of them because the programmes were so badly put together
Managerial orientation	When managers' need to implement the latest management philosophy takes the emphasis away from the customer	The national charity that put so much effort into being the first in the sector to be accredited under the people management standard ISO 9000, Investors In People, and then the Business Excellence Model, that its change-weary staff failed to respond to a major change in the needs of the people it existed to help
Professional orientation	When professionals in an organisation do not listen to service users because they believe that they know best	The consultant who did not listen to the concerns of a patient because he knew what the problem was and the appropriate treatment, but did not understand the patient's distress, caused by ignorance of the terminology he was using

the customer perceives to be most important. The outcome will be one of three states:

- expectations met: the customer will be satisfied;
- expectations not met: the customer will be dissatisfied;
- expectations exceeded: the customer will be very satisfied, but will probably increase their expectations to take into account the new level of quality they have received; in future, the customer will probably need to perceive that the product is being delivered to this new level of quality just to be satisfied.

Parasuraman *et al.* (1991) showed that customers have two levels of expectation, adequate and desired: the first is what they find acceptable and the second is what they hope to receive. The distance between the adequate and the desired levels is known as the *zone of tolerance*, and this can expand and contract according to circumstances. The two levels may vary from customer to customer, and from one situation to another for the same customer, depending on what else has happened to them that day, whether they are in a hurry and so on. You can probably remember situations in which you have accepted services or products which in other circumstances you would have refused or been disappointed by. The zone of tolerance is shown in Figure 17.2.

If we accept that this is how customers subconsciously evaluate products and that there is some tolerance in their evaluation, we can start to see what is meant by responsiveness to customers. Ideally, organisations, and more particularly their employees, will always try to operate within a customer's zone of tolerance. To do this, managers need to understand what customers want from their organisation and whether or not their customers' expectations are being met.

If an employee realises that a customer is dissatisfied, they should, if they are responsive to the customer's needs, attempt to 'recover' the situation. Of course, it is not always possible to rectify the situation immediately: other people

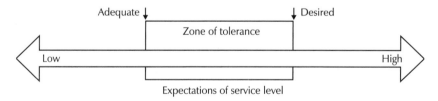

Figure 17.2 The zone of tolerance

Source: Parasuraman *et al.* (1991, p. 42).

may need to be involved, or the resources may not be available. However, even if the response cannot be immediate, it is important that the organisation encourages feedback from staff and customers, so that lessons can be learned.

CUSTOMER EXPECTATIONS: BRANDS AND BRAND VALUE

A brand name can be a good way of differentiating a product. If two products are similar, customers are more likely to buy the product with the brand name they know, rather than the one they have not heard of, as a surer way to having their expectations fulfilled.

An interesting example of how important brand image is can be seen from taste tests carried out by Coca-Cola and Pepsi. Respondents were asked to decide which of the two cola drinks they preferred. When they were allowed to see the brand of the drink there was a marked preference for Coca-Cola – 65 per cent preferred it. However, when the respondents were blindfolded the distinction between the two brands was reduced significantly. In this test 51 per cent of testers preferred Pepsi (De Chernatony and McDonald, 1998, p. 11). The differences between the two sets of results suggest that customers 'taste' both the drink and the brand image. The brand image adds value to the product or service in the mind of the customer.

Branding can provide benefits for both buyers and sellers. Customers benefit because they can immediately identify specific products that they do and do not like. Without brands, product selection would be quite random, with customers having to read the packaging every time to find out about each product and how it matched with what they wanted. Creating brand loyalty permits companies to charge a premium price for a product. For example, the manufacturers of Nurofen, a pain-relieving product, charge more than the manufacturers of generic products which use the same active ingredient (ibuprofen).

Arnold (1992) claims that three important principles have emerged from research into brand performance:

1 *Market leaders and superior brand positions are interlinked*: top brands are virtually all leaders, or joint leaders, in their markets. This is not just because the companies spend a lot on advertising or because the brands have a good name or are inherently better quality products. It is the perception of quality by the customer which is important.
2 *Market-leading brands tend to have higher profit margins*: market leaders command a price premium and therefore make higher profits. Arnold

reports surveys that conclude that in the UK the market leader returns a profit margin six times that of the number two in the market. Leading brands also demonstrate greater resilience during recessions or price wars. Perceived superior quality is reflected in consumers' willingness to pay more.

3   *There is no such thing as a brand life-cycle*: once a leading brand is established with a loyal customer base, there is no reason why that position cannot be maintained almost indefinitely. Brands are larger than products. They can be updated regularly and altered in almost any aspect to maintain their relevance to the market.

There are a number of successful brands in sport and fitness, for example Nike (footwear and clothing), Marin (mountain bikes), Virgin Active (health and fitness clubs), Lucozade (sports drinks) and PGL (youth activity holidays). For a brand to be successful, it must:

- deliver *functional* benefits to meet the market need at least as well as the competition does;
- offer *intangible* benefits over and above the basic benefit of the core product;
- comprise various benefits which are *consistent* with each other and present a unified character or identity;
- offer *special features* that customers want, that is, something valued and which customers judge nobody else can offer.

The most successful brands have an appeal that can cross borders and cultures and combine physical, rational and emotional (psychological) appeal. The blend must be distinctive and, particularly in sport and fitness, it must have a clear identity which offers benefits of value to customers.

MARKET RESEARCH

Finding out what people think of an organisation – its brand, services and those of its competitors – is known as market research. It can be used as a means of helping organisations forecast the future of the environments in which they operate. It is only on the basis of a sound description of current reality that we can plan for change.

Market research provides managers with basic data and information to help them understand their customers, markets, suppliers, competitors, external factors and trends. Data is defined simply as raw, undigested facts (an example

Figure 17.3 The three key elements of market research

Source: Open University Business School (2001).

of data is the number of people using different brands of running shoes). Information, on the other hand, is data that has been made sense of, generally by combining and comparing it with other data (for example that blue and white is the most popular colour of running shoes sold to adults between the ages of 20 and 40). Decisions may follow (a company may decide to launch a new brand of running shoe taking account of information about population segments, customers' preferences, competitors' products and much else besides). Figure 17.3 shows this diagrammatically.

People do not realise that many of their activities represent research. For instance, the accounts department of a fitness organisation which produces a pattern of memberships gained and lapsed may not regard the results as 'proper' research. However, they do yield invaluable data on customers, which, if accurate and representative, can be used to improve understanding. Indeed, informal but informed analysis and judgements are frequently as valuable as formally commissioned surveys of customers.

In many cases, informal information can be of value to other parts of the organisation connected to the customers. Many smaller organisations hold regular meetings where everyone from the receptionist to the managing director takes part in the information-sharing process.

It will be useful for you to be clear about the difference between primary and secondary data when finding out more about customers and their needs. Secondary data already exists: sales and customer information, previous surveys and studies, published reports, data or statistics. The advantages of secondary data are that it is readily available – especially with increasing electronic access – and that it is free or costs relatively little. The disadvantage is that it may not include the exact information that you need for your purposes. Primary data, on the other hand, is derived from specially commissioned surveys or studies. It can be tailored to your exact needs, but these methods are both time-consuming and expensive. It makes sense, therefore, to ensure that you have searched all the secondary sources before committing yourself to primary market research.

Of course, both primary and secondary data have to be generated in the first place. Research methods can generally be divided into qualitative methods and quantitative methods. In simple terms, qualitative market research methods (such as interviews) are used to explore the attitudes and behaviours of customers. Quantitative methods (such as surveys) apply numerical values to measure aspects of customer behaviours and attitudes such as using a five-point scale to rate satisfaction or the extent of agreement with a statement.

SUMMARY

Marketing is a way of harmonising the needs and wants of the customers with the resources and objectives of an organisation; therefore one of the primary ways of bringing about this harmony is to get to know the customer. In this chapter this understanding of customers has been developed by ideas from the seven Cs of the marketing mix, the concepts of customer orientation, customers expectations and brand value. The final section of the chapter considered an outline of the role of and terms used in market research.

REFERENCES

Arnold, D. (1992) *The Handbook of Brand Management*, London: Century Business/Economist Books.

Berry, L. L., Zeithaml, V. A. and Parasuraman, A. (1985) 'Quality counts in services too', *Business Horizons*, May–June, pp. 44–52.

Borden, N. H. (1964) 'The concept of the marketing mix', *Journal of Advertising Research*, 4, June, pp. 2–7.

De Chernatony, L. and McDonald, M. (1998) *Creating Powerful Brands in Consumer, Service and Industrial Markets*, Oxford: Chartered Institute of Marketing/Butterworth Heinemann.

Finkelman, D. and Goland, A. (1990) 'How not to satisfy your customers', *McKinsey Quarterly*, Winter, pp. 1–13.

McCarthy, E. J. (1960) *Basic Marketing*, Homewood, IL: Irwin.

Open University Business School (2001) 'Book 3: Valuing your customers', *Managing Customers and Quality*, Milton Keynes: The Open University.

Parasuraman, A., Berry, L. and Zeithaml, V. A. (1991) 'Understanding Customer expectations of service', *Sloan Management Review*, Spring, pp. 39–48.

Zeithaml, V. A. and Bitner, M. J. (2003) *Services Marketing*, 3rd edn, New York: McGraw Hill Companies, Inc.

CHAPTER 18

SATISFYING CUSTOMERS IN SPORT AND FITNESS

Glynis Young and Ben Oakley

This chapter aims to develop an understanding of customer satisfaction and unravel the range of components that contribute towards it. It will draw upon your own experiences in purchasing goods or services and assumes that you also have some experience of using a sport or fitness facility. Whether your experience was positive or negative probably depended on many factors, and our objective here is to help you understand those factors and why they may vary from one situation to another.

When people purchase a service, they do so with a set of expectations of what they are likely to receive. What customers expect and what they receive are often two different things; sometimes this leads to a customer's delight and sometimes to disappointment and frustration. In other words the customers' perception of what they receive often does not match what they have been expecting. Organisations which aim to please their customers and retain them have to understand what it is that customers want, how customers form their opinions and what the organisation can do to make sure those expectations are met or perhaps even exceeded.

Following a more detailed discussion on customer expectations (that links with Chapter 17), we then move on to consider a 'quality gaps model' that helps to identify how there might be gaps in service provision between customer expectations and what is delivered. The concluding part suggests which components deserve the particular attention of sport and fitness facility-operators if they wish to close the gaps and ensure customer satisfaction.

CUSTOMER EXPECTATIONS

Customer expectations vary depending on matters such as what they have been told by friends or colleagues (word of mouth), how much is being charged, how important the purchase is to them and how urgently the service is needed. All these factors lead customers to have different levels of expectations.

> Customer expectations are beliefs about service delivery that function as standards or reference points against which performance is judged.
>
> (Zeithaml and Bitner 1996: 76)

For example, we expect that if we arrive at an upmarket, expensive fitness club at the time of our booking, our personal trainer will be ready for us and the exercise programme offered will have been carefully planned to meet our specific needs, and that all the staff, as well as the trainer, will be friendly and efficient. On a more complex level, another expectation might be a dynamic picture of the future which is continuously adjusted to take into account our changing moods and states of mind as well as new information and experiences. Reading a good or poor review of the club, or learning that someone influential has trained there recently, or learning that your personal trainer has been replaced, or having an argument with one of the other members who goes at the same time as you can influence your expectation of how your next session is likely to be.

Expectations range from the very high or ideal to the absolute minimum acceptable level, as outlined in Figure 18.1 and Parasuraman et al. (1991) referred to this as the zone of tolerance (see Chapter 17). It may be worth reflecting on the different values and beliefs that underlie the different levels of expectation; these are partially revealed by the examples given in the table. Note that different individuals will often have very different perceptions.

CUSTOMER REQUIREMENTS

Research suggests that customers evaluate service along a range of multiple factors relevant to the context. Parasuraman et al. (1988) point to five elements that customers take into account when considering service:

1   *Reliability*: 'Will it continue to do what I expect?' Clearly, customers will

Level of expectation	Example	
Ideal expectations	I am organising a very prestigious award ceremony with dignitaries and press attending so everything must be perfect.	**HIGH** ▲
'Should' expectations	The sports coach should be good given the amount s/he charges.	
Previous experiences	The clubhouse facilities were great the last time I visited.	
Acceptable expectations	As long as the court is ready and the changing rooms clean, it will be acceptable to me.	
Minimum tolerable expectations	The clubhouse is rundown and the equipment is old, but I still go because the squash court is usually available and the membership fee is cheap.	▼ **LOW**

Figure 18.1 Possible levels of customer expectations

Source: adapted from Zeithaml and Bitner (2003).

value a coaching service that keeps its promises and continues to give good tips and advice.

2 *Responsiveness*: 'Will the service be prompt in responding to requests?' Often customers have specific issues that need solving so this is about attentiveness and promptness.

3 *Assurance*: 'Do the employees seem knowledgeable and inspire trust and confidence?' This becomes more important if the service involves a degree of uncertainty or risk. In sport and fitness credentials, reputation and safety considerations will often help inspire confidence in a service.

4 *Empathy*: 'Is the attention given caring and individualised to my needs?' This involves treating customers as individuals and would include aspects such as remembering a client's name and any previous problems or achievements.

5 *Tangibles/physical evidence*: 'Does the physical appearance of the facility and personnel generate a feeling of quality?' Since a service is not as tangible as a product the appearance of facilities, equipment, personnel and communication materials all help convey messages about the organisation and its products.

Zeithaml and Bitner (2003) suggest that the relative significance of these five elements may vary according to different businesses. There is no current research that identifies which of these elements is more important in a sport and fitness setting, but we can relate findings from investigations into similar industries that identify the vital role played by people in sport and fitness, particularly with respect to *responsiveness*, *assurance* and *empathy*. Multi-site branded operators of health and fitness facilities also pay a great deal of attention to the *reliability* and consistency of service experiences and the environment in which they are delivered (*tangibles/physical evidence*).

QUALITY GAPS

Shortfalls in quality are likely to arise when there is a gap between what customers expect and what they consider they are getting. When such gaps exist it is almost bound to lead to customers' dissatisfaction. Parasuraman *et al.* (1985) identify the main points where gaps between customers' expectations and their perceptions of a product or service may arise (see Figure 18.2). Box 18.1 illustrates this model.

BOX 18.1: JUDGING THE GAPS

The head coach of an Olympic sports team referred a young athlete, who had suffered a recent knee trauma, to a sports injury 'assessment centre' for a comprehensive assessment in four areas – psychological, core stability and flexibility, peer support network and medical – before making a decision about the athlete's future. The young athlete was a promising young talent who was devastated by her injury so close to Olympic selection but the athlete still thought playing in the final stages of the tournament might be possible; the coach wanted to advise the athlete appropriately about her chances of selection and whether she should stay with the squad whilst recovering or go away for specialist treatment. In this case, the head coach was a customer relying on the expertise of a number of different experts under the umbrella and assurance of the assessment centre and its manager.

Gap 1: between customers' expectations and managers' perceptions of customers' expectations

This gap can be seen when a manager does not know what a customer expects.

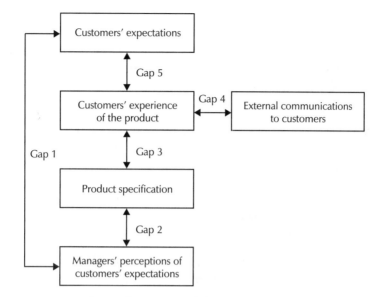

Figure 18.2 The quality gaps model

Source: adapted from Parasuraman *et al.* (1985).

Assessment centre example: The managers of the assessment centre considered the quality of the reports to be the most important aspect of the assessment. However, the customer – the head coach – looked for promptness, the clarity of the recommendation and the pros and cons of various options. The managers failed to understand the benefits sought by their customer.

Gap 2: between the managers' perception of customers' expectations and the product specification

This gap can be seen when managers do not draw up an appropriate specification to show clearly what they intend a service to be, leaving the employees who deliver the service unsure what is intended.

Assessment centre example: In this case, those who carried out the assessment were not sure what the managers had undertaken to do for the head coach, i.e. which components made up the report.

Gap 3: between the service 'product' and customers' experience of it

This gap can be seen when a product is not delivered as specified. There are many reasons why this can happen. Perhaps demand has been greater than anticipated, or perhaps resources are constrained. It should be remembered that it is the customers' experience of the product that is important. This can be affected by many intangible factors, which can be especially important in service delivery. In the assessment centre example, this gap took the form of an incomplete assessment.

Assessment centre example: The assessment centre had indicated that a psychological report would form part of its report, but the psychologist got his dates muddled. There was not time to rearrange the date, and the assessment omitted a psychological report.

Gap 4: between customers' experience and external communications to customers

This gap can be seen when an organisation cannot deliver what it promises in its advertising or other promotional activity. If they want satisfied customers, organisations should promise only what they can deliver.

Assessment centre example: The head coach had started to use the assessment centre because its multi-disciplinary team had claimed it could produce 'comprehensive reports' comprising many aspects. The centre's failure to include one aspect (the psychological report) because of its dependence on an unreliable external provider meant that it failed to deliver what it had promised.

Gap 5: between customers' expectations and customers' experiences

Customers' overall expectations are affected by their own experiences, the recommendations of others and the claims of suppliers. Remember that customers' experiences are determined by their perceptions and not by those of the supplier of a product or service. It is essential for suppliers to see things from their customers' standpoint.

Assessment centre example: After the accumulation of quality gaps, the overall impression was of failing to deliver in Gap 5 at a crucial time; the assessment centre therefore found that it received less work, having not lived up to the head coach's expectations and thereby acquiring a reputation for poor quality.

The quality gaps model provides a useful extension to our thinking about expectations since it suggests how the different parts of an organisation's activities contribute to meeting (or not meeting) customer expectations. Of the five gaps that are identified in the model, Gap 5 (between customers' expectations and their experiences) is the most significant since a gap here will make satisfaction unlikely. Gaps 1, 2, 3 and 4 all contribute to the overall perceptions of the 'customer gap' (Gap 5), and there is an important role in gaps 2 and 3 for a clearly understood vision of the product specification.

In terms of service quality, therefore, it is essential to set clear specification standards and monitor them so that the required standard of service, once achieved, can be maintained. To achieve this it is vital to ensure that the standards are customer driven, which means that the organisation must seek to find out from their customers what is really important to them, which will enable an accurate measure of service quality to be established.

CLOSING THE GAPS

So far we have investigated some of the theory behind the components of customer satisfaction; but what should sport and fitness operators concentrate on in striving to satisfy more customers and to close the quality gaps? Here, we will briefly outline some of the main items that are linked to recognised industry quality standards in sport and fitness (see Quest 2007 for further details). To link theory with practice we will also indicate which gaps such actions are mainly designed to close from the quality gaps model (Gaps 1–5).

A good starting point is for an organisation to understand its customers, the way the market is segmented and, most pertinently, *their needs and wants*. This will require sound market research which includes systems that encourage and engage with customer feedback (Gap 1).

Acting upon this information, *systems* and *processes* need to be designed with an appropriate specification so that the staff who deliver them know what is expected (Gap 2). Think, for instance, of the design of entry procedures and the payment system in a busy facility and how these are put under considerable strain at peak times. Clemmer makes the point that managers need to recognise 'the 85/15 rule: 85 per cent of service breakdowns originate in an organisation's systems, processes and structure' (2007, p. 16). For example, the *process* of regular service and maintenance of gym equipment – rather like a car's engine oil or tyre pressure – is important since if neglected it can lead to eventual breakdown; the *system* of ordering spares in maintaining gym equipment needs to take account of the delays that might be caused if spares are not available promptly; and the *structure* concerns which level of management needs to be informed of such matters in order to deal with problems efficiently. If these procedures fail, equipment will be out of service frequently, affecting customer perceptions.

Since sport and fitness services are heavily reliant on *people* to deliver their product, a focus on staff represents an investment in the organisation. Staff have a crucial role to play in Gap 3 of the model, when a product is not delivered as specified. The failure to deliver services as designed can result from a number of factors originating in an organisation's personnel, but these can be avoided by a combination of the following:

- recruiting the right people with service skills;
- using effective staff training;
- promoting empowerment;
- involving people in the organisation's strategy;
- rewarding good service.

A focus on the way an organisation *communicates* with its customers, and in particular, the way in which it creates levels of expectation of the service (Gap 4) is an important principle. Communication consistency, marketing, service guarantees and branding are all closely connected with this notion of creating appropriate expectations, and therefore the messages conveyed by promotional material and websites have particular importance.

The appearance, cleanliness and ambience of the physical environment, typically the car park, reception, changing rooms and the sport facilities themselves, contribute greatly to customer perceptions. The overall 'customer gap' (Gap 5) has many contributing factors but the state and design of the buildings play a role in shaping customer expectations and mood.

SUMMARY

This chapter set out to examine the factors that contribute to positive or negative customer experiences and why they may vary from one situation to another. The idea of customer expectations lies at the core of understanding customer satisfaction. This concept was developed further by identifying five different quality gaps in service provision. The role of people and their interpersonal skills has also been outlined, as in the sport and fitness industry people deliver so much of the 'product', particularly in coaching settings and personal training. However, it must be remembered that every person with whom a customer comes into contact has the potential to enhance the customer's experience or make it less enjoyable, and this includes every single employee from the receptionist and instructional staff to the directors in the board room.

Good management plays a major factor in achieving customer satisfaction. One of the main leadership roles managers play is in developing a genuine customer focus throughout an organisation and a focus on continual improvements by learning from past service failures, and in closing quality gaps. The combination of managers' commitment to customer oriented systems and ways of working and employees who acknowledge their own crucial role in interacting with customers forms the foundation for satisfying customers.

REFERENCES

Cleminer, J. (2007) 'Business is like tennis – if you don't serve well, you lose', *Fitpro Business*, April/May, p. 16.

Parasuraman, A., Zeithaml, V. A. and Berry, L. L. (1985) 'A conceptual model of service quality and its implications for future research', *Journal of Marketing*, 49(4), September, pp. 41–51.

Parasuraman, A., Zeithaml, V. A. and Berry, L. L. (1988) 'SERVQUAL: a multiple-item scale for measuring consumer perceptions of service quality', *Journal of Retailing*, 64, Spring, pp. 12–40.

Parasuraman, A., Berry, L. and Zeithaml, V. A. (1991) 'Understanding customer expectations of service', *Sloan Management Review*, Spring, pp. 39–48.

Quest (PMP Consultancy) (2007) *Welcome to the Quest and National Benchmarking Service Website*, accessed July 2007, available from: http://www.questnbs.info/.

Zeithaml, V. A. and Bitner, M. J. (1996) *Services Marketing*, 2nd edn, New York: McGraw Hill Companies, Inc.

Zeithaml, V. A. and Bitner, M. J. (2003) *Services Marketing*, 3rd edn, New York: McGraw Hill Companies, Inc.

CHAPTER 19

THE RULES OF CUSTOMER CARE

Leigh Robinson

Customers need to be valued and nurtured and there is a considerable amount of advice available both online and in the academic literature about how this might be achieved. A review of the literature identified a number of common themes in the writings on customer care (Beech and Chadwick, 2004; Business Link, 2007; Cardwell, 1994; Checketts, 2006; Clutterbuck, 1991; Cook, 2002; Customer Care Institute, 2007; Colombo, 2003; Oakland and Beardmore, 1995; Robinson, 2001; Robinson and Wolsey, 1996; Sayers, 1991; Torkildsen, 1993; Williams and Buswell, 2003). In this chapter, I have chosen to present these themes as 'rules' of customer care as they categorise and summarise contemporary thinking in this area. I have chosen themes that focus on services and service delivery in a competitive environment as these areas particularly apply to sport and fitness.

RULE 1: GIVE CUSTOMERS WHAT THEY WANT

The first rule of customer care is to ensure that the organisation delivers services that customers want. People will only come to the organisation if it has something to offer that they feel they want or need and that they cannot get from a competitor. This is known as the organisation's *unique selling proposition* (USP). A USP for a sport and fitness organisation could be its location, a swimming pool, the price of membership or the fact that it provides activities for children. The organisation needs to identify and protect its USP in order to give customers what they want.

The market research aspect of finding out what customers want is a large topic in its own right which will not be covered in this short chapter. My point here is that it does not really matter how the information is collected; the important point is that it is collected and then acted upon. The following list reiterates the information that managers should know about their customers for customer care purposes:

- *who they are*: demographic details such as age, gender, family life-cycle and income all help to create a picture of customers, allowing services to be designed to specifically meet any needs that arise because of these demographics.
- *what they do*: the occupational status, occupations and hobbies and interest of customers. This will allow the organisation to deliver services around working arrangements which also allow other interests to be met.
- *why they buy*: why customers choose a particular sport and fitness organisation. Understanding this makes it easier to match their needs with the benefits the organisation has to offer.
- *what they expect*: often different from what customers want. Customers create their own mental picture of sport and fitness organisations from promotional material, past experience and talking to others. This means that there will often be expectations of the organisation that have to be met, even if they are not directly related to the needs of the customer. For example, a customer may expect a sport and fitness organisation to have a spa and sauna, even if they have no intention of using it. If these facilities are not available, the customer may perceive the quality of the organisation to be poor.

RULE 2: VALUE STAFF

An essential component of customer care is having motivated, well-presented and approachable staff who are able to communicate with customers and have the authority to deal with customer requests. This empowerment of staff will motivate staff to deliver the service expected of customers and is important because empowerment allows people to 'grow and develop to become more autonomous and take more responsibility for their own actions' (Senior, 1997, p. 300).

Sport and fitness organisations need to operate fair recruitment and selection procedures to ensure that the right people are recruited, along with good staff development provision so that their skills remain up to date (see Chapter 22 for further discussion of staff training).

More importantly, however, the way staff are treated at work will be reflected in the way they treat customers, which means that managers must find ways of demonstrating that they value their staff. There are a number of ways of doing this, such as:

- giving regular constructive feedback;
- allowing staff to make decisions about their work;
- giving staff appropriate responsibility to carry out their work;
- treating staff fairly and equally;
- paying staff fairly;
- providing opportunities for team building and social activities, such as staff events and parties.

Staff who feel valued and fairly treated will be motivated to do their best for the organisation and deliver good levels of service to customers.

RULE 3: GIVE GOOD SERVICE EVERY TIME

Frequent service breakdowns indicate to customers that the organisation does not really care about them. Staff are essential in this regard, but it is also important to have good operating procedures that can help staff deliver customer care.

Consequently, all sport and fitness organisations should have a clearly thought out Manual of Operating Procedures (MOP) that sets out how the organisation should be run and the standards that are considered necessary to deliver good customer care. The MOP should set out such things as the maintenance systems and processes for key equipment, the control of numbers in busy classes, staff recruitment and training policies, as well as complaint handling procedures. This can then be used to set standards, monitor performance against a set specification, achieve consistency across departments or sites and train new staff members. It is the way that customer focused standards are designed and implemented that is important.

RULE 4: KNOW HOW GOOD THE ORGANISATION IS

Assessment of satisfaction is fundamental to customer care. Not knowing if services that customers want are being delivered, or if these are being delivered at an acceptable level, is likely to lead to customer dissatisfaction. Alternatively, if customers are happy, investing in new services or equipment may be an unnecessary expense. Any sport and fitness organisation's market research must determine how good they are.

Sport and fitness organisations should not rely on one measure of performance in order to determine how good they are. For example, Esporta health and fitness clubs obtain feedback on performance from their extensive performance management system, customer panels in each club and a centrally administered complaints procedure. Reliance on one measure of performance is likely to provide an inadequate picture and prevent the organisation from clearly knowing how good it is.

An organisation's own research and feedback mechanisms provide one source of data but for impartial assessment against recognised industry standards a UK-wide system has been developed called Quest. Launched in 1996, Quest has been supported and promoted by a wide range of organisations such as the four home country Sports Councils, the Institute of Sport and Recreation Management (ISRM), ISPAL and the Fitness Industry Association. There is a Quest scheme for facility management and for sport development.

The Quest scheme for facility management identifies 22 critical management issues that are grouped into the following four areas:

- facility operation;
- customer relations;
- staffing;
- service development and improvement.

A key strength of this system is that it requires managers to address all aspects of their operations and customer satisfaction. The process involves a self-assessment, followed by a visit from a trained assessor and another from a mystery customer, when an assessor visits the facility to use it in the guise of a customer.

In the 'customer relations' section of the report which the organisation receives there are scores and feedback to the organisation in customer care, research, customer feedback, marketing/pricing and reception/administration. Facility managers feel that the main benefit of Quest is its potential for reviewing procedures and getting feedback on these (Robinson and Crowhurst, 2001).

RULE 5: FEEDBACK AND COMPLAINTS ARE A LEARNING OPPORTUNITY!

It is a real challenge to maintain top quality service standards all of the time. Even if standards are maintained at a fixed level, customer expectations evolve and change over time and gradually aspects of the service may not be as appropriate as they could be (see Chapter 20). The way in which complaints are handled or the procedures for ensuring 'service recovery', as it is sometimes is known, have a long-term impact on customer loyalty and satisfaction. Research has shown that if an organisation deals effectively with a complaint, customers become more loyal to the organisation (Hess *et al.*, 2003; Karatepe and Ekiz, 2004; Plymire, 1991).

Customer feedback or complaints provide a goldmine of valuable information – direct to the company from the customer. Professor John Murphy of the Manchester Business School states that 'feedback from customers is akin to free market research – it should be freely solicited' (Ideascope, 2007). Experience suggests that most people simply walk away from a service rather than complain about it. An organisation should therefore ensure not just that making a complaint is an easy and straightforward matter but that it is actually encouraged as a learning opportunity.

The feedback mechanism should, if needed, be able to identify aspects of a service across a number of sites that are continually falling below par, or particular times of the day when special attention is needed in certain areas. Sport and fitness organisations which genuinely seek feedback offer a range of avenues for encouraging customers' responses such as a feedback form, a phone line, an online or text system, or simply encouraging customers to speak to the staff and vice versa.

There are a range of checklists and advice in the literature and online about staff handling complaints from the theoretical to the more practical. The following is a summary of the more practical advice for dealing with verbal complaints, where, above all else, excellent communication skills and an empathetic, calm, confident disposition are required by staff who work directly with customers. Staff training in such matters is obviously a crucial ingredient. Here stages of verbal complaint handling have been summarised as:

1 *Acknowledgement*: letting customers have their say and acknowledging their problem by not arguing or being defensive is the general tenor of much advice. Normally recognising the problem and using appropriate

phrases such as 'sorry to hear what's happened' are reported as being helpful.

2   *Respond and act quickly*: complaining customers are reported to want quick responses. Building and maintaining rapport is also a commonly reported theme and this is achieved by careful listening and establishing facts by questioning effectively and having an open mind. The skill of summarising the problem and connecting issues back to the customer to check understanding is often emphasised. Ideally organisations will have suitably trained and empowered front-line staff to enable them to take ownership of the problem and, where procedures allow, to solve problems as they occur.

3   *Generate and communicate alternative solutions and actions*: alternatives for resolving the complaint need to be identified. One option for helping resolve issues may be an offer of financial compensation to customers for significant breakdowns in service; another option is a complimentary use of a service. Much of the advice suggests the value in establishing what expectations the customer has and focuses on what can be done by staff in the short term. The importance of fairness and following through on agreed actions with customers and colleagues is also a recurring theme since it demonstrates the integrity of the organisation.

In the literature on complaint handling the importance of feeding back information to the organisation to learn from and prevent service failure in the future is commonly advocated. It is also worth reflecting that those selected for key front-line service positions should be recruited on the basis of their appropriate communication and people skills, such is their importance to shaping perceptions of the organisation in service recovery situations.

CONCLUSION

Sport and fitness organisations will have their own customer care procedures and policies that will reflect the particular circumstances of their organisation and customers. For example, if the organisation is focusing on providing activities for families it may have policies that cater specifically for customer care for children and ensuring their safety. Procedures are also likely to vary depending on the services and facilities offered and an organisation with a swimming pool will have different policies from an organisation which also has tennis facilities. Nonetheless, these five rules provide the basis for the delivery of customer care and should therefore underpin individual organisations' policies.

REFERENCES

Beech, J. and Chadwick, S. (2004) *The Business of Sport Management*, Harlow: FT Prentice Hall.

Business Link (2007) 'Manage your customer care', available from: http://www.businesslink.gov.uk, accessed 12 February 2007.

Cardwell, M. (1994) *Customer Care: Strategy for the 90s*, Cheltenham: Thornes.

Checketts, D. (2006) *Customer Astonishment: 10 Secrets to World Class Customer Care*, Bandon: Robert D. Reed Publishers.

Clutterbuck, D. (1991) *Making Customers Count: A Guide to Excellence in Customer Care*, London: Mercury.

Colombo, G. W. (2003) *Killer Customer Care*, Newburgh, NY: Entrepreneur Press.

Cook, S. (2002) *Customer Care Excellence: Create an Effective Customer Service Strategy*, 4th edn, New York: Kogan Page.

Customer Care Institute (2007) 'Customer care news', available from: http://www.customercare.com, accessed 12 February 2007.

Hess, R. L., Ganesan, S. and Klein, N. M. (2003) 'Service failure and recovery: the impact of relationship factors on customer satisfaction', *Journal of the Academy of Marketing Science*, 31(2), pp. 127–145.

Ideascope (2007) The 7 Habits of Highly Effective Customer Feedback Series: Habit No. 1 Listens More than Speaks, available from: http://www.ideascope.com/info/doc/7HabitsWeek3.htm, accessed July 26 2007.

Karatepe, O. M. and Ekiz, H. (2004) 'The effects of organisational responses to complaints on satisfaction and loyalty', *Managing Service Quality*, 14(6), pp. 476–486.

Oakland, J. and Beardmore, D. (1995) 'Best practice customer service', *Total Quality Management*, 6(2), pp. 135–148.

Plymire, J. (1991) 'Complaints as opportunities', *Journal of Services Marketing*, 5(1), pp. 1–19.

Robinson, L. A. (2001) 'Quality management and the public services', in Wolsey, C. and Abrams, J. (eds) *Understanding the Leisure and Sport Industry*, Harlow: Addison, Wesley, Longman.

Robinson, L. and Crowhurst, M. (2001) *Quality Programmes in Public Leisure Services*, Melton Mowbray: ISRM.

Robinson, L. A. and Wolsey, C. (1996) 'Considerations in developing a PSO in leisure services', *Local Government Policy Making*, 23(1), pp. 65–70.

Sayers, P. (1991) *Managing Sport and Leisure Facilities: A Guide to Competitive Tendering*, London: E. & F. N. Spon.

Senior, B. (1997) *Organisational Change*, Harlow: Prentice Hall.

Torkildsen, G. (1993) *Guide 4: Focusing on Customers*, Torkildsen's Guides to Leisure Management, Essex: Longman.

Williams, C. and Buswell, J. (2003) *Service Quality in Leisure and Tourism*, Wallingford, Oxon: CABI Publishing.

CHAPTER 20

CUSTOMER RETENTION
A business school perspective[1]

Tom Power (editor)

INTRODUCTION

Customer retention or loyalty is about relationships between individuals and companies or organisations. This chapter takes a business school perspective on the subject by discussing different approaches to customer retention and the role of rising expectations amongst customers. Throughout reference is made to sport and fitness facilities, with a particular focus on memberships of such facilities or clubs. This introductory section leads into the topic by considering what loyal customers and suppliers would say about each other and the costs associated with recruiting new customers.

Ideally, loyal customers would say the following about suppliers of sport and fitness:

- I trust their intentions and practices.
- They try to understand and provide what I need.
- They are interested in me.
- They value my custom for more than simply how much money they get from me.

In turn, the suppliers ideally would say the following of loyal customers:

- They are likely to use us again.
- They are unlikely to be easily tempted away by a competitor.
- They speak well of us to other potential customers.

[1] This chapter is an edited and adapted version of OU Business School Certificate in Management Programme, B630 *Managing Customers and Quality*, Book 3 *Valuing your Customers* (2001), Milton Keynes: The Open University.

- They are understanding and tolerant when we explain any difficulties we have in providing our products or services.
- They trust our understanding of their needs.
- They tell us what they think.

Reichheld (1996) believed customer loyalty based on repeat sales and recommendations was the foundation of growth in market share and profitability. If new loyal customers are acquired more quickly than existing ones are lost, the customer base grows in quantity and quality. The defection of customers, he says, is like a leaky bucket. The bigger the hole, the harder you have to work to fill it up and keep it full.

Even if you can 'fill the bucket as fast as it leaks', new customers are often not as profitable as existing ones. During the first year a new customer can cause a loss – or at least very low profits – for the following reasons:

- new customers need to be recruited, which may involve advertising costs or sales staff;
- new customers' financial arrangements need processing, which may include credit evaluation;
- new customers do not know how an operator's system works; they will often have to ask for help, requiring more staff time and intervention;
- new customers may not have found and taken advantage of extra services and facilities (such as clubs within clubs, events, personal training, catering) that generate additional income.

The interest in customer loyalty, or retention, as it is known, is also partly a response to increasing fragmentation in modern societies. When people were more stable, and moved house, moved round the country and changed their jobs less often, many consumer transactions such as shopping and leisure pursuits were conducted on a more local basis, so less effort was needed to secure loyalty. Now that people have a wider choice of options it is more difficult for organisations to secure customer loyalty so they have to look harder for ways to achieve it.

LIFETIME VALUE

The benefits of loyalty can be measured through considering the 'lifetime value' (LTV) of customers, which can be defined as:

the value that a customer has to a business over the expected lifetime of the relationship, measured in terms of financial contribution.

(Stewart, 1996, p. 27)

Put simply, in the context of a sport or fitness facility LTV is an attempt to work out how much money a customer contributes to the facility over the period of their membership. In the short term, the cost of acquiring a customer (perhaps including advertising, free visits, the time of sales staff and instructors) may exceed the revenue earned from that customer, making their membership unprofitable. But over a longer period, as the costs of maintaining that customer reduce, we then see an entirely different picture.

For example, if a health club estimated that, in advertising, sales and instructor time, recruiting a new member cost £200, and if the member's fees were £50 a month, it would take five months for each new member to generate a profit. In the first three months, the new member would represent a net cost. This suggests that it may be more cost effective to retain an existing customer than recruit a new one.

APPROACHES TO CUSTOMER RETENTION

We now turn to three broad approaches to retaining customers. All are based on the idea of relationship marketing. The first concerns the increasingly sophisticated use of customer databases to track and maintain relationships with customers. The second deals with customer relationship management. The third considers the characteristics of the loyal customers that organisations seek.

Tracking customers

Holiday companies, supermarkets, banks and other industries design the content, frequency and type of incentives in their mailshots and other communications with their customers according to the available information about their purchasing behaviour. In the sport and fitness industry, customer databases are increasingly being used to maintain customers' loyalty. The aim is to encourage a feeling of connection between clubs and their customers, and to tailor provision to the needs of the clients.

Customer relationship management

Customer relationship management (CRM) has emerged as a broad heading for some approaches and techniques to achieve long-term developing relationships between organisations and their customers or members. The starting-point is an appropriate form of relationship.

CRM can feature one of three basic types of relationship, and this depends on the type of product or service that is being offered (see Table 20.1). In other words, some transactions and customers are to do with a one-off exchange – say a taxi ride in a town you are visiting for the first and possibly last time – and merit little or no CRM beyond the period of the transaction. Other one-off purchases, perhaps a coffee and a sandwich while visiting that town, are not prime targets for CRM. The intermediate category – transaction plus technical advice – is still transaction-based, but with scope for adding services that can secure some degree of loyalty; an example of this might be a golf driving range that offers coaching as an additional service.

In a partnership-based relationship the customer's needs over a long period are met by an array of different products from the supplier as the customer evolves through different stages. For example, you might start to visit your local leisure centre because it has squash courts and you enjoy playing with a work colleague. You just pay for the court time you use. As you get older and perhaps start a family you begin to use the leisure centre for other activities, such as badminton, table tennis for the children, gymnastics for one child and swimming for another. Now you pay an annual subscription which covers your whole family. As time goes by, you start to attend keep-fit classes and yoga. The children leave home and you retire, so you and your partner have a membership that allows you to use the centre during the week for a reduced rate. As your needs change, so the leisure centre continues to provide different products that will suit your needs.

Table 20.1 Relationship types

Type of relationship	Product offer
Transaction-based	Single product
Transaction plus technical advice	Product and service 'bundles'
Partnership-based	Based on products and services changing as customers' life stages evolve

Source: adapted from Ernst & Young (1999, p. 3).

These categories should not be seen as always separate but more as a spectrum. The growth of technology and the provision of information tools based on it have been a huge bonus for the development of CRM within organisations.

CHARACTERISTICS OF LOYAL CUSTOMERS

Reichheld (1996) suggests there are three categories that organisations should focus on in acquiring loyal customers:

- Those customers with an inherent tendency to be predictable and loyal, whoever they end up doing business with. They prefer long-term, comfortable and stable relationships and are uninterested in spending their time researching available alternatives. Poor service will not necessarily result in their switching.
- Those customers who are more profitable than others.
- Those customers who identify most strongly with your distinctive features and for whom these have the most appeal. What distinguishes you from your competitors cannot appeal equally to all your customers and will not necessarily meet all your potential customers' needs. Customers strongly attracted to your organisation are more likely to be loyal.

Clearly, the more customers that can be attracted who fall into one or more of these categories, the better an organisation's chance of retaining them.

Customers' changing expectations

Why do customers' expectations change, how do they change, what causes the changes and how can we find out about those changes? These are important questions, which can be answered by organisations only if the people within them observe what customers expect and want.

How do customers' expectations change?

We have suggested that customers' expectations do not remain static for very long. They are constantly changing. Not only do they change but they also increase over time. For example, customers generally are unlikely to ask a company to reintroduce a product that was withdrawn from the market 15 or more years ago – customers used to a modern swimming complex are unlikely to be satisfied with a single unheated open air pool.

Customers' expectations change *and* increase – customers demand more from products over time, not less. Customers expect things to improve. They expect their products to do more than they did before, and they expect more and more choice.

Similarly, when organisations set themselves targets, they usually set targets higher than the ones they set the year before. The same targets would not be considered challenging or acceptable; their employees are expected to achieve more than they did the year before. We live in an environment where this is normal practice.

Organisations may feel that they are constantly having to respond to these increased expectations, but they are actually a part of the reason that the expectations are increasing. As soon as organisations improve a product, their customers become accustomed to the improvement and expect it to be standard. They then start to expect further changes and improvements; so their expectations rise again, and the organisations respond again. If no organisation responded, customers would have to put up with what was available or do without. However, this is unlikely to happen.

In the commercial world, organisations are constantly trying to find ways to add value. If they can see a chance to do so ahead of other organisations, they are likely to take this chance. Other organisations will follow, and the stakes will have risen for everyone. It may be in the organisation's best interests to agree with others that they will make no changes; but this also is very unlikely to happen, as all organisations want to gain customers, and taken too far this type of collusion would result in a cartel, which is unacceptable in most economies because it is associated with price fixing.

Customers may accept a difference between what the private and public sectors provide, but their expectations may be influenced by what is happening in the private sector. People expect computerised systems, helpful staff and detailed information from sport and fitness centres, whether they are public or private. All organisations need to know how their customers' expectations are changing.

What causes the change in expectations?

We have already said that a general desire that things should get better drives people to expect more. Quite often people find it difficult to say exactly what else they expect from a product, but they are sure something is possible. One factor that may prompt changing expectations is the improvement in technology that allows enhanced products to be made available.

For example, it is unlikely that gym users asked for exercise records and machines to be computerised and networked. Rather, they expressed the desire for their training routines to be easier to remember and record and for the gym equipment to be easier to use and set up. Manufacturers responded to this by developing computerised exercise stations that could automatically recall and configure themselves for each member's desired settings, resistance, sets and repetitions, as well as guiding the user through how to carry out the exercise and reporting on their performance. Consumers have come to expect changes and improvements in all areas of their lives.

In this example we can see that developments in technology – specifically linked to computer technology – have led to improvements in the quality of the service available to customers.

Many organisations are enabling their customers to choose how they access services, for example by enabling booking through face-to-face, telephone or online facilities, but the next stage is to empower customers so that they can tailor what they receive to suit them precisely. People can access websites and order CDs made up of tracks of their own choice from the banks of music available. This empowers customers to obtain the products they want immediately and simply.

Moynagh and Worsley (1999) believe that customers will increasingly take choice for granted. In fact, in many instances customers already believe there is too much choice; what people want now is to be able to select experiences that suit them exactly:

> consumers will no longer clamour for more choice. They will take choice for granted. Instead, they will want help in knowing how to choose – or even to have their choices anticipated. 'Don't confuse me with choice; just give me what I want.'
>
> (Moynagh and Worsley 1999: 10)

Whilst this is a much more difficult proposition for many organisations, in sport and fitness settings this could be interpreted as a move from making a wide range of training activities available to using the expertise of the coach or instructor to provide the very best training programme tailored to the particular circumstances and goals of an individual.

The expectation–experience gap

The difference between what customers expect and what they experience is an important concept in customer satisfaction (see Chapters 17 and 18). If their expectations exceed their experience, they are likely to defect. If their expectations match their experience, they are satisfied customers. If their experience exceeds their expectations, they become loyal customers.

McCarthy (1997) terms the difference between expectation and experience the 'E-gap'. He qualifies the model a little: when the E-gap is positive (i.e. experience exceeds expectation) this *promotes* customer loyalty. When it is negative (experience falls below expectation) loyalty is *eroded*.

For every organisation, once someone has experienced a positive E-gap, it is expected to be matched when they have their next contact with the organisation. If it is not matched again, its absence will produce a negative effect. This requires a continuous improvement curve and in part explains why customer satisfaction is so difficult to achieve.

Spiralling expectations

A health and fitness club at the 'upper end' of the market has a policy of monitoring customer satisfaction with its services through surveys and focus groups. This has led to improvements in its services, such as:

- providing online booking for classes and treatments;
- updating and restyling the wet room areas;
- increasing the frequency of updating workout programmes;
- changes to the social activities programme.

The manager claims to have a generally loyal membership, but a recent experience has shown how customers' expectations are rising. On the members' survey, they had always had a question 'How satisfied are you with locker-room and washroom areas?' The manager had recently found several members had ticked 'not very'. First the manager checked with the cleaning supervisor that these areas were being cleaned as normal, and it was confirmed that they were. The members were then contacted, and it transpired that the customers' definition of 'satisfactory' and the company's had diverged. Customers were becoming used to branded luxury toiletries, individual linen towels and similar small touches in the washrooms of hotels and restaurants that they frequented. The absence of these in the club facilities was leading to dissatisfaction.

SUMMARY

We have discussed the factors that are important in considering the balance between acquiring new customers and retaining existing ones. The emphasis has been moving away from conventional marketing, with its concentration on obtaining new customers, towards customer relationship management since the cost of obtaining new members is normally greater than that of retaining existing ones. The process of rising customer expectations, the role of new technologies and the importance of ongoing consultation with customers have been recognised.

REFERENCES

Ernst & Young (1999) *E-commerce: Customer Relationship Management, 1999 Special Report Technology in Financial Services*, New York: Ernst & Young.

McCarthy, D. G. (1997) *The Loyalty Link*, New York: John Wiley.

Moynagh, M. and Worsley, R. (1999) 'This century was off-the-peg: the next will be tailor-made', *Brand Strategy*, 22 November, pp. 9–10.

Reichheld, F. F. (1996) *The Loyalty Effect*, Boston, MA: Harvard Business School Press.

Stewart, M. (1996) *Keep the Right Customers*, Maidenhead: McGraw-Hill International.

CHAPTER 21

CUSTOMER RETENTION
A manager's perspective

Mark Talley

INTRODUCTION

For those who run sport and fitness facilities, competition for prospective members has never been greater. Two key factors have contributed to this situation:

1   The provision and quality of health and fitness facilities has increased enormously over the last 15 years.
2   Despite this increased provision and a renewed government focus on improving the health of the nation (particularly focusing on smoking, alcohol, obesity and physical activity), the proportion of the population who use such facilities remains relatively static. Some 47 per cent of the population have never been a member of, or used, a club or centre (Leisure-net HAFOS Solutions, 2005).

This means that new members are harder (and more expensive) to find than ever before. As a result, facility operators are starting to consider retention more seriously, concentrating on keeping the members they already have as long as possible.

Retention is ultimately the direct result of appropriate customer service. Improving retention means greater service and an enhanced experience for members. Every member of staff has a direct impact on retention. It is vital that every fitness professional understands the role that they play and the importance of every interaction with the customer.

This chapter provides an overview of the importance of retention and presents a retention model based on research, best practice and the professional experience of the author. It is up to the reader to select which ideas and processes they consider to be most appropriate in the battle to keep members longer.

DEFINING AND MEASURING RETENTION

Let's start by trying to understand the way retention is both defined and measured.

> Retention is simply about keeping the members or customers you have for a longer period of time.

In simple terms, consider the impact of succeeding in retaining one member for one month longer. In a club that charges £50 per month for membership, the financial impact is an additional £50 of income. If the club has, 3,500 members and is successful in retaining half of the members for one month longer, then the financial impact would be an additional £87,500 of income.

If the company has 20 clubs and achieves the same level of success in each club the financial impact is an additional £1.75 million. This does not include additional secondary spend on items such as food and beverage and personal training, or any membership referrals of friends/family as a result of satisfaction with the service they receive. Clearly, retention has important financial consequences for facility operators.

Unfortunately, the health and fitness industry has no single accepted method to measure retention (the proportion of members who stay with a club) or attrition (the proportion of members who leave). This makes the comparison of performance between clubs and operators difficult, as there is no central pool of data against which to benchmark.

Researching retention

Whilst there has been extensive research which has focused on behaviour change and exercise adherence in relation to individuals, scientifically conducted research on health club retention and attrition has been almost non-existent. Only in recent years has information been available with which effective operational and business decisions can be made. The UK has led the way in this recent work, with the Fitness Industry Association commissioning ground-breaking work in the area since 2000.

The guidance which follows draws heavily upon the findings of the FIA research reports, which are summarised in the Appendix to this chapter.

Managing retention

In this part of the chapter a model for retention management is presented, which follows the member journey, from pre-joining to the termination of membership, as shown in Figure 21.1.

Although there is no one single solution to the issue of retention, there are numerous strategies and processes that an operator can employ. Every operator needs to determine the retention initiatives that will produce the best results for them. Effective retention management relies on systems and processes to deliver appropriate service, some of which begin even before a member has joined.

MEMBER JOURNEY PART 1: TARGETING

Certain types of member groups have better retention than others. Older members, family members, racquet members (tennis, squash), and members that live closer to the club generally stay at clubs longer. For example:

> Annual retention rates for family users are 15 per cent higher than for single or joint members.
>
> Members aged 35 years and over have annual retention rates 1.5 times higher than members aged 16–24 years.
>
> (FIA, 2001b)

Knowing the retention characteristics of different types of members and matching these to the facilities and programmes that the club offers means that member prospecting and outreach can be targeted at attracting those members that are likely to stay longer.

MEMBER JOURNEY PART 2: SELLING

The tactics, strategies and processes used by sales teams can have a significant impact on retention. Below, six items that are often claimed to contribute to the

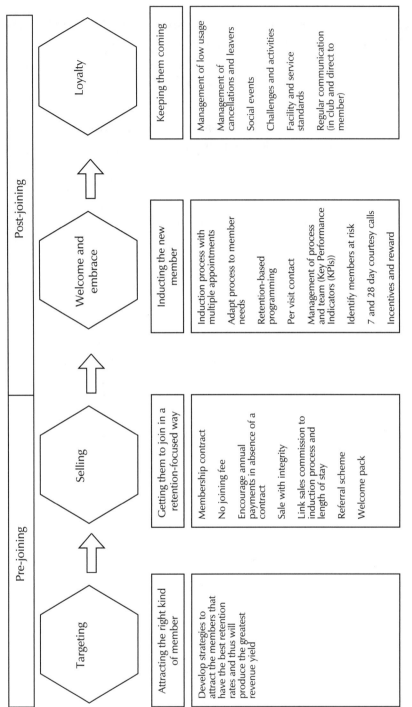

Pre-joining

Post-joining

Targeting

Attracting the right kind of member

Develop strategies to attract the members that have the best retention rates and thus will produce the greatest revenue yield

Selling

Getting them to join in a retention-focused way

Membership contract

No joining fee

Encourage annual payments in absence of a contract

Sale with integrity

Link sales commission to induction process and length of stay

Referral scheme

Welcome pack

Welcome and embrace

Inducting the new member

Induction process with multiple appointments

Adapt process to member needs

Retention-based programming

Per visit contact

Management of process and team (Key Performance Indicators (KPIs))

Identify members at risk

7 and 28 day courtesy calls

Incentives and reward

Loyalty

Keeping them coming

Management of low usage

Management of cancellations and leavers

Social events

Challenges and activities

Facility and service standards

Regular communication (in club and direct to member)

Figure 21.1 The member journey – a model for retention

relationship between membership, sales and retention are discussed against recent evidence.

The membership contract

The presence of a membership contract improves retention:

> Attrition rates for those members who sign a membership contract are almost half that of those who do not.
>
> (FIA, 2005)

The findings of a recent study completed by Fitness New Zealand have shown that the length of the contract is directly related to retention. Over 50 per cent of the members studied had contracts of between 12 and 23 months, with over 27 per cent having contracts of 24 months or more. The members on the shorter contracts had attrition rates almost five times higher than those on the longest contracts (Fitness New Zealand, 2006).

A membership contract is a vital part of retention management, and consideration should be given to extend contract periods beyond the traditional 12-month duration.

The joining fee

A joining fee does not have a significant impact on retention. In the absence of a contract the joining fee may have a limited effect, but is likely to have a far greater effect as a barrier to people actually joining in the first place, as shown by the FIA research *Winning the Retention Battle*, parts 4–6 (FIA, 2002b, 2002c, 2002d).

A joining fee is generally ineffective at improving retention (FIA, 2005). It is frequently used as a discounting tool (see below) for the sales team to provide an added member incentive at point of sale.

Payment method

Payment method, contracts and joining fees tend to be very inter-related. Contracts generally require automated monthly payment, and frequently as an incentive to sign up for a contract the joining fee will be discounted or dropped. In the absence of a contract, members who pay annually tend to have better retention than those who pay monthly (FIA, 2002b).

The sales process

In such a competitive marketplace, it is the norm for membership sales to be driven by discounting and special offers. This tends to result in customers who are less committed to the facility they have joined. A retention focused sales process will be results-driven rather than price-driven. The discounting of fees should be the exception rather than the norm. In my experience, a sale based on a thorough needs analysis and belief in a quality product will have a lifespan longer than one influenced by a heavy discount.

Often, in a club environment, there is a conflict between the sales team and those responsible for delivering follow-up service. Promises are made in order to close a sale which cannot be delivered by the rest of the team, even to the extent of selling services that are actually not provided.

Where a club has an induction programme for new members, the sales team must sell the programme and ensure that new members sign up to the programme at the point of sale. Failing to do this significantly reduces the chances of the new member completing the programme.

Selling for retention is about selling with integrity, really seeking to understand what the prospective member needs and matching the quality of facility and service to those needs. In the ideal world operators should consider linking part of the sales commission into two other steps in the process: sign-up for service induction programmes and the period of time those members actually stay. Such an incentive, if it could be tracked, would encourage the sales process to be results-driven rather than price-driven.

Membership referral schemes

The FIA research (2001a, 2002b, 2002a–d) shows that members who join with family have retention rates 15 per cent higher than those that join as individuals. In my experience, the retention effect of having social networks with other club members also applies to those who join with friends or business associates; these members also tend to stay longer than those who join alone.

Offering membership referral incentives to new members at point of sale will not only increase the numbers of members, but is likely to increase the length of stay of those members concerned.

Welcome pack

A welcome pack should be sent to new members, which includes:

- further information about facilities and programmes;
- Refer a Friend information (known as customer referral);
- vouchers for personal training, health and beauty, free beverages, etc.

A welcome pack should aim to increase the perception of value for money, help the new member to further justify the purchase and create an opportunity for cross-selling of services.

MEMBER JOURNEY PART 3: EMBRACE

The induction and socialisation process for new members is critical to retention. Visits to the club in the early weeks of membership are a key predictor of membership retention.

> During 80 weeks of follow-up, members who visit at least once per week in the first month of membership stay on average 13 weeks longer than members who don't visit that often.
>
> (FIA, 2001b)

> Members using the club less than once per week in the first 3 months of membership are twice as likely to leave as those visiting just once per week.
>
> (FIA, 2005)

The FIA research has shown us that an induction, personal exercise programme and follow-up appointments are all associated with lower attrition. Members who receive all three leave at a rate half that of members receiving fewer appointments (FIA, 2005). Discussion of these crucial early membership weeks is structured around two headings:

- content of induction and follow-up appointments;
- management of the induction process.

Content of induction and follow-up appointments

Number of appointments

Industry practice with regard to inductions is varied but most new members joining a facility receive no more than a basic equipment induction and basic exercise programme. The minimum level of service for a new member should be at least one personalised one-to-one consultation and personal programme, followed by at least one follow-up in the early weeks. A more effective benchmark would be one in which three appointments are allocated in the early weeks, and the possible content of these is shown in Figure 21.2.

Generally, the more appointments attended, the greater the subsequent frequency of visits during that period. At the end of the induction process, the member must be confident that they will continue to retain their membership and visit at least once every two weeks.

Personalisation of the process

Often fitness professionals fail to tailor consultations and subsequent programmes to the needs of the individual. Despite a needs analysis being completed by the sales team, each member is sometimes treated in exactly the same way as the next, regardless of experience and level of fitness.

Clearly needs differ, and the induction process should be tailored to the individual. Unless the induction process is personalised, the individual's perception of value and service will be compromised at an early stage.

Appointment 1	Appointment 2	Appointment 3
Within 7 days of joining	2–4 weeks after joining	4–8 weeks after joining
Up to 1 hour	10–13 minutes	Up to 1 hour
Needs analysis and some exercise instruction	Discussion and some exercise instruction	Discussion and some exercise instruction

Figure 21.2 Possible appointment structure involving three appointments

Exercise programming

There are two key areas within an exercise programme set for a new member that are important in determining whether a member sticks to it and whether they continue to attend.

The first key area is that too many sessions are often prescribed too early; often fitness professionals and members are impatient for results and too much exercise is prescribed too soon. This results in a frequency of exercise unrealistic for the member's lifestyle.

Industry experience suggests that in the early weeks visiting once per week is key to promoting retention. However, although a once per week exercise frequency will have little physiological impact and produce few, if any, fitness improvements, this visit frequency will be very realistic for most members and its achievement will enhance confidence. The more confident a new member is, the greater the likelihood of them staying, increasing their visit frequency and starting to achieve fitness goals.

The second important aspect of an exercise programme is that members should feel that they have some choice in and influence over the components of their programme. The more choice a person has, the greater the feeling of control and the more likely they are to put in and maintain their efforts in the face of obstacles. Encouraging members to try different exercises and choosing exercises based on likes and dislikes can have a dramatic impact on visits.

Evidence of this is provided in Figure 21.3, which summarises the findings of a study that investigated the extent to which the perception of activity choice

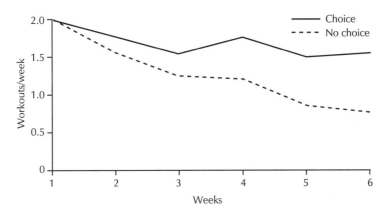

Figure 21.3 Effects of perceived activity choice on exercise behaviour

Source: Thompson and Wankel (1980).

influenced the frequency of exercise in a sample of people who had recently joined a health club. At the end of a six-week programme participants who perceived a degree of choice and control exercised twice as frequently as those who did not.

Programming for retention should therefore focus on a realistic exercise frequency and on providing choice in exercise options. Both of these will help to build a new member's confidence so that they can succeed. Increased confidence will lead to increased visits and will ultimately improve retention. Programming for retention is often about psychology rather than physiology, and sometimes taking a much longer-term view on health and fitness improvements.

Per visit communication

Communication with a fitness instructor at each visit, even a simple 'hello' or 'goodbye', strongly influences a member's perception of customer service.

> The leaving rate for members who are spoken to only 'rarely' or 'never' is 50% higher than for members who are spoken to during every visit.
>
> (FIA, 2005)

Research, such as that by Lombard et al. (1995), has shown that exercise adherence, in terms of those completing a set number of sessions per week, improves as a result of the amount of contact participants have with a fitness professional. Put simply, the more often staff talk to members, the longer they are likely to stay. In Figure 21.4 the results of a 24-week walking programme are presented. The group of people that had frequent contact with a fitness professional (feedback and goal setting conversations, in particular) was more likely to adhere to the set programme of 3 × 20 minute sessions per week than other groups involved in the research.

The traditional approach to interaction focuses around exercise correction – highlighting to the member that they are doing something wrong. Whilst this is important for member safety, it needs to be balanced with a more positive approach. Providing positive feedback gives the single greatest opportunity to have an impact our members. This type of interaction should far outweigh criticism. The focus needs to be on recognising good technique, effort, attendance and progress and general conversational skills.

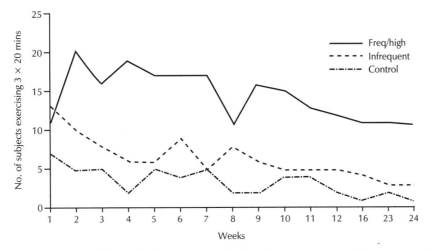

Figure 21.4 Effects of frequent professional contact on follow-up and adherence

Management of the induction process

Measuring induction

To have maximum effect and influence on the greatest number of members, the induction process needs to be effectively managed.

The purpose of the induction process over the first 8–12 weeks is to promote realistic visit frequency, which in turn is the key to members staying longer. Subsequently there are two ways that the process can be measured:

1   Percentage of new members achieving a visit frequency of once per week. This is the most direct indicator of the success of the process. However, if the systems in a club are not robust enough to measure visit frequency, then an alternative measure is needed.
2   Percentage of new members attending each of the induction appointments. Attendance at consultations is directly related to visit frequency over the first 8–12 weeks. Therefore if we cannot measure visit frequency directly, measuring the induction appointment uptake is the best alternative.

The fitness team must be accountable for achieving set targets with the new members joining the club. To be effective, each member of the team should be allocated new members who they manage through to completion of the induction process. Instructors' performance can then be measured against such targets (e.g. 90+ per cent completion of second consultations), or ranked to show the best or worst performing instructors in relation to getting clients to attend consultations. This caseload management approach requires instructors to keep in regular contact with members to ensure that they complete the process.

Member courtesy calls

Ideally new members should receive a courtesy call after the first 7–10 days to welcome them to the club, answer any questions or queries and invite them to attend the next new members' evening.

Areas for discussion include:

- progress of induction;
- receipt of their welcome pack;
- usage;
- social events and programmes.

An additional courtesy call should also be made after the first month, when the member is in a better position to provide feedback about their experiences. The organisational challenge is to make sure such calls are made, and at a time convenient to the customer (often in the evenings for those at work).

Managing those members at risk of leaving

A member should be defined as 'at risk' if:

- they fail to attend the first appointment;
- they fail to attend the club in the first two weeks;
- they fail to attend the club at least once every two weeks in the first 8–12 weeks.

The club needs to put systems in place to identify members at risk, make contact with them and provide an incentive for their attendance.

Incentives and rewards

Consideration should be given to providing incentives for attendance over the early months. Incentives can be linked to either actual visits or the completion of all the induction appointments.

Rewards will depend on the resources available, but examples include:

- complimentary personal training sessions;
- free products such as bags, water bottles and towels;
- guest passes;
- discounted memberships;
- vouchers to redeem in retail outlets.

The combination of both the content of induction and the management of the systems/processes involved in induction is vital in the early membership weeks. The second point requires managers to put in place well-designed systems to track customers and instructors.

MEMBER JOURNEY PART 4: LOYALTY

On completion of the first 8–12 weeks, if these have been managed correctly, the new members should be motivated and confident. However, members constantly evaluate value for money and any cause for dissatisfaction will tend to have a cumulative effect until a decision to leave is reached.

Six strategies can be employed in this 'loyalty period' to enhance retention. They are outlined next.

Management of low usage

The first sign of possible membership cancellation will be reduced visit frequency. This provides the trigger for a club to act. Ideally, any member who has not attended in the previous two weeks should be identified and contacted. However, this is very resource intensive and a more manageable option would be to identify those who have not attended in the previous month.

The choice regarding type of contact is broad and includes email, letter, phone, postcard or even text. Ideally, the contact will result in a dialogue to discuss reasons for the low usage. Where appropriate, incentives should be used to encourage the member's return, such as further appointments with the fitness team, personal training sessions or vouchers for food and beverage or health/ beauty or guest passes.

Management of cancellations and leavers

Although members who rejoin the same club are more likely to leave than those joining for the first time, given sufficient resources an attempt should be made immediately to rescue those members who leave. Members who give notice to leave, cancel direct debits or whose membership renewal is overdue should be contacted and reasons for wanting to leave explored. Some of the reasons may be minor and easily rectified.

Social events

Whilst not appropriate in every club and for every member, social activities, such as family fun days, frequently provide an extra reason for a member not to leave. Clubs within clubs – cycling, triathlon, running, rambling – run and organised by the members and supported by the club itself, are also a possibility.

Challenges and activities

The traditional approach to fitness challenges and activities within the club is to focus on achievement and competition, such as how fast you can run a mile and how fast you can row 1,500m. This type of challenge tends to be completed by the fittest members and those who attend the most often.

A more effective approach to enhance retention is one that focuses on visit frequency, for example offering a reward for all those members who complete 8 workouts in 8 weeks. A challenge passport can be stamped at each visit, providing an opportunity for interaction.

Facility standards

Numerous facility and operational factors can contribute to members satisfaction. The marketing mix (7Cs) framework (discussed in Chapter 17) provides a perspective on the range of interrelated factors that might be addressed to help maintain high facility standards.

BOX 21.1: THE MARKETING MIX (7Cs) FRAMEWORK

- *Customer needs and wants*: designing all the elements of a product or service so that the final offer will satisfy the customer.
- *Cost*: the customer will consider many factors when deciding if a product or service is value for money.
- *Convenience*: the delivery of products and services to customers involves factors such as quality, access and availability, reliability and the need to develop good customer relationships.
- *Communication*: organisations need to ensure that customers know about the benefits of products and services and where to obtain them.
- *Contact*: all the people who play a part in service delivery.
- *Context*: the physical environment in which the service is delivered.
- *Conducting the process*: the actual procedures, mechanisms and flow of activities by which the service is delivered; the service delivery and operating systems.

However, industry experience suggests that the final C of 'conducting the process' is particularly relevant here since clubs must have robust procedures for maintaining standards, ensuring quality and addressing any issues quickly.

Regular communication

Members value communication throughout the life of their membership. All too often the first communication that they receive is the letter informing them that their membership fees are due. In club and out of club communication should be designed to inform the member of activities, events, improvements and news. Many clubs produce a monthly or quarterly newsletter (note that communication is also one of the 7Cs).

The health and fitness industry has a lot to learn from other industries. Digital marketing technology now allows companies to target both customers and prospective customers much more accurately utilising text and email. Database management allows companies to evaluate buying behaviour and specifically communicate information regarding offers, programmes and promotions to those who have purchased similar items in the past or have profiles most suited to the offers. The supermarket industry has been at the forefront of this technology.

CONCLUSION

In the competitive health and fitness marketplace, across both private and public sectors, the attraction of new members and users is increasingly difficult. Operators are becoming more interested in retention-based activities to retain both new and existing members for a longer period of time.

However, despite this, much work still needs to be done. A consistent and accepted definition of retention needs to be universally agreed. Understanding the motivations and behaviour of the health and fitness consumer is still largely in its infancy when compared to other sectors, requiring further research. The research reviewed does, however, provide data with which operators can start to make business decisions, as well as giving practical advice on what initiatives are likely to make a difference. Many operators have started to adopt some of the ideas, and information is now freely available from organisations such as the Fitness Industry Association in the UK, International Health, Racquet and Sportsclub Association in the US and Fitness New Zealand.

Whilst these initiatives are positive, across the industry retention initiatives are still rarely resourced or prioritised to the same extent as new member acquisition. A new mindset is required that moves the industry from being an equipment and facility rental business to becoming a people business.

Whilst systems and processes can be devised to allow a quality of service that will influence a member to stay longer, the deciding factor will always be the staff members who deliver the service. As the health and fitness industry becomes increasingly technological in its equipment and information systems, it is important to remember that 'high touch' is just as important as 'high tech'.

Employers are looking for fitness professionals who really can help them make a service difference, not just advise and guide on the technical aspects of health and fitness. Technical skills are a given – regulation of the industry means that it is easy to identify the technical competency of a fitness professional. Service skills and the ability to make a member feel special are much harder to develop and measure, but ultimately lie at the heart of effective retention practices.

APPENDIX 1: FIA RETENTION RESEARCH REPORTS

Why People Quit (FIA 2000)

This study was the catalyst for further work and highlighted a number of reasons why members allowed their membership to lapse. These reasons are summarised in order of importance below:

- cannot afford fees
- change of workplace/working hours
- poor value
- overcrowding
- loss of motivation
- injury/illness
- bad atmosphere

Whilst this work was useful at the time, many factors were highlighted that were outside the club's control, such as a change of workplace or working hours, change of home, injury, illness or family difficulties. The work was limited in that it did not provide guidance as to how clubs could practically improve their retention.

Winning the Retention Battle, parts 1–3 (FIA 2001a, b, 2002a)

Between November 2001 and January 2002, the FIA published three reports presenting the findings of the first ever industry-wide study of membership retention rates. Over 67,000 adult member records were analysed across 64 clubs. Part 1 begins to provide standard methods for defining retention. Parts 2 and 3 look at factors that affect retention and how these can be used to identify members at risk of leaving.

The headline findings were:

- Members aged 35 years and over have annual retention rates 1.5 times higher than members aged 16–24 years.
- Retention rates for family users are 15 per cent higher than for single or joint members.
- Paying a joining fee improves both short-term and long-term retention.
- Annual payments – making an annual membership payment improves retention.

247

- Private clubs have higher retention rates than local authority facilities and hotel-based clubs.
- Members who visit at least once per week in the first month of membership stay on average 13 weeks longer than members who do not visit that often.
- Even low users who subsequently increase their usage during their first three months have a higher retention rate than those who do not.

Winning the Retention Battle, parts 4–6 (FIA 2002b, c, d)

In 2003 the FIA published the second series of three reports, presenting the findings from a qualitative research study in which current club members and ex-members were questioned about their views and attitudes at different stages of their membership.

These parts focus upon the perspectives of members: prior to joining; early membership experiences; reasons for leaving.

The headline findings were:

- Annual contracts or annual fees are effective in keeping members for the duration of their membership.
- A joining fee was less acceptable than an annual contract, increasing retention but having a negative impact on sales.
- The first few months are a crucial time when staff can have their greatest impact on retention.
- Members constantly evaluate the per visit cost.
- Reduced visit frequency is an early indicator of membership termination.
- Major factors causing members to leave include:
    - the quality of the physical environment (facilities, maintenance, cleanliness);
    - the quality of service environment (opening hours, staff turnover, instructor quality);
    - the quality of the social environment (atmosphere, inclusivity, ethos);
    - perceptions of value for money.

Revisiting the Retention Battle (2005)

In 2005 the FIA published their final report, *Revisiting the Retention Battle*, which focuses on the early health club experiences of members and their association with short-term attrition. Data for 1,000 health club members across four clubs were analysed and telephone interviews conducted. This focused on all the areas covered in the previous reports, and is arguably the most comprehensive study currently available on retention/attrition in the health and fitness industry to date.

The headline findings were:

- A contract is associated with lower attrition.
- A joining fee is associated with higher attrition (contrary to previous research).
- Men have lower attrition rates than women (contrary to previous research).
- Over 35s have lower attrition than those younger.
- Members rejoining the same club are twice as likely to leave as members who are completely new to the club.
- Members using the club less than once per week in the first three months of membership are twice as likely to leave as those visiting just once per week.
- Members who had not visited in the last two weeks were three times more likely to leave than members who had used the club in the last week.
- Every visit during which a member does not get spoken to increases the chance of that member leaving.
- An induction, personal exercise programme and follow-up appointments are all associated with lower attrition. Members who receive all three leave at a rate half that of members receiving fewer appointments.
- Members who were confident they would retain their membership had lower attrition in the first six months than those who were less confident.

REFERENCES

Fitness Industry Association (2000) *Why People Quit – UK Health and Fitness Clubs. A Survey of Lapsed Members*, London: Fitness Industry Association.

Fitness Industry Association (2001a) *Winning the Retention Battle – Reviewing the Key Issues of UK Health and Fitness Club Membership Retention*, pt 1, London: Fitness Industry Association.

Fitness Industry Association (2001b) *Winning the Retention Battle – Reviewing the Key Issues of UK Health and Fitness Club Membership Retention*, pt 2, London: Fitness Industry Association.

Fitness Industry Association (2002a) *Winning the Retention Battle – Reviewing the Key Issues of UK Health and Fitness Club Membership Retention*, pt 3, London: Fitness Industry Association.

Fitness Industry Association (2002b) *Winning the Retention Battle – A Member's Perspective – Pre-Joining*, pt 4, London: Fitness Industry Association.

Fitness Industry Association (2002c) *Winning the Retention Battle – A Member's Perspective – Early Exchanges*, pt 5, London: Fitness Industry Association.

Fitness Industry Association (2002d) *Winning the Retention Battle – A Member's Perspective – in the System*, pt 6, London: Fitness Industry Association.

Fitness Industry Association (2005) *Revisiting the Retention Battle – Members' Early Health Club Experiences and Their Association with Short Term Attrition*, London: Fitness Industry Association.

Fitness Industry Association and the Leisure Database Company (2005) *The State of the UK Fitness Industry 2005*, London: Fitness Industry Association.

Fitness New Zealand (2006) *National Retention Research*, London: Fitness Industry Association.

Lombard, D. N., Lombard, T. N. and Winnett, R. A. (1995) 'Walking to meet health guidelines: the effect of prompting frequency and prompt structure', *Health Psychology*, 14(2), pp. 164–170.

Leisure-net Solutions (2005) *Health and Fitness Omnibus Survey* (HAFOS), Norwich: Leisure – net Solutions.

Thompson, C. E and Wankel, L. M. (1980) 'The effects of perceived activity choice upon frequency of exercise behavior', *Journal of Applied Social Psychology*, 10 (5), pp. 436–443.

CHAPTER 22

STAFF TRAINING AND DEVELOPMENT

Providing for quality service provision in sport and fitness

Debbie Lawrence

INTRODUCTION

Staff training and development activities have an integral role in building a customer-focused workforce within the sport and fitness industry. Individuals and teams need to be knowledgeable, skilled and committed to an ethic that prizes the delivery of an outstanding quality of service.

Commitment to service quality and customer experience is essential for organisations to thrive in changing economic and social conditions. For individual employees, knowledge of what customers want, effective communication skills and a willingness to respond to meet customer needs are vital ingredients for success.

This chapter focuses on training and development activities to promote service quality in sport and fitness facility management. It explores the value of staff training and development for promoting customer service. It discusses different types of activity, including induction and socialisation. A model of practice is proposed for implementation and evaluation of service provision that identifies training and development needs. It also discusses a range of training methods. Examples from within sport and fitness facility management are provided throughout.

THE VALUE OF TRAINING AND DEVELOPMENT

Without committed staff, organisations cannot exist in the competitive market. Staff training and development can contribute to building a person centred and customer focused organisational culture and philosophy. They have the potency to reflect the values of senior management and their commitment to 'investment' in people. A congruent commitment to quality needs to be reflected from the highest levels within the organisation and these must be communicated to all involved with sincerity and meaning. As Zeithaml and Bitner suggest: front-line service providers need to 'experience the same values and behaviours' (2003, p. 332) from their line managers if they are to deliver high quality service to external customers.

Training and development activities can also help to secure the loyalty and commitment of the workforce. Training and development activities provide an indicator of an organisation's commitment to invest in their people. This can potentially reduce high staff turnover rates. Training and development initiatives (induction, socialisation, coaching and mentoring) can raise individual and team awareness of opportunities for career development and progression. This can act as a motivational tool for individuals wishing to achieve professional success.

Staff training and development activities also offer the opportunity for individuals to have a 'voice' within the organisation. The potential for involvement and making a contribution can help to build a collaborative work force. A collaborative team effort is essential to provide the highest possible quality of service. Individuals working together with a shared mission are more effective in meeting the changing demands and diversity of needs within the community. Staff training and development activities provide an opportunity for managers to receive feedback and gather ideas and invest these within the organisational mission and goals.

Each of the above features can contribute to an organisation's success. As Zeithaml and Bitner suggest: 'Successful companies invest heavily in training and make sure that training fits their business goals and strategies' (2003, p. 331).

Greenwich Leisure Ltd (GLL) (see Chapter 2 for further background) have a 'people vision' embedded into their corporate strategy. They invest heavily in training and development across all levels. Each working role is aligned to a specific 'training academy' (managers, recreation assistants, customer services advisers, fitness instructors, etc.). Each academy defines the 'competences' for the specific role and provides an ongoing training route for developing knowledge, skills and a focus on customer service. The academy provides an assessment strategy that involves: self-assessment; manager assessment; individual learning plans; opportunities to fill knowledge and skills gaps; and, in some instances, a specific exam.

TYPES OF TRAINING

Staff training provides the foundation for developing and maintaining a knowledgeable, skilled and customer orientated workforce. Authors such as Zeithaml and Bitner (2003, p. 330) suggest that once organisations have hired the right employees they must work with them to ensure high quality service provision.

Different organisations will offer different types of training. The training available may relate to the following:

- the functioning of the organisation;
- building positive relationships with customers;
- improving team well being and functioning;
- developing individual qualifications and skills.

Induction training

Induction training provides a simple yet essential welcome for an individual to the organisation and their work team. An effective induction process can help new employees to cope with the anxieties created by making a transition to a new working environment. It is the first step towards helping them to socialise and establish a sense of belonging within an organisation.

An ineffective induction process can contribute to an individual feeling unhappy, demotivated and abandoned. If these feelings remain unresolved, the new employee may be unclear about their working role and may start looking for another job.

Being left alone with an induction handbook after a quick tour of the building is hardly sufficient 'induction' to support an individual. The induction process needs to be tailored to the specific needs of an individual. It needs to start on their first day and continue until they feel comfortable to manage in their new working role.

Fowler (1996) suggests that induction information can be structured into four main areas. These are offered as a starting point for induction activities:

- *individual*: hours of work, holiday provision, flexi-time, training and development, sickness and absence, dress code, payment methods, etc.;
- *work/job*: health and safety, standards and targets, specific roles and responsibilities, use of equipment and any mentoring/coaching available;

- *department*: introducing and meeting key contacts, knowledge of how departments communicate and any connection between duties;
- *organisation*: mission statement and specific targets, policies and practice (equal opportunities, grievance, etc.), pension schemes.

Socialisation

Socialisation extends beyond induction and involves the transition from being an 'outsider' to becoming an 'insider' within the organisation. It relies on inter-action with colleagues and how an individual interprets their experience of work-specific situations. Managers need to have awareness of the socialisation process to assist new staff through the transition.

Wanous (1992) offers a four-stage model to assist with conceptualisation of what the 'socialisation' process may involve:

1   *Confronting and accepting reality*:

   - acceptance of expectations about the working role and organisation;
   - resolution of initial conflicts between personal and organisational values;
   - recognition of aspects of self that are acceptable and 'fit' within the organisation.

2   *Achieving role clarity*:

   - clarifying work role;
   - understanding how work performance will be reviewed;
   - learning to work within the structure and cope with ambiguities.

3   *Integration – coming to terms with context*:

   - learning the behaviours that fit with the organisational culture;
   - resolving conflicts between work and home;
   - increasing commitment to work;
   - establishing an altered self-image, new relationships and values.

4   *Detecting signposts of successful socialisation*:

   - achieving dependability and commitment;
   - feeling high satisfaction;

- mutual acceptance;
- job involvement and motivation.

Interventions that may assist with socialisation include training activities that involve specific work teams.

A MODEL OF PRACTICE

Staff training and development should be part of a cyclical process of ongoing discovery, experience and reflection. The process is represented in Table 22.1.

Review and evaluation

The starting point for any training provision is to review current practice and skill levels to identify possible 'skills' gaps. Organisations must continually reflect on standards and find ways of responding to changing customer expectations and external trends. The review process needs to involve feedback from the following people:

- *customers*: to identify the 'customer experience'; information can be gathered via questionnaires/suggestion boxes/mystery shoppers;
- *front-line service providers*: to identify current practices and potential areas for development;
- *supervisors and managers*: to identify strengths, weaknesses, opportunities and threats within current service levels, with recommendations for training and development needs amongst all team members;
- *directors and strategic planners*: to establish:

  - benchmarks for quality achievement;
  - action plans to achieve quality;
  - appropriate monitoring systems to review process.

GLL work within a framework of ongoing 'reflective practice' – they continually evaluate their services and develop strategies to build a workforce that 'has the drive to be the best' (Greenwich Leisure Limited, 2007).

Table 22.1 A model of cyclical staff training and development

	Review and evaluation	Goal setting	Action planning	Action
Key questions	▦ Where is the organisation now? ▦ What are the main skills gaps amongst staff?	▦ Where does the organisation want to be and by when?	▦ How can the organisation close gaps in skills, knowledge, attitudes? ▦ What training/development methods would be most effective?	▦ How will training be implemented and the effects monitored at all levels?
Key activities	▦ Gathering feedback	▦ Establishing objectives and measurable targets	▦ Selecting appropriate type(s) of training, training methods and support relevant to the needs of individuals at different layers within organisation	▦ Implementing training with reflection in action, and provision of additional coaching/mentoring to integrate learning into practice ▦ Monitoring and reviewing performance after training to make recommendations for future activities

Source: adapted from Petty (2004).

Goal setting

On completion of the review, feedback needs to be translated into measurable and achievable targets for all levels of service provision (front-line providers to senior directors). The acronym of SMART objectives can provide the benchmark from which to monitor future service provision. This commonly used acronym helps to ensure that goals and objectives fulfil their purpose, in that when objectives are set they are:

- specific
- measurable
- achievable and agreed
- realistic and
- time-framed (i.e. a date is set).

Action planning

Strategies and methods for closing any learning gaps need to be identified. There are a variety of training methods. The method selected will be determined by a number of factors. These include:

- the subject area and learning domain targeted;
- effectiveness of methods for promoting learning;
- resources (training budget and level of involvement required);
- development options (a range of possibilities are available, including individual coaching/mentoring – it all depends on the above factors).

Subject area and learning domains

Understanding the desired aim and purpose of the training is essential in establishing the appropriate method of delivery. What is it that team members should be able to do or know when they have completed the training? How will learning be monitored and measured? For example, will they be able to:

- know something (*cognitive learning domain*), developing knowledge? For instance being able to recognise the reasons for providing a quality service to customers;
- perform a task or do something (*psychomotor learning domain*), developing

skills? For instance being able to communicate effectively with customers (listening etc.);

▪ respond effectively in situations *(affective learning domain)*, developing attitudes? For instance having an internalised and heartfelt sense of value, respect and caring for the 'experiences' of all customers.

Training and development provide a foundation for continued learning in each of these three major learning domains. The first two domains are arguably the easiest to train in and learn. The latter domain is developed and possibly acquired through experience and inspiration and is very much the reflection of an individual's commitment to the life-long learning process. See Box 22.1 for an example that illustrates the three learning domains further.

BOX 22.1: AN ILLUSTRATION OF THE THREE LEARNING DOMAINS

▪ I may be able to comprehend the reasons for providing customer care; I have knowledge – cognitive awareness.

▪ I may be able to maintain eye contact, stand with open body language and show agreement by nodding my head in the right places – psychomotor/skill acquisition.

▪ However, the extent to which I use, apply and integrate this knowledge and skill when working with customers and clients can depend very much on what I feel about myself (esteem) and customers and the organisation; and, furthermore, the extent to which I value the organisation, customers and myself – affective learning. The affective domain also represents the extent to which I feel a valued member of the team.

As a way of validating this assertion a successful US airline has the motto 'you can train skills, you cannot train attitude' (Southwest Airlines, cited in Cook, 1997, p. 150). The airline uses stringent recruitment and selection procedures to ensure it gets the right people working with it.

In recognition of these issues, Greenwich Leisure Limited have recently developed and are piloting their 'Inspire' programme, which was launched in April 2007. During the first six months each team member will follow a 'working whilst learning' programme. They will be supported by mentors, given hands-on training by managers and provided with the opportunity to gain additional industry qualifications. The potential for a salary increase is offered as an incentive for staff who complete their training successfully and reach the role-model standards for their specific job at the end of the six month training scheme (Greenwich Leisure Limited, 2007). Opportunities available after the six month period include: graduation, additional mentoring, deployment to a specific centre, the opportunity to become an Inspire role-model trainer, salary increase and promotion.

Effectiveness of methods for promoting learning

There are a variety of different learning activities that trainers can use to engage and enthuse learners. Ideally, the methods selected should be varied to accommodate different learning preferences, provide a holistic and interesting learning experience and promote learner involvement. A range of possible activities are listed in Table 22.2. Usually a combination of two or more activities is used in any one session to create variety.

It is worth considering data before selecting specific methods. The Audiovisual Association (in Cook 1997, p. 152) suggests that people learn most through incoming sensory data that is visual (what they see) (see Table 22.3). In addition, learners remember different quantities of information from different sources (see Table 22.4). The data would imply that the most effective learning occurs from observing and being involved in the process. Reading manuals and being lectured or talked at are less effective at promoting 'learning'.

Since the goal of learning is to bring about 'change' in knowledge, skill or attitudes (Reece and Walker, 2004) it is essential to use methods that involve learners as these are more effective for promoting both learning and change.

Further considerations for training may include:

- providing a structured and logical order, starting at a meaningful point and developing from the known to the unknown (cognitive strategies);
- respecting all learners, reflecting empathy, non-judgement and positive regard and providing a safe and non-threatening learning environment (humanistic strategies);
- offering praise, encouragement and reward (behaviourist strategies).

Table 22.2 Example learning activities broadly categorised under three headings

Learner centred	Learner and trainer centred	Trainer centred
Reading	Discussion	Demonstrations
Debates	Question and answer	Explanations
Practical sessions	Learning using information or computer technologies	Presentation
Application of theories		Simulations
Personal research	Structured workshops	
Games and simulations	Skills practice workshops	
Case studies		
Group work		
Role play		
Problem solving		

Source: adapted from Petty (2004).

Table 22.3 Learning through different sensory sources

Sensory information	% of learning
Taste	3
Touch	6
Smell	3
Hearing	13
Sight	75

Table 22.4 Recall of information from different sources

Learning source	% of information remembered
What we read	10
What we hear	20
What we see	30
What we see and hear	50
What we say	80
What we say and do	90

Source: Cook (1997, p. 152).

Readers interested in exploring different learning theories are directed to Petty (2004), Reece and Walker (2004) and Curzon (2004). Specific delivery methods are discussed in the sections which follow.

Resources

Most organisations establish a budget for staff training as part of their strategic plan. The training budget will influence the type of training that is made available and whether this occurs on or off the job. The level of involvement (time commitment) required from individual team members will potentially add to the cost of training.

Blended learning packages

Mixing attendance, on the job and some distance learning study may offer a more cost effective and time efficient way of providing training within larger organisations.

Internal training

Accessing training internally may be more cost efficient than accessing training from external sources.

Cascading

External training can be attended by managers and then delivered to other levels of an organisation. This can provide a number of benefits. At a surface level, it enables training to be scheduled at convenient times for the work team. At a deeper level, involving managers in actual delivery of training enables them to receive feedback and create open discussion and dialogue. This can help them to review and develop a greater understanding of service provision and barriers to achieving high level service.

Development options

Different types of training will be appropriate for different needs. The type of training implemented will need to take into consideration the work role and the individual's level of development.

Cook (1997, p. 146) suggests that the priority subject information for managerial training may include leadership, quality and teamwork, whereas, the priority subject information for other team members may include customer care, quality and teamwork.

The learning needs of the individuals at whom the training is targeted will also need to be considered. (Readers are recommended to refer back to the previous section 'Effectiveness of methods for promoting learning' (on p. 259) to consider the most appropriate methods.)

Lectures and talks

These require a greater involvement from the speaker/trainer (planning, delivery and evaluation) and lower levels of activity from attendees (trainer focused learning). The cost of sending all team members to attend a lecture within working hours needs to be accounted for. However, lectures can enable a large audience to be reached in one sitting. The disadvantages of lecturing as a method may include: staff attention span; low opportunities for interaction and questions; and how effectively the lecturer engages the audience.

Work-based NVQ/apprenticeship

National Vocational Qualifications (NVQs) reflect an individual's competence to perform their working role. They will require a greater involvement and commitment from the trainee (student or trainee focused learning) and also from line managers. The time and support needed for individuals to achieve these qualifications – collecting evidence, coaching and support, work-based assessment and verification – also need to budgeted and accounted for.

Ongoing support (role models, coaching and mentoring)

One-off training events with no follow-up review and no ongoing support will have less impact then training that is supported – in action. Cook suggests: 'the best training in the world will fail without the managers' praise, encouragement and good communication' (1997, p. 150).

Managers will need additional training to know how to support staff. Within the person-focused organisation leadership training may involve movement away from bureaucratic leadership styles (leader decides and tells) and towards democratic leadership styles (leader consults and asks), with the aim being to empower individuals and promote responsibility.

debbie lawrence

- *Role models*: this is a powerful socialisation quality that managers need to exhibit. Cook asserts that contradictory behaviour from managers can kill the positive effects of training; 'words and deeds need to match' (1997, p. 151). This includes the manager's attitude to training and development activities. What people do is overwhelmingly more influential than what they say (Petty, 2004, p. 19).
- *Coaching*: this is a method of imparting knowledge and skill from a more experienced practitioner to a less experienced practitioner. Effective coaching involves the coach and trainee:

  - spending uninterrupted time to identify and plan strategies to meet the agreed developmental need;
  - coaching through a specific task or role – this offers both the opportunity to discuss other solutions and ways of working;
  - reviewing the process and identifying further ways of working together.

- *Mentoring*: this involves aspects of both coaching and role-modelling, the main difference being that a mentor would not be an individual's line manager and would therefore have no 'reporting' duties. Informal and unstructured mentoring is often visible in many organisations, with a senior, more experienced individual supporting the development and growth of a younger and inexperienced protégé. More recently, larger organisations have developed structured and formal mentoring schemes. The benefit of a structured scheme is the provision of equal opportunity and access to mentors for all employees.

Action

The next stage of the model is to implement the training and reflect on its impact. Coaching and mentoring are useful during this stage to support any teething problems and promote further integration and development of skills/knowledge. Coaching and mentoring also offer support during the 'socialisation' process.

Review and evaluation, completing the circle

There are a number of ways of monitoring the impact of training. Evaluation forms can be completed after training sessions as a method of gathering feedback regarding the impact of training and how it was received. Observations of practice can be conducted as a method of checking that knowledge is being applied to practice (skills). The ongoing support process should enable remaining skills gaps to be identified and acted upon.

Appraisal system

This is another way of involving team members in the review process. Appraisals can be used to identify where individuals perceive themselves to be and where they would like to be, and the additional skills and qualifications that need to be achieved for them to reach their goals. Appraisal can be also be used to negotiate targets to work towards service objectives and as means of recognising achievements. A further opportunity of the appraisal process is that it can enable individuals the opportunity to feed back to other team members and managers. Open communication amongst work teams can potentially enable specific issues to be identified and consequently managed and dealt with. Issues that remain unvoiced and unresolved arguably create discord amongst work teams and can contribute to dysfunctional teamwork.

CONCLUSION

Staff training and development are of paramount importance in sustaining an organisation and in managing changing customer expectations. The very fact that staff are often a principal part of the service offering in sport and fitness demands this investment in people.

A customer focus needs to be embedded within the organisation's mission statement and should be reflected in the criteria used to recruit and select staff. Customer orientation also needs to be embedded within competency frameworks that reflect the skills, knowledge and attitudes required for different working roles.

Constant review and evaluation of service provision to internal and external customers provide a foundation from which future practice (service provision, staff training and development) can evolve.

An ethos that reflects the value of people is essential for success. Service providers (internal customers) who perceive themselves as valued and valuable (intrinsic and extrinsic) are more likely to reflect these values to service users (external customers).

REFERENCES

Binden, A. (2007) *GLL Management and Leadership Development*, London: Greenwich Leisure Limited.

Clutterbuck, D. (1991) *Everyone Needs a Mentor: Fostering Talent at Work*, London: Institute of Personnel Management.

Cook, S. (1997) *Customer Care*, London: Kogan Page.

Curzon, L. (2004) *Teaching in Further Education*, 6th edn, London: Continuum.

Edwards, J. (1991) *Evaluation in Adult and Further Education*, Liverpool: WEA.

Fowler, A (1996) *Employee Induction: A Good Start*, London: Institute of Personnel Development.

Greenwich Leisure Limited (2003) *The GLL Management Academy – Realising Future Potential*, Senior Management Group Paper, London: Greenwich Leisure Limited.

Greenwich Leisure Limited (2007) *INSPIRE. Campaign to Inspire GLL Talent*, London: Greenwich Leisure Limited.

Kerry, T. and Shelton Mayes, A. (1995) *Issues in Mentoring*, London: Open University/Routledge.

Kram, K. (1988) *Mentoring at Work. Developmental Relationships in Organizational Life*, Lanham, MD: University Press of America.

Petty, G. (2004) *Teaching Today*, 3rd edn, Cheltenham: Nelson Thornes.

Reece, I. and Walker, S. (2004) *Teaching, Training and Learning*, 5th edn, Sunderland: Business Education Publishers Limited.

Wanous, J. P. (1992) *Organisational Entry: Recruitment, Selection and Socialisation of Newcomers*, 2nd edn, Boston, MA: Addison-Wesley.

Zeithaml, V. A. and Bitner, M. J. (2003) *Services Marketing; Integrating Customer Focus across the Firm*, 3rd edn, New York: McGraw-Hill.

CHAPTER 23

PROFIT FROM GETTING CLOSE TO YOUR MEMBERS[1]

David Minton

Introduction

What is so valuable about a name and address? Well, member data could be your most powerful weapon if it is viewed as the strategic tool it is capable of being. Profiting from a better understanding of members is an underpinning principle of customer oriented organisations.

Technology will undoubtedly help in the struggle to understand our members better but it is only a tool for getting it right. Having the right business approach is the important precursor. The value placed on the information members provide daily and the level of member information used in business decision-making will make a significant difference to the success of your sport or fitness facility (termed 'club' from here onwards).

PROFITING FROM INFORMATION

Looking outside our industry, it is easy to see retail companies like Tesco benefiting from their investment in systems which have been established to gain long-term member insight. Their success is being linked to their loyalty 'Clubcard' which provides extensive member data, helping Tesco managers predict future demand and trends, ultimately selling more through better targeting and thereby enabling Tesco's profits to soar. Sir Terry Leahy, Tesco Group Chief Executive, called this 'building the business backwards from the member'.

Astute business managers know they should base their business on their members' needs, so what is stopping more companies from putting the theory into practice?

---

[1] Edited from Minton, D. (2006) 'Profit from getting close to your members' in Algar, R. (ed.) *Mastering Health Club Management*, pp. 24–31, Brighton: Oxygen Consulting.

In many clubs no one individual is responsible for the data. Information may be stored on different databases or on incompatible systems in different departments. Company takeovers may have led to two systems being operated without good effect. Businesses may not be supporting the staff properly with training. There may be little or no reward for staff to gain member insight. What really happens to member 'complaint' information? Whatever the reason, it is time to use the flow of valuable member information in your organisation. Open up the communication pipeline to your members and you will reap the rewards.

USE MEMBER DATA TO BENEFIT ALL

For a long time small clubs have successfully used their knowledge of members so that they can almost instinctively adapt their classes, programmes and marketing communications according to their members' needs. This helped small clubs maximise their marketing spend to the full, enjoy high levels of loyalty and produce rapid results.

Today any size of organisation can gain these advantages and more by using the techniques of member profiling, user-friendly software and the important interpretation of the information.

Using member data for profiling delivers a better understanding of your members, their lifestyles and their motivation towards using your facilities. This empowers you to sell to them successfully, retain them and to attract prospects like them.

All club personal benefit from an understanding of the general market that they are operating in, their catchment area and their competitive environment. This detailed information is an important element in staff inductions and ongoing training. Knowledgeable staff are more motivated and hence better at delivering good member service.

THREE IMPORTANT STEPS

There are three important steps to follow to get to know your member base better:

1   profile your members to establish your best members;
2   define the club's potential;
3   decide which groups to target.

Step 1: profile your members

Understanding who your members are enables you to target others like them. However, membership profiling can go beyond this. Knowing who your most loyal members are enables you to segment your membership base and to target your efforts appropriately. Retaining the best members and attracting more people like them is the end goal. Profiling will establish the differences for you between higher and lower value members, giving you more opportunities to target your communications.

Member intelligence can easily be passed on to staff using geo-demographic reports which use information derived from the Census, as well as lifestyle and life-stage data to group people according to similar characteristics, attitudes and habits. This information is then applied to geography, where households or individuals are coded. This enables report users to gain an insight into the composition of an area where different groups of people are clustered. It also identifies the different types of people that are club members, and importantly where more of these types of people can be located.

More on profiling

There are two major products available for profiling customers, both promoted by leading international companies specialising in providing information, analytical and marketing services to help manage businesses. A company called CACI produces Acorn and Experian produces MOSAIC. Both products were originated by a UK professor, Richard Webber, who produced the first area classifications from the 1971 Census.

The two classification systems are very similar. CACI has been in the market for 28 years and Experian developed a product at a later date. The two classifications use 'categories', 'groups' and 'types' to define the segments of the population. The types provide a picture of the general characteristics of those living in the area. This chapter will refer to the MOSAIC system throughout since it is favoured by the Leisure Database Company.

MOSAIC combines over 400 separate data sources and divides the UK adult population into 61 different types and eleven groups, covering the full spectrum of British and Northern Irish society. In addition to the UK Census, data sources for MOSAIC include the electoral roll, Experian's lifestyle information, house price data and Office of National Statistics local area data.

MOSAIC is designed to identify groupings of consumer behaviours for households and postcodes. These classifications paint a rich picture of UK consumers in terms of their social demographics, lifestyle, culture and behaviour to provide organisations with a detailed view of UK consumers.

A MOSAIC report shows the number of people living within a specific area broken down by 11 MOSAIC Groups and 61 Types (see Box 23.1 for an example of 3 MOSAIC Groups).

BOX 23.1: A 'SNAPSHOT' OF THE MOSAIC PROFILE FOR LEOMINSTER LEISURE CENTRE, HEREFORDSHIRE

Facility membership

6,400 members.

Core catchment area

Within 22 minutes driving time – 28,554 people reside (an extremely rural catchment area).

Key customers in catchment area/MOSAIC Groups

K (Country Dwellers) 46 per cent

MOSAIC Group 'Pen' portrait:

Genuinely rural neighbourhoods where houses have names not numbers and where agriculture and tourism are significant sources of local employment. All areas suffer poor access to shops, post offices, schools . . . and are heavily dependent on cars for work and leisure. To most *Country Dwellers* small scale is still beautiful; people are expected to help their neighbours and many attempt to hold out against the depersonalising aspects of a mass consumption society.

B (Suburban Semis) 9.6 per cent

MOSAIC Group 'Pen' portrait:

Suburban Semis represent the bedrock of middle class suburban taste. Within these neighbourhoods are found middle aged, middle income families, where parents often commute to work in middle management jobs in large service organisations. Living in satellite villages or in

---

well-established suburbs, these people live organised and agreeable lives and have time and income to pursue a wide variety of home based leisure interests. Most are owner occupiers and have had children; many of the houses are inter-war semis with their own garages and reasonably sized gardens.

C (Blue Collar Owners) 9.6 per cent

MOSAIC Group 'Pen' portrait:

Blue Collar Owners comprise the less expensive neighbourhoods of owner occupier housing where skilled manual and junior white collar workers take pride in the exercise of practical skills in the home and garden, where sensible and self-reliant people have worked hard to achieve a comfortable and independent lifestyle. Relatively few ethnic minorities or single people reside in *Blue Collar Owners* areas. Children tend to leave school early to get a job, whilst continuing to live at home. Family incomes are relatively high due to the large number of adults working and the absence of expensive mortgages.

Population characteristics

- *Age*: numbers in the 20–30-year-old band are up to 30 per cent down on the national average; numbers in all bands over 50 are well above average.
- *Retirement*: 24.9 per cent of the population of Herefordshire are of retirement age (well above the national average of 18 per cent) (Herefordshire County Council, 2001).
- *Car ownership*: 18.2 per cent of the population of Herefordshire are without cars, which is well below the national average of 26.8 per cent (Herefordshire County Council, 2001).
- *Wealth*: not an affluent area – numbers of MOSAIC group A (High Income Families) are less than half the national average; group D (Council House Owners) well above average.

Source: Halo Leisure (2007); Debenham (2002) MOSAIC Pen Portraits

A MOSAIC report enables clubs to decide on a realistic catchment area within which to market. A club can therefore make some basic judgements as to the types of people that would be most likely to visit their facilities. A MOSAIC map (see Chapter 4 for an example) shows where these people live, providing valuable information about where to target marketing activities. Finding out which postal geographies contain high numbers of target types opens up the possibility of highly effective leafleting and local paper advertising.

Once a club reaches a reasonable stage in membership volume and income, activity to generate new members can become more targeted. An in-depth understanding of members is very beneficial as it provides an understanding of which future groups of people have the highest propensity to join and where members travel from. This provides the basis of the club's core catchment area.

Step 2: define the club's potential

Many operators employ companies like the Leisure Database Company to profile their membership base and produce a geo-demographic member profile report showing the actual breakdown of members by their MOSAIC Group and characteristics. A penetration summary comparing members to the total population (using MOSAIC Group and Type) can also provide an awareness of the penetration rates (as a percentage) that are being achieved within the core catchment and gives information about the potential membership for the club. Management can use this current status compared with potential analysis as a performance measurement and to help set realistic targets for growth as well as understand any investment decisions required.

Using the two comparative reports, clubs can formulate very detailed knowledge as to the types of members that are most likely to join, and use this knowledge to maximise sales budgets by targeting similar people within the catchment area.

Drive time and distance decay graphs can also be studied, which show how far people travel and how much time they spend getting to the site (see Figure 23.1). A club can now look at the areas they are actually pulling from to decide whether the initial core catchment area that was identified needs to be adjusted.

In-depth analysis of members also gives a club the details of who are its most loyal and highest value members (in terms of spend – including membership fees and longevity of membership) by membership and MOSAIC Type. It is important that the club collect as much data as possible about its members and their behaviour patterns within the club.

An understanding of members' habits and behaviours will enable operators to anticipate needs and ensure that they communicate to members in the most relevant media. This is information that can be assessed when staff talk with members about what local media they read or listen to.

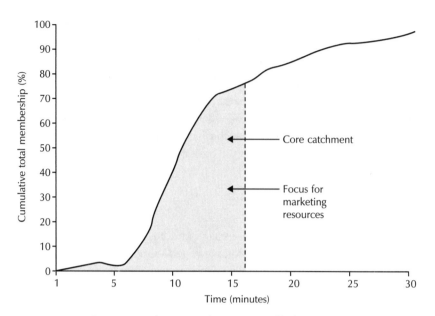

Figure 23.1 Drive-time decay graph (time travelled)

When a club is considering introducing a new product or service these will need to be tested against the known needs of the various member groups to establish whether the new products and services will be valued by members.

Step 3: decide which groups to target

The profiling and catchment area analysis identifies the various members and local populations available to you (see Figure 23.2). Critically the success comes in selecting the small number of member groups to really focus on. In the case of Leominster (Box 23.1), three groups represent 65 per cent of the population.

Once the club has reached a high level of membership there is no longer the need to be driving volume into the club. A highly targeted approach to sales and retention is required which no longer focuses purely on membership numbers.

Segmenting the club's offering becomes highly relevant at this stage to ensure that the club is being used at maximum capacity and that the highest amount of revenue is being driven out of usage. Having identified the types of members that are the most valuable in terms of length of membership and spend and their referral capacity, the focus switches to optimising off-peak times.

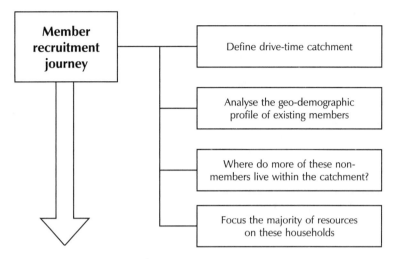

Figure 23.2 Targeting marketing activity

Driving income-generating off-peak memberships and concurrently phasing out discounted memberships is an important strategy. If, for example, student members have unlimited access to the club, then this category should either be capped or a new student membership created that only allows access at off-peak times. Setting sales targets for specific membership categories as well as for membership revenue ensures the club is implementing its strategy for membership mix. The importance of retention is paramount (see Chapters 20 and 21), ensuring that existing members are happy with their club and rewarded for their loyalty.

Analysing your own club is vital but do not stop there: analyse competitors too. Sales staff especially need an awareness of the competition and should be able to identify and communicate their club's unique qualities. These may change over time so repeat this exercise at least twice a year.

SUMMARY

The use of geo-demographic profiling with tools such as MOSAIC can provide rich insights into customers of sport and fitness facilities. It supports the idea of understanding your customers and, in particular, it is important at the very least to have full knowledge of local population characteristics, the extent of a facility's catchment area and the drive time to the facility.

REFERENCES

Debenham, J. (2002) *Understanding Geodemographic Classification: Creating the Building Blocks for an Extension – Appendix 1 'MOSIAC Pen Portraits',* Working Paper 02/01, University of Leeds, School of Geography, Available from: http://www.geog.leeds.ac.uk/wpapers/, accessed August 2007.

Halo Leisure (2007) *Halo Leisure Marketing Plan 2007/08,* internal document, Leominster: Halo Leisure.

Herefordshire Country Council (2007) *Census of Population 2001: Key Statistics for Herefordshire Country (with Comparative figures for England and Wales,* available from: http://www.herefordshire.gov.uk/council_gov_democracy/council/4768,asp,accessed November 2007.

Helpful links

MOSAIC pages of the Experian web site: www.experianmarketingsolutions.co .uk/ Products/Data_Integrity/Enhance/Mosaic.aspx

Link to the CACI Acorn web pages: www.caci.co.uk/acorn/

CHAPTER 24

TURNING MEMBERS INTO RAVING FANS[1]

Duncan Green

INTRODUCTION

Member acquisition costs are significantly greater than those of retaining existing members. This is not to understate the importance of sales and marketing in running successful health clubs but to realise that improving the member experience makes selling memberships easier in an increasingly competitive market.

By far the most effective and the least expensive means of achieving local awareness and member acquisition is through member referral (i.e. word of mouth). It is no surprise that the smart operators spend time, effort and money in ensuring a memorable member experience which enhances the referral potential.

What exactly constitutes a very high quality service in a health club? Research into the field has identified three levels of service that apply to any business regardless of sector (Smith, 2001).

LEVEL ONE SERVICE

Level one business is characterised by a lack of consistency in service delivery and staff operate without any clear structure or process. Invariably, this means staff are forced to invent the components of the experience on an ongoing basis. Sometimes this works but on many occasions it falls short of members' expectations.

---

[1] Edited from Green, D. (2006) 'Turning members into raving fans' in Algar, R. (ed.) *Mastering Health Club Management*, pp. 80–100, Brighton: Oxygen Consulting.

Level one service businesses can be characterised as being *personality-led*. Unfortunately the transient nature of club staff means that when staff turnover occurs the bond between club and member is broken. This can radically change the experience for the member and attrition often follows.

Many health clubs have adopted the principle of process-driven service in the operation of formal sales systems and increased efficiency and productivity have occurred as a result. The same cannot be said for the way most clubs deliver fitness supervision and general member communication programmes. From the outset of a new membership, many clubs set themselves up to fail by making claims about what they will deliver when they are not sufficiently organised to deliver it.

This retention process starts at the 'orientation' session performed almost universally in the industry on new members. With the members having made the financial commitment to enrol and with motivation at a high level, the event is a key opportunity to inform members of the club's service plan and in doing so raise member expectation.

Clubs should use the opportunity to explain the following by way of a structured presentation covering:

- what will happen to the member today;
- how the member's programme has been designed;
- the benefits that a member can expect to see;
- how the club will monitor the intensity of the programme;
- what happens after the first session;
- the member support services;
- the member incentive schemes.

Future member bonding with the club is largely dependent on the goodwill established at this session. However, even when this is achieved it is likely to be short-lived as further contact is unlikely.

LEVEL TWO SERVICE

In recent years innovative operators have designed a clearly defined member journey – a timetabled series of qualitative and quantitative moments of staff interaction and member communication tailored to meet the individual needs of the member.

A high-performing club ensures that member needs and expectations are properly evaluated at the outset and periodically thereafter by a range of measures performed at strategic points throughout the membership term. With this intelligence, a club is able to deliver a tailored series of suitable events and experiences which have the consequence of further raising member expectation. When expectations are met, the relationship between club and member is enhanced.

The importance of *training staff* to deliver consistently high levels of member service is therefore critical to the success of any club but this can only happen when those interactions are predictable, structured and systemised.

Defining the member service in a health club

The types of processes that clubs should consider in building a member service strategy include:

- inbound call handling
- front desk welcome
- bookings policy
- touring a prospective member
- prospective member tracking
- member orientation sessions
- exercise programming
- maintaining exercise records
- member follow-up and support
- member communication services
- member record-keeping
- programme developments
- club retail
- staff interactions
- member incentive programmes

LEVEL THREE SERVICE

This is where consistent processes fuse with attentive, well trained staff, who assist members in achieving their goals. The increased esteem of the member is linked indelibly to the club and the staff that helped to make it possible. This is

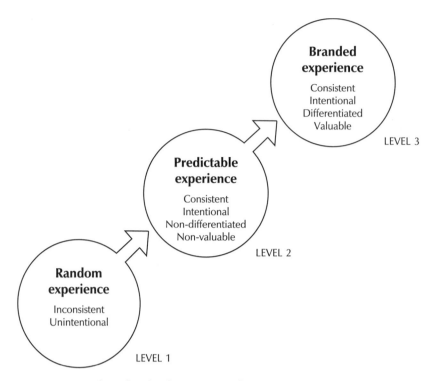

Figure 24.1 Three levels of service excellence

Source: Smith (2001).

the 'branded experience' (see Figure 24.1). It is where members are given time and attention and are made to feel important. These are vital ingredients in achieving long term member loyalty and the products of effective communication systems. No business can remain at level three for any sustainable length of time without first going through level two.

There are many staff in the health club industry who have the power to interact positively with members and to be 'nice'. Unfortunately this is not enough. Without a consistent approach, a member's loyalty to the club is determined by the weakest club relationship, rather than the strongest.

If a level two service business is about defining member services by appropriate processes and systems, then the level three focus is in ensuring that staff are suitably prepared to add the intangible value to the experience.

STAFF ROLE IN DELIVERING SERVICE

Clubs need to ensure that suitable attention is placed on the following:

- recruitment strategy
- training strategy
- motivation strategy
- communication strategy
- evaluation strategy

Recruitment strategy

Clubs must ensure that they recruit the right staff with the right type of personalities, experience and background for the job.

Qualifications are important in building credibility for the club but this is no substitute for personality. The adage 'Nobody cares what you know – until they know you care' applies for any member-focused business. The perfect solution is to recruit staff with the requisite knowledge together with the ability to empathise, lead and communicate with people of the club's target membership profile.

Training strategy

From the orientation presentation to the rebooking of programmes, it is a prerequisite for a level three business that staff consistently deliver the highest standards of service. This is based on good management practices and training. Training should be task-specific and evaluated to ensure that performance is achieved. The use of presenters, scripts and tests ensures staff knowledge of the business processes (see Chapter 22).

Motivation strategy

The long-term retention of staff is a key factor in building member loyalty. Staff are motivated by a complex combination of intrinsic and extrinsic factors that management needs to be aware of:

- *intrinsic factors*: 'the urge to do a good job', which can be reinforced by evaluating success along objective lines, role feedback from the manager, member testimonials and usage reports;

- *extrinsic factors*: 'what's in it for me?' – personal financial reward, promotion opportunities, peer group recognition.

Communication strategy

Successful organisations are those that demonstrate the ability to make swift operational changes when required, and to communicate these changes effectively to staff.

In order to achieve this an organisation needs:

- effective staff structures – facilitating staff empowerment and career advancement;
- effective communication that allows for rapid operational improvement, while maintaining a feeling of buy-in from all staff. Successful clubs also encourage regular team and project meetings;
- clearly defined job roles which ensure higher levels of staff confidence;
- clearly defined objectives with an agreed set of consequences and rewards acknowledged by all staff.

Evaluation strategy

Finally the club should be evaluating the usage patterns and feedback of its members in relation to the service plan and evaluating qualitatively the work of staff. This carries sound benefits for the club such as:

1   ensuring adherence to the strategy;
2   confirming performance standards;
3   motivational back-up for staff who know they are doing a good job;
4   further developing and enhancing the member–service journey based on member results and feedback.

TAILORING THE MEMBER JOURNEY

If the key to a successful club is robust processes and systems, what exactly must these deliver to members? A key feature that characterises exceptional service is that the member journey is tailored to the needs of distinct groups. An effective club manager recognises that segmenting members is the route for a more focused service offering and is a building block for cultivating member loyalty.

The business needs to have some means of analysing the expectations of members with a view to matching differing needs to the service strategy. Assuming that the basics of cleanliness, functioning equipment, polite staff and effective management are met, what do clubs have to do to identify and service the differing needs of their members?

IDENTIFYING MEMBERS' NEEDS

Many clubs utilise some form of prescriptive entry-level interview process which identifies factors such as:

- geo-demographic profile;
- exercise history;
- exercise aims;
- estimated usage patterns;
- level of motivation to achieve the desired goal;
- current attitude to health and fitness.

When a member joins, their motivation to succeed and support requirements as a new user can be very different from those of more experienced members.

THE MEMBER QUADRANT MATRIX

Where members sit within this matrix is dependent on how they score against two parameters (see Figure 24.2). Their degree of *self-motivation* (vertical axis) determines the likelihood of them adhering to an exercise programme without any input from the club. Members who score highly on this will need few or no motivation strategies or incentives from the club, while those at the lower end will need greater support.

The horizontal axis is a member's *experience and knowledge* of the product and is defined by their ability to self-manage the whole process of using the club. This experience extends not just to the member's ability to confidently operate the fitness equipment but also includes critical knowledge of exercise programming, and the ability to self-manage personal progress and goal setting. There are also

turning members into raving fans

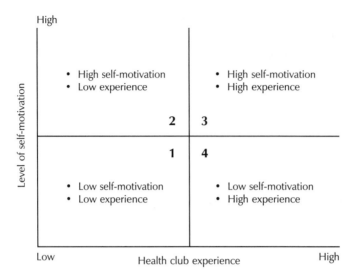

High

Level of self-motivation

- High self-motivation
- Low experience

- High self-motivation
- High experience

2 | 3

1 | 4

- Low self-motivation
- Low experience

- Low self-motivation
- High experience

Low   Health club experience   High

Figure 23.2 The member quadrant mix

operational issues such as locker usage, class bookings and achieving rapport with staff members.

Lack of experience can lead to feelings of unease and anxiety. The initial aim of the club should be to ensure that members are made comfortable, which is achieved by providing sufficient support.

THE FOUR TYPES OF MEMBER

It is important to remember that this is a dynamic model and that members will probably show the characteristics of at least one other segment during their membership. Members' motivation levels will fluctuate for a variety of reasons, which is why it is important to implement a member communications strategy to detect any significant changes in member motivation and make the necessary interventions.

Group one: inactive partners

This is the smallest group represented on the matrix. Typically, these individuals lack club experience and a motivation to exercise and are typically recruited by a club on the back of a more active partner. They are notoriously difficult members to service and maintain.

Group two: enthusiastic beginners

Members in this group are characterised by a high motivation to exercise and achieve a specific goal. However, they have little experience of how to operate equipment or how programmes are constructed. They are relatively stable members providing they are integrated properly. While motivation remains high the only issue for this group is whether the club can integrate them through adequate education ensuring that they achieve a feeling of belonging. Their motivation is derived from a range of catalysts, from health scares and relationship breakdowns to pending events such as holidays and weddings where they will be particularly body-conscious.

A successful educational process will ensure that the individual moves to quadrant three, where they can self-manage their visits to the club.

Group three: motivated minority

Members in this group are very knowledgeable and committed exercisers and their club of choice is dictated by factors such as location, equipment, facilities and price. They require little in the way of integration from the club but attendance levels should be monitored as motivation can wane through injury, or if usage patterns are significantly disturbed.

Group four: reactivated users

Members in this group are possibly returning to an exercise programme but with a history of non-adherence, together with experienced lapsed members who, for a variety of reasons, have lost the motivation to attend. To make them stable members, the club has to ensure that motivation is maintained by utilising short-term programmes, recording results and highlighting improvement. They can be attracted by results-based, low commitment membership offers. However, they can be encouraged to rejoin on longer commitment schemes if the club can convince them to continue attending through its retention programmes.

It is possible for quadrant three individuals to lose motivation and to drop into quadrant four, as a result of the usage pattern being disrupted for some reason such as an injury, holiday or some other enforced layoff, which fosters a feeling of frustration at not being able to train as before. If a club's motivational strategy is effective, then members in the fourth quadrant can become more stable quadrant three members.

QUADRANT IDENTIFICATION

High-service clubs need to uncover where the prospective member is positioned in this matrix. The sales presentation can then be tailored to match the anticipated needs of the member. In my experience, a club can significantly improve member retention by segmenting members in this way. However, because a member's motivation to exercise is subject to change, it is important that a club's communication plan permits a regular and ongoing review of where a member currently sits in this quadrant in order to avoid attrition.

SUMMARY AND KEY ACTIONS

In this chapter we have introduced the importance of enhancing the member experience to create a club that can outperform its rivals. The three levels of organisational (club) service have been outlined, ranging from the random (level one) to the consistently differentiated experience (level three). A level three club psychologically connects with members to assist in them in achieving their goals. A club creates raving fans when a manager recognises that exceptional service is delivered by providing staff with effective leadership and sufficient resources. The member quadrant matrix has been introduced to illustrate that the degree of self-confidence and previous health club experience that a member possesses should be used to determine the support provided.

REFERENCE

Smith, S. (2001) *Experiencing the Brand – Branding the Experience*, London: Ferum Corporation, available from: http://www.brandchannel.com/images/papers/ETB_UK.pdf.

INDEX

Routledge Sport